THE BUSINESS ENVIRONMENT

W. Körner

Study Course 530
Distance Learning Division

ISBN 1 85369 087 2
Revised and reprinted 1992

THE AUTHORS

Wolfgang Körner Lic. econ., PhD, was born in Germany in 1952, attended primary school in Germany and secondary school in Turkey, studied economics at the University of Zurich and did a teacher training course at Jordanhill College of Education in Glasgow. He taught at Zurich University from 1973 to 1977 and at Glasgow College from 1977 to 1989, and now works as a freelance.

David Green LLB, FCII, Solicitor, who contributed Part IV of this book, began his career in the life underwriting department of the Prudential Assurance Company Ltd (now part of Prudential Corporation plc) in 1967. After qualifying as a Fellow of the CII, he transferred to the Solicitors Department of the Prudential after obtaining an external law degree of the University of London. He qualified as a solicitor and was admitted to the Roll of Solicitors in 1982. Since then, he has specialised in company and commercial law. He advises the Prudential Group on a wide range of corporate matters. He has been an Examiner of the CII since 1982, and since 1987 has been a Joint Secretary of the Examiners Committee.

Keyed by the CII Distance Learning Division
Page make-up by Goodfellow & Egan, Cambridge
Production Services by Book Production Consultants, Cambridge
Printed and bound in the United Kingdom by
BPCC Hazell Books, Aylesbury HP20 1LB

CONTENTS

CONTENTS

4
THE NATURE OF COMPETITION

5
NATIONAL INCOME AND RELATED CONCEPTS

6
TWO ECONOMIC PROBLEMS INFLATION AND UNEMPLOYMENT

CONTENTS

PART II

The Operational Environment

9

TYPES OF BUSINESS: INTERACTION BETWEEN A BUSINESS AND ITS ENVIRONMENT

CONTENTS

CONTENTS

13

BASIC ACCOUNTING

14

FINANCIAL ANALYSIS, CONTROL AND PLANNING

15

CAPITAL MARKET FINANCE NEEDS

CONTENTS

PART IV
The Legal Environment

16
TRADING ORGANISATIONS

17
COMPANY MANAGEMENT

18
INSURANCE COMPANIES

PART I
THE ECONOMIC ENVIRONMENT

1

BASIC ECONOMIC PROBLEMS AND SYSTEMS

A   Basic economic problems

B   Economic systems

C   How it works

A

BASIC ECONOMIC PROBLEMS

We usually take it for granted that we can walk into a shop and buy all the things we want. However, we find the goods we have decided to buy only if the shop has bought the right mixture of goods, and this in turn is possible only if producers (sometimes spread over many different countries) have produced just the goods we want to buy. Who organises all this? Who decides that those Japanese cameras, Spanish oranges and so on should end up in a shop in Britain rather than in some other part of the world? While occasionally there may be a shortage of one product or a glut of another, such aberrations are usually ironed out fairly quickly, and the normal situation is that producers produce just about the quantities consumers want to buy, and this applies for every one of the thousands of goods we find on display in the shops.

By generalising these questions we arrive at the three basic economic problems which every society must solve, no matter what its state of development or whether it operates under a capitalist or communist system. These three basic questions are:

1 **What goods shall be produced?**
2 **How shall those goods be produced?**
3 **For whom shall those goods be produced?**

Let us look at each of these questions in more detail.

A1   WHAT TO PRODUCE?

First, **what** should be produced? Should we try to produce all the goods we want to consume and leave the rest of the world alone, or should we specialise in some goods and import the rest? If we choose the latter, what goods should we specialise in and what should we import? Different countries have made different decisions in this

LEARNING OBJECTIVES

After studying this chapter, you should be able to:

▷ name the three basic problems every economy has to solve;

▷ name the two main economic systems;

▷ explain the features of a mixed economy;

▷ categorise a given country with regard to its economic system.

regard. Britain, for example, has been a net importer of food for at least a century, specialising instead in the production of industrial goods at first, and now increasingly in services (more about this in the chapters on gross national product and the balance of payments). Denmark and New Zealand, on the other hand, are net exporters of foodstuff and net importers of manufactured goods.

A2 HOW TO PRODUCE?

Once we have decided **what** we want to produce, we have to decide **how** we want to produce those goods. For instance, a modern economy cannot function without electricity, so we will have to produce so many million kilowatt-hours of it every year to keep our economy going. However, **how** are we to produce that electricity? A number of methods are known; we can, for example, produce it from nuclear power, in coal- or oil-fired conventional thermoelectric power stations, or from waterfalls. Again, different countries have reached different decisions. In Scotland and France, nuclear power is the main source of electricity generation; in England and Denmark coal predominates; and in Canada and Austria about two thirds of all electricity comes from hydroelectric power stations.[1] An important part of the 'how to produce?' question is the extent of mechanisation we want. To tear a house down, you can employ twenty strong men, give them a big hammer and tell them to get on with the job. Alternatively, you can let one man do the job with a bulldozer. In developing countries, production is usually a lot more labour-intensive than it is in developed countries, even if the same end product is involved.

A3 FOR WHOM TO PRODUCE?

Having decided what our economy should produce and how those goods and services should be produced, we have to decide the **'for whom?'** question. Who is to get the benefit of the goods and services produced? In a stone age village at the seaside or near a river where some of the villagers engage in fishing, somebody must decide how the fish caught by the villagers is to be dis-

tributed. Should every fisherman be allowed to catch as much as he likes and to keep his entire catch, or should he have to give some or all of his fish to the village chief to distribute among the villagers according to merit, need or some other criterion? In a modern economy the same problem arises, albeit in a different form. Here the question is: how should the national income be distributed among the population? (We will see later that national income is basically the same as the value of all the goods and services produced.) Should a bus driver earn more or less than, or the same as, a schoolteacher? Again, different countries have made different decisions. According to a survey published by the Union Bank of Switzerland,[2] a London Transport bus driver earns roughly the same as a London primary teacher. In Paris and New York, the bus driver earns about ten per cent more than the teacher, whereas in Zurich and Tokyo the teacher is better off than the bus driver (by 14% and 35%, respectively).

B
ECONOMIC SYSTEMS

We have now discussed the three basic economic problems every society must solve. The next question is: how are these decisions made, and who makes them? Who or what is it that decides whether we should produce all the food we need or whether we should produce other things and import the food? How do we reach a decision on whether we should produce electricity from coal or from nuclear energy, or whether a primary teacher should earn more or less than, or the same as, a bus driver?

Basically, there are two different methods of deciding the 'what, how, and for whom' questions. One is to let the **government** alone decide these issues. Countries where such matters are decided by the government alone are called **planned economies**. The other method is to leave these decisions to the **market mechanism** alone: to the interaction of supply and demand. Countries which rely on the market mechanism to decide the 'what, how, and for whom' questions are known as **market economies.**

B1 THE MIXED ECONOMY

In reality, no country is completely in the one camp or the other; all real world economies are **mixed economies,** but one of the two systems (planned or market) usually predominates. Britain, for instance, is predominantly a market economy, but that does not mean that there is no government intervention in the British economy. A building company could not, for example, build houses in Hyde Park or on farmland somewhere between London and the south coast, even if building such houses would help to alleviate the shortage of reasonably priced residential property in the London area. You are only allowed to build houses on land which the government has decided should be used for that purpose; if the government has decided that land should be used for agricultural or recreational purposes, it cannot be used for house-building. So, Britain is predominantly a market economy, but there is nevertheless a certain amount of government intervention, especially in areas like land use, social security, defence, law enforcement, and education. The Soviet Union, on the other hand, is predominantly a planned economy: questions like what, how, and for whom to produce are decided mainly by the government. However, there is some market-related activity even in the Soviet Union. For example, members of collective or state farms are allowed some land for private use where they can grow what they like, either for private consumption or for sale. The last couple of years have seen an expansion of the market element in most communist countries, although government planning still predominates.

C
HOW IT WORKS

How then do these two systems, the planned economy and the market economy, decide what, how, and for whom to produce? The basic principle of the planned economy is easy to understand: the government decides what to produce, it lays down what methods of production should be used, and it decides what the distribution of income should be like. The whole programme is usually embedded in a five-year plan; production units (like farms or factories) are given production targets (instructions as to how much they should produce), and are expected to adhere to these targets. If you listen to Soviet news broadcasts in December, you will regularly hear reports like 'Production unit XYZ has fulfilled its annual production target on 10th December, and the goods it will produce between now and the end of the year will allow it to over-fulfil the plan by so and so many per cent.' Of course, it also happens that production units are not able to achieve their target output.

In Britain, we have nothing of this kind. Nobody tells a farmer in this country whether he should use his land, labour and machinery to grow wheat, potatoes or vegetables: the farmer himself decides.

Q What will the farmer take into account in deciding what to grow?

A He will grow what he thinks it is in **his best interest** to grow.

(Wealth of Nations)

As the Scottish economist Adam Smith put it more than 200 years ago, 'it is not to the benevolence of the baker, the butcher and the brewer that we owe our meal, but to their regard for their self-interest.'[3] The basic idea of the market economy is to let everybody produce what he wants, and people who favour the market system believe that if the market is allowed to operate, people's self-interest will see to it that all the jobs society wants to be done will be done. To quote Adam Smith again,

Every individual endeavours to employ his capital so that its produce may be of greatest value. He generally neither intends to promote the public interest, nor knows how much he is promoting it.

He intends only his own security, only his own gain. And he is in this led by an *invisible hand* to promote an end which was no part of his intention. By pursuing his own interest he frequently promotes that of society more effectually than when he actually intends to promote it.'[3,4]

Such a system where everybody is guided by his own interests may seem pretty chaotic: how can it possibly coordinate the plans of consumers and producers, so that producers produce what consumers want to buy? How does the 'invisible hand' referred to by Adam Smith work? To answer this question, we have to look in some detail at **supply and demand.**

References

1 Sources: Fischer Weltalmanach 1989 (Frankfurt, Germany), and the annual reports of the South of Scotland Electricity Board, the Central Electricity Generating Board, and Electricité de France.

2 Union Bank of Switzerland: Prices and Earnings Around the World, Zurich 1988.

3 Adam Smith : The Wealth of Nations (1776).

4 By 'invisible hand' Smith means that this process works automatically, without any individual, government or other organisation consciously planning or organising it.

1

SELF-ASSESSMENT QUESTIONS

1. Which are the three basic economic problems every society must solve?

   What to produce

   When to produce it for

   How to produce it

2. What is the difference between a market economy and a planned economy?

   Planned all aspects controlled by Govt

   Market allows the forces of Supply

   + demand to control it

3. What does it mean to say that Britain is a mixed economy?

   Some aspects Govt Controlled

   but Market force play a

   Major role

4. Which of the following countries is closest to the model of a planned economy?

   (a) Britain.
   (b) The USA.
   (c) The Soviet Union.

   (C) Soviet Union.

5. Which of the countries listed in question 4 is closest to the model of a market economy?

   USA

1
ANSWERS TO SELF-ASSESSMENT QUESTIONS

1/6

1. The problems are: what goods to produce, how to produce them, and for whom to produce them.

2. In a planned economy, decisions on the basic economic issues are made by the government alone. In a market economy, these issues are settled by the working of supply and demand.

3. In Britain, the market mechanism is allowed to settle most economic issues, but there are certain areas where it is seen as proper for the government to intervene.

4. The Soviet Union, although it is currently moving away from this system.

5. The USA.

2

SUPPLY AND DEMAND

LEARNING OBJECTIVES

After studying this chapter, you should be able to:

▷ explain the relationship between the price of a product and the demand for and supply of it;

▷ explain how prices come about if the market is allowed to operate;

▷ give two reasons for implementing government price controls;

▷ explain the effects of government price controls;

▷ list the advantages and disadvantages of government price controls;

▷ name two factors other than the price which affect the demand for and supply of a product;

▷ explain what can cause shifts in supply or demand curves;

▷ explain how the market decides the 'what, how, and for whom' problem.

A
DEMAND

Suppose you are in a shop buying some food for your dinner, wondering what vegetables to buy. You see some nice cabbages on the shelves. Will you necessarily buy one of those cabbages? You will probably check the price before you put one into your shopping basket. If you find the price reasonable you will perhaps take a cabbage. However, if the price is higher than you expect, you are likely not to buy cabbage: you will probably prefer to buy some other vegetable. Other people may of course have different views on what is a 'reasonable' price for cabbage. Somebody who is poorer than you are may decide not to buy at a price which you still find acceptable, and somebody who is richer than you are will perhaps still buy cabbage even if you find the price too high. This, however, does not change the fact that there is a relationship between the **demand** for cabbage and the **price** of cabbage: **the higher the price, the fewer people will be prepared to buy, and the lower the price, the more people will be prepared to buy.**

Let us assume that we have studied the relationship between the price of, and the demand for, cabbage in a particular week in a certain part of the country, and have found the following relationships:

Price of cabbage (pence per kilo)	Demand for cabbage (kilos)
5	3,000
10	2,500
15	2,000
20	1,500
25	1,000
30	500
35	0

Suppose cabbage is very cheap (say, 5 pence per kilo). At such a low price, even the poorest can afford to buy it, and all other vegetables are a lot more expensive. So, many people will want to buy cabbage, which means the demand for it will be high (3,000 kilos in our example). If the price rises, some people will no longer want to buy cabbage. Either they can no longer afford it, or they prefer to buy some other vegetable. So, the higher the price, the lower will be the demand. This is reflected in the table above.

We now know what quantities of cabbage people want to buy at various prices. Does this allow us to find out what the price of cabbage will be? Using the numerical relationship above, will 3,000 kilos of cabbage be bought and sold at 5 pence per kilo, or will 500 kilos change hands at 30 pence per kilo?

We cannot answer this question from the information we have so far. The above table just tells us how much people would like to buy at various prices. However, it does not help the public that they want to buy a huge quantity of cabbage at some ridiculously low price (say, 5 pence per kilo) if no farmer is willing to produce any cabbage at that price; maybe because it does not even cover his costs of production. Therefore, to find out what the price will be, we have to take into account the supply as well as the demand.

B
SUPPLY

We have seen in the previous section that buyers want low prices: the lower the price, the more they will want to buy. However, producers have just the opposite preference. Low prices mean low income for the producer, so at low prices it is not terribly attractive to produce the product in question, and so few people, if any, will be prepared to produce it. The higher the price, the more profitable production becomes, and so more people will want to produce that product. **Low prices lead to a low quantity of supply; high prices lead to a high one.** Using the same method as in section A, let us assume we have found the following relationship between the price of cabbage and

the quantity of cabbage which farmers are willing to produce:

Price of cabbage (pence per kilo)	Supply of cabbage (kilos)
5	0
10	500
15	1,000
20	1,500
25	2,000
30	2,500
35	3,000

We have seen in the demand section that people want to buy a huge quantity of cabbage if cabbage costs 5 pence per kilo. Will they be able to get all that cabbage at such a low price? The table above gives the answer: they won't. The supply at that price is zero, which means no farmer is willing to produce any cabbage if all he gets for it is 5 pence per kilo. Let us assume that farmers whose land is particularly well suited for cabbage production can produce it at 7 pence per kilo. They will obviously not produce cabbage if they get only 5 pence per kilo for it; there is no point in producing something at a cost of 7 pence and then selling it at 5 pence (remember the story on self-interest at the end of Chapter 1). If cabbage can be sold only for 5 pence per kilo, the farmer will use his land, labour, machinery and so on to produce other things.

If the price now goes up to 10 pence, however, those farmers who can produce cabbage at a cost of 7 pence will make a profit. Consequently, some of them may start growing cabbages, and according to our example 500 kilos are supplied to the market. Farmers whose land is not quite so suitable for growing cabbages and whose cost of production is, say, 12 pence per kilo will of course still not produce cabbage even at a price of 10 pence per kilo; they can only be tempted into cabbage production if the price goes above 12 pence. This example shows that the higher the price, the more farmers will find it profitable to grow cabbages, so more of that vegetable will be produced as prices rise: **higher prices lead to a larger quantity of supply.**

C
SUPPLY AND DEMAND COMBINED

Now, the same question as before: does this relationship between prices and supply tell us what price will come about and what quantity of the product will be traded at that price? Again, the answer is no. The supply table in section B tell us only how much farmers are willing to supply at various prices. However, just as it does not help consumers that they want to buy large quantities at low prices, so it does not help producers that they want to sell large quantities at high prices. In our example, farmers want to sell 3,000 kilos of cabbage if the price is 35 pence per kilo. However, farmers can sell only if consumers are prepared to buy, and at 35 pence per kilo consumers just say, "Keep your cabbage." Demand is zero; see section A.

So, we will not find out what price will come about if we look **only** at demand or **only** at supply; we have to look at both. Combining what we already know about supply and demand, we get the following relationships:

Price of cabbage (pence per kilo)	Demand for cabbage (kilos)	Supply of cabbage (kilos)
5	3,000	0
10	2,500	500
15	2,000	1,000
20	1,500	1,500
25	1,000	2,000
30	500	2,500
35	0	3,000

We now see straight away that prices like 5 pence or 35 pence per kilo will not satisfy anybody. Low prices may seem fine from the consumers' point of view, but at prices like 5 pence per kilo (in our example) no farmer is willing to produce, and the cheap food you cannot get will not make you very happy. If consumers want cabbage, they will have to offer farmers a higher price, otherwise supply will be insufficient to meet the demand.

Q   What do you think will happen to prices if demand exceeds supply, and why?

A   If at any given price (say 5, 10 or 15 pence in our example) demand exceeds supply, some people will not get what they want, and some of the disappointed customers will start offering higher prices to get what they want: **if demand exceeds supply, prices are pushed up.**

Starting at the other end, we can see that prices like 35 pence or 30 pence per kilo cannot establish themselves in the market either. At such prices farmers are willing to produce large quantities, but there are not enough buyers. If farmers want to sell their output, they will have to lower the price to attract more buyers: **if supply exceeds demand, prices fall.** Such a fall in price will mop up the existing excess supply by increasing demand, and it will reduce production in the future.

Now we have all the information we need. We have seen that prices rise as long as demand exceeds supply, and prices fall when supply exceeds demand. It follows that there is only one price at which market conditions are stable, and that is the price at which supply equals demand. This price is known as the **equilibrium price.** In our example, supply equals demand at a price of 20 pence per kilo. At that price, supply and demand are both 1,500 kilos.

So, the price comes about by the interaction of supply and demand, and the market mechanism, if allowed to operate, will automatically bring about the price at which supply equals demand.

D
SUPPLY AND DEMAND CURVES

The equilibrium price can also be found by means of supply and demand curves. Instead of showing the relationship between price, supply and demand in the form of a table (as in sections A, B and C) we can use diagrams. Using the data in section A we get the following:

Demand curve for cabbage

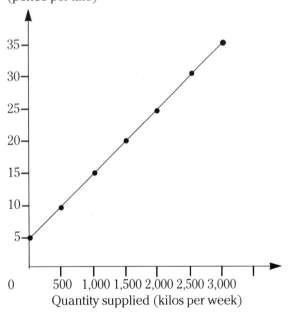

We can now do the same for supply, using the data in section B:

Supply curve for cabbage

By the way, the term demand or supply **curve** is used even if the resulting 'curve' is a straight line. Whether we get a curve or a straight line depends on the product in question. In the examples here, straight lines are used for simplicity.

The fall of the demand curve (from left to right) reflects the fact that demand increases as price decreases, and the reason for the slope of the supply curve is that supply increases with the price.

We have seen earlier that if we want to draw conclusions about market conditions, we have to look at supply and demand together, rather than studying each in isolation from the other. So, let us combine the demand and the supply curves in one diagram. We then get the following:

Demand and supply curves for cabbage

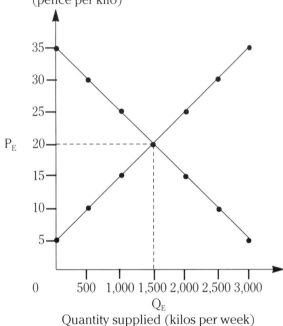

This diagram shows even more clearly than the table in section C how supply and demand interact. There is only one price at which supply equals demand, and that, as we already know, is the **equilibrium price (P_E)** which will establish itself in the market. In our example we get an equilibrium price of 20 pence per kilo, and an **equilibrium quantity (Q_E)** of 1,500 kilos. (Practices like temporary low-priced offers, made for promotional purposes or to enter a market for the first time, are ignored here.)

Now let us go back to the beginning of Chapter 1. We asked there why we usually find in the shops what we want to buy; who organises production so that the quantities produced are roughly in line with the quantities customers want to buy; and so on. We now see that those questions really boil down to asking: who or what makes sure that supply equals demand? Now we know the answer: **it is the price which makes supply equal to demand.** If at any time the demand for a certain product exceeds the supply of that product, the price will go up.

This will encourage production (increase supply) and discourage consumption (demand will fall as some people no longer want to buy the product at the higher price). Eventually, supply will again be equal to demand. Note that it was not necessary for the government or anybody else to intervene in this process. Whatever the weaknesses of the market mechanism may be, it has the advantage of determining prices in such a way that supply equals demand. Every producer can sell as much as he wants, and every consumer can buy as much as he wants, provided he is willing and able to deal at the market price.

E

GOVERNMENT PRICE CONTROL

The point mentioned in the last sentence of section D has often been used to attack the market mechanism: "OK, you can buy whatever you like, but only if you are willing and able to pay the market price. What happens if you cannot pay the market price?"

? Spend a minute or two thinking about possible responses or solutions to this problem. What **does** happen if one cannot afford the price set by the market?

The response depends largely on the type of good we are talking about. If an average wage earner cannot afford a diamond ring because the equilibrium price of diamonds is too high for him, nobody will be terribly concerned about this since one can live perfectly well without such jewellery. However, if the product in question is some basic foodstuff, housing or some other essential item, the story is rather different. In cases where, for whatever reason, market forces have pushed prices of essential commodities to levels beyond

the reach of average wage earners, governments have often been tempted to intervene. Let us now look at the effects of such government intervention. Suppose the diagram below represents the supply and demand curves for a certain product:

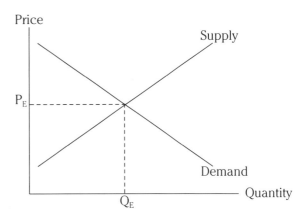

If the market mechanism is allowed to operate freely (i.e. without government intervention), the product in question will be traded at the equilibrium price P_E. At that price, both supply and demand amount to the equilibrium quantity Q_E. If the product in question is an essential item and the government thinks P_E is too high a price, it may intervene and set the price at a lower level. That is, the government dictates a maximum price (below P_E) and makes it illegal to buy or sell the product for more than that price.

What are the effects of such a measure? Why does the government not legislate all prices down in this way? The answer to the second question is that imposing maximum prices has some unintended (and undesirable) side-effects. Our supply and demand curves show what they are.

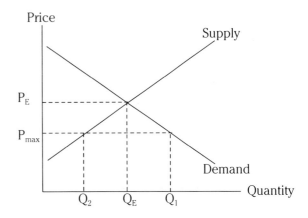

We already know that in the absence of government price controls the price will be P_E (see diagram above). If the government now imposes a maximum price P_{max} at a level below the equilibrium price P_E, what will happen to supply and demand? Well, demand will increase and supply will decrease. The reason for this is that at a lower price more people will want to buy the product, but producing it becomes less rewarding for producers.

So, starting in an equilibrium position where supply equals demand (both are Q_E), demand will rise (to Q_1 in the diagram above) and supply will fall (to Q_2). The diagram shows at one glance that the lower price leads to problems. At the lower price, supply no longer equals demand: people now want to buy quantity Q_1, but producers are only prepared to supply quantity Q_2. Demand exceeds supply. This means that not everybody who wants to buy the product in question will be able to get it, even if he is willing and able to pay the price set by the government.

So, when advocating legislative action to bring prices down, one should keep in mind that lower prices are not the only results of such measures: if the government imposes a maximum price below the market equilibrium, shortages are the inevitable consequence because demand will exceed supply.

Who will get the desired products in such circumstances and who will go without varies from case to case. Since the price is no longer allowed to allocate the goods, some other allocation mechanism must be found. This could be first come, first served: come early in the morning or whenever the lorry with the supplies arrives and you will get something; come two hours later and the shelves will be empty. Another possibility is to introduce a rationing system of some kind, as for example the food rationing system many European countries (including Britain) used during the Second World War. In 1989 meat, butter, rice and cooking oil were rationed in parts of the Soviet Union.[1] Yet another allocation mechanism is to introduce waiting lists. If you want the product, your name is put on a list and you will get your supply once your turn arrives. This system is used in Britain at

the moment for allocating council houses, and some East European countries use it to allocate cars.

A discussion of the consequences of the legislative imposition of maximum prices would be incomplete without mentioning the even less desirable side-effects such measures may have. If they do not get what they want by legal means (since demand exceeds supply), some people will try to get the product in question in other ways, be it by bribing officials to put their name at the top of the waiting list, or by trying to tempt producers to sell to them rather than to other people by illegally offering to pay more than the maximum price allowed. So, corruption and black markets have often been the consequence of government price control.

So far, we have talked of government imposing a price **below** the equilibrium in order to protect consumers. We still have to discuss another form of price control: if the government thinks that the market price is too low to give producers a 'reasonable' income, it may fix a minimum price below which the product must not be sold. The consequences of such a measure are easy to see:

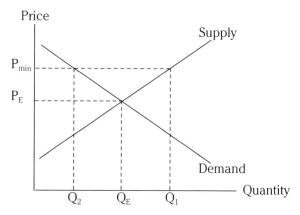

If the government sets a minimum price P_{min} at a level higher than the equilibrium price P_E, supply will rise (to Q_1), and demand will fall (to Q_2). Just as maximum prices below the equilibrium lead to an excess demand, so minimum prices above the equilibrium lead to an excess supply: to the production of goods which nobody wants to buy. The 'butter mountains' and 'wine lakes' of the EC can serve as examples.

F

OTHER DETERMINANTS OF DEMAND

There are other factors which influence demand for a good. These are now discussed.

F1 PRICES OF OTHER GOODS

In the previous section we saw how the price of a product affects the supply of, and the demand for, that product. However, price is not the only factor affecting supply and demand. Suppose the price of coffee goes up substantially. Some people will decide that coffee is now too expensive for them and stop buying it. The demand for coffee has fallen because the price of coffee has gone up.

Nothing new in that, but what we have said so far is only part of the story. The people who no longer drink coffee will presumably want to drink something else instead; maybe tea. If this happens, the demand for tea rises, not because of any change in the price of tea, but because of the rise in the price of coffee. Thus **the demand for one product may change because the price of some other product has changed.**

Whether an increase in the price of the one good will increase or decrease the demand for the other depends on what kind of goods we are talking about. If the two goods are **substitutes** (like tea and coffee, or butter and margarine), an increase in the price of the one will increase the demand for the other: if butter becomes more expensive, some people will eat less butter and more margarine. However, some goods are not substitutes, but **complementary goods.** This is the case, for example, with petrol and cars. If petrol prices went up to £5 a gallon, some people could no longer afford petrol, and if you cannot afford petrol, there is of course no point in having a car. Thus a rise in the price of petrol may reduce the demand for cars.

Finally, the two goods may be **unrelated.** If peanut prices go up, people will hardly want to buy more or fewer fridges as a result, so in this case the price of the former has no effect on the demand for the latter. (This, at any rate, is true for Britain. It may not be true for countries like Senegal or the Gambia where peanuts are the main export product and where, consequently, peanut prices play an important role in the national economy.)

F2 INCOME

If your income goes up, you can buy more than you could in the past. Therefore, a rise in your income may increase your demand for a product even if the price of that product has remained unchanged. A rise in incomes in real terms (i.e. after allowing for inflation) will increase demand overall. This, however, does not mean that the demand for each and every product will go up as incomes rise; the demand for some products may even fall. For example, somebody may buy a black and white television set because he cannot afford a colour set. If that person's income goes up, he may buy a colour television set instead, which means the demand for black and white television sets would fall. Generally, a rise in incomes will increase the demand for luxury products and reduce the demand for cheap substitutes (so-called inferior goods). In developed countries, the demand for basic foodstuffs is unlikely to be affected by rises or falls in income: would you buy more bread or onions or potatoes if your income went up?

F3 TASTES AND FASHIONS

This is an item which is difficult to measure and which may change erratically and for no apparent reason. Still, such changes affect the demand for goods and services. If people become more health-conscious they may reduce their consumption of tobacco, alcohol and animal fats, and eat more fruit and vegetables. Tastes and fashions are particularly important in the clothing industry. Textile retailers often find that garments which sold well in the past are no longer in demand because fashions have changed.

G

OTHER DETERMINANTS OF SUPPLY

Supply is also affected by a large number of factors. If wheat prices rise, wheat production becomes more profitable, so farmers will want to produce more of it. However, where will they grow that wheat? Unless they have unused land, they can only produce more wheat by growing it on land where they grew other crops in the past. In other words, higher wheat prices increase the supply of wheat, but reduce the supply of some other crop: **the price of one good affects the supply of other goods.** In agriculture, the weather is an important determinant of the quantity of output, and so is farmers' access to fertilisers and other chemicals. Costs of production, such as material and labour costs, affect industrial production as does competition from abroad. At the turn of the century about half of the world's ships were built on the Clyde. Now shipbuilding is a declining industry in Britain (and the former shipbuilding areas have high unemployment rates) because countries like Brazil and South Korea can produce many types of ship more cheaply.

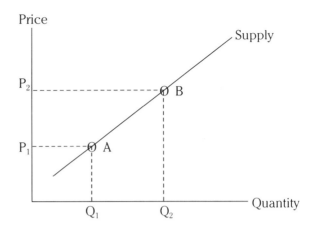

In sections F and G, however, we saw that demand and supply are affected not only by the price of the product in question but also by a large number of other factors. If any of these other factors changes, the entire supply or demand curve shifts to the left or to the right. This will be explained in more detail below.

H
SHIFTS IN SUPPLY AND DEMAND CURVES

If the price of the product in question changes, we move up or down along the existing demand or supply curve (see section D). The diagrams below show how we move from point A to point B on the same curve if the price goes up from P_1 to P_2.

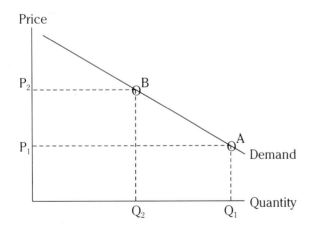

H1   SHIFTS IN THE DEMAND CURVE

Suppose the diagrams below represent the supply and demand for pork and beef.

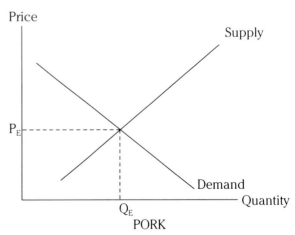

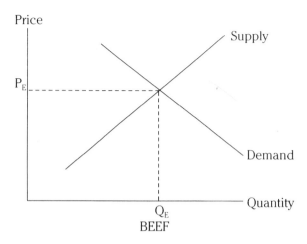

BEEF

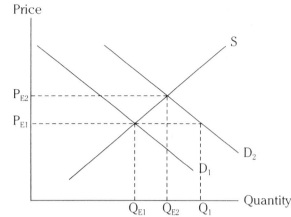

Both markets are in equilibrium (supply equals demand) at their respective equilibrium prices.

Q Can you state briefly what will happen to the demand curves if, due to a change in tastes, people suddenly want to buy more pork and less beef?

A Very briefly, the demand curve for pork moves to the right, and that for beef moves to the left. Now let's look at this process in a little more detail.

Taking pork first, at any given price people want to buy more pork than before. This implies a shift of the demand curve to the right, as shown in the diagram below.

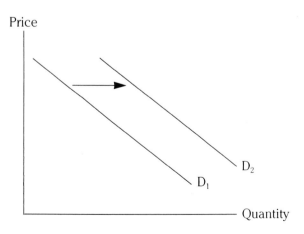

If we combine this with the (unchanged) supply curve, we see what effects such a change in tastes will have on the market:

The market used to be in equilibrium at price P_{E1}. After the shift of the demand curve, however, demand exceeds supply at that price (demand is D_2 whereas supply is Q_{E1}), which means the price will rise (see section C). That rise will continue until a new equilibrium level has been reached. According to the diagram above, the new equilibrium price is P_{E2}.

Why this price rise? Well, people want more pork, so they have to provide farmers with an incentive to produce more. The higher price makes pork production more profitable, so more pork will be produced, which is exactly what consumers want. In the diagram above, the equilibrium quantity goes up from Q_{E1} to Q_{E2}. Now the market has found a new equilibrium. People wanted more pork, and the market has provided more pork. The price rise is the signal to farmers that they should produce more of that product, and as we can see such an adjustment takes place quite automatically, without any need for government or other intervention.

Let's not forget the beef market, however. What will happen there? Well, pork has become more popular, and beef less so. Therefore, people will want to buy less beef than before at any given price: the demand curve for beef shifts to the left.

Price

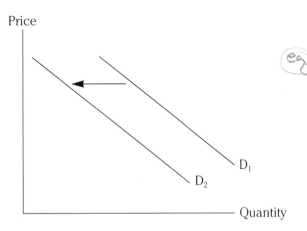

If we now bring the supply curve in, we see the effects of this change:

Price

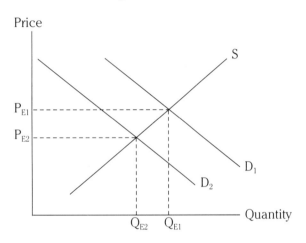

After the demand curve has shifted to the left, there is an excess supply of beef at the old equilibrium price P_{E1}. This will push prices down until a new equilibrium is found at P_{E2}. At that price, of course, beef production is less profitable than it used to be, so some farmers will give it up and so the equilibrium quantity falls from Q_{E1} to Q_{E2}.

Summarising, we can say that if people want more pork and less beef, pork prices will rise and beef prices will fall. After these price changes, pork production is more profitable and beef production less so; therefore farmers will react by producing more pork and less beef, which is exactly what consumers now want.

H2 SHIFTS IN THE SUPPLY CURVE

In analogy to these shifts in the demand curve, we get a shift in the supply curve if any of the determi-

nants of supply other than the price of the product in question changes. Suppose that due to some technological progress, such as more productive machinery or more effective fertiliser, industry can produce more of some product. We will then have a larger supply than before at any given price. This means that the supply curve has shifted to the right:

Price

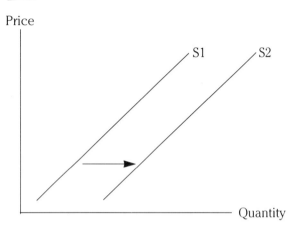

If we link this with the demand for the product in question, we see the consequences of such an increase in supply:

Price

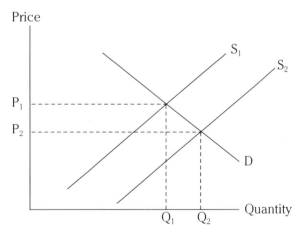

The old equilibrium price is P_{E1}. After the increase in supply to S_2, however, there is an excess supply at that price. This excess supply pushes the price down until a new equilibrium is found. In the diagram above, this is the case at P_{E2}. So, **an increase in supply leads to a fall in prices.** This explains why farmers have often had the experience that bumper crops lead to lower prices.

A fall in supply (caused by factors other than the price of the product in question) shifts the supply curve to the left, and **leads to a higher equilibrium price.** You can use the diagram above as an illustration, by assuming that supply has fallen from S_2 to S_1.

I
'WHAT, HOW, AND FOR WHOM' AGAIN

Before we apply the principles of supply and demand to insurance, let us go back briefly to the question we raised earlier: how does the market system solve the 'what, how, and for whom' question?

We have seen in this chapter how the market decides what to produce; supply and demand determine what quantity will be produced and at what price the output will be sold, and this holds good for every single product. But how does the market decide **how** to produce things? Well, essentially in the same way as it decides what to produce: namely, by means of prices. Just as there are prices for cabbage or motor cars, so there are prices for coal, uranium (think of the question whether to produce electricity from coal or from nuclear energy), labour, machinery, and so on.

The prices for those items determine which method of production is the **cheapest,** and that is the one which will be used if the market is allowed to operate. As for the **distribution of income,** this is again determined by prices. Just as there is a supply of, and a demand for, cabbages, so there is a supply of, and a demand for, various kinds of labour, capital (both physical capital like machinery and financial capital like bank loans) and land. These items are known as **factors of production:** more about them in Chapter 5. So, in a market economy, wages for the various types of work are determined by supply and demand. If certain skills are in short supply, people who have those skills will be able to earn more than people whose skills are no longer in demand.

People sometimes wonder why chairmen of large companies earn hundreds of thousands of pounds per year. Now that we know how prices come about in a market economy, that question is easy to answer: there are very few people who have the ability to hold such large organisations together and to give them some sense of direction. Consequently, the few who have such abilities can sell their labour at very high prices. If everybody had leadership abilities like Napoleon, company chairmen would not earn any more than anybody else. So, in a market economy, the competition-based price mechanism decides the 'what, how and for whom' problem in an impersonal, automatic way; acting like an 'invisible hand', as Adam Smith put it in 1776.

Reference

1   Source : BBC World Service, 3.4.1989

2
SELF-ASSESSMENT QUESTIONS

1. List a few items which affect:
   (a) the supply of;
   (b) the demand for;
   a given product.

   (a) Price of good, availability of Subs

   (b) Cost of producing/ Size of market/ Selling Price

2. Why does your company not double the price of its products?

   Would lose customers to competition

3. How do prices come about in an uncontrolled market?

   Interaction of Supply + Demand

4. Why are house prices higher in London than they are in most other parts of the UK?

   Demand is greater

5. Why are there waiting lists for council houses but not for owner-occupied houses in Britain?

   Demand greater than Supply

6. Explain the reason for the overproduction of certain farm products in the EC.

   State Subsidies + min price mean people produce more than customers willing to purchase

7. How do you think a rise in the price of coffee will affect the demand for tea?

    Inc it as they are Subs

8. How does a pure market economy decide whether to produce electricity from coal or from nuclear power? How would this decision be made in a planned economy?

    Market — by Supply + Demand
    Planned — Govt decision

2/15

ANSWERS TO SELF-ASSESSMENT QUESTIONS APPEAR OVERLEAF

2

ANSWERS TO SELF-ASSESSMENT QUESTIONS

1   (a)   The obvious example is the product's price. You might also have mentioned the price of other goods, and costs of production.

(b)   Again, the product's own price is a crucial factor. Others include prices of various kinds of other goods, people's income, and changing tastes or fashions.

2.   If you double your prices, your competitors are likely to take away all your customers.

3.   Prices will settle at the 'equilibrium' level where supply matches demand.

4.   Demand for housing in London is higher than elsewhere.

5.   Many people cannot afford to buy a house of their own. So, demand for such housing is lower than for cheap, rented accommodation, for which there are more potential tenants than houses.

6.   Minimum prices have been set for some products, above the equilibrium level, which encourage farmers to produce more than the market demands.

7.   The demand for tea should increase, as these are to some extent substitute goods.

8.   A pure market economy will make this decision on grounds of cost alone: people will choose the cheapest way of producing electricity. In a planned economy, other issues, such as political considerations, will come into the reckoning.

3

SUPPLY AND DEMAND APPLIED TO INSURANCE

A   The demand for insurance

B   The supply of insurance

In Chapter 2 we discussed supply and demand in general. Let us now apply these to insurance.

A
THE DEMAND FOR INSURANCE

What affects the demand for insurance? After all, it is not necessary for survival, so why do people buy insurance at all? To answer this question it is useful to look first at the kind of service provided by insurance companies.

A1   ATTITUDE TO RISK

Unlike many other industries, the insurance industry does not supply tangible goods, like food or clothing or motor cars. What insurance 'supplies' is a variety of **services,** and the main service provided by insurance companies is that of a **risk transfer mechanism.** Almost everything is exposed to risks of one kind or another. A building may be destroyed by fire; personal possessions may be lost or stolen, goods may be damaged while being transported; an individual may be unable to work after an illness or accident, and so on. Insurance cannot, of course, remove these risks. If you take out fire insurance, that does not mean that your house will not burn down. What insurance can do, however, is to transfer the financial burden resulting from that fire from the owner of the destroyed house to an insurance company. If your house burns down and you are not insured, you have to pay for the rebuilding yourself; if you are insured, your insurance company will pay that bill for you.

The main factor affecting a person's demand for insurance is that person's **attitude to risk.** Without insurance, few people would have enough money to buy another house if fire destroyed their current one, and many small businesses would simply have to cease trading if a fire destroyed their premises (leading to a loss of output and employment). Therefore, many people want to transfer to an insurance company those risks which they cannot or do not want to handle themselves. There are, of course, individual differences here. Some people want to take out insurance against just about every risk they may be exposed to. On the other hand, there are people who do not care about the future: some seem to think they are somehow immune from risks (the 'it won't happen to me' syndrome), while others are not aware of some of the risks they are exposed to. The last point (**risk awareness**) is quite an important one. If you are not aware that you are exposed to a certain risk, you will of course not take out insurance against that risk. In Britain, medical services are provided by the National Health Service, and some people may believe that this is so all over the world. If such a person goes to the USA on holiday and needs medical services while he is there, he will be in for a nasty shock, because he will get a bill from the doctor or hospital which he will have to pay. If you know before you go that there is no National Health Service in the USA, you can of course take out medical insurance (or simply travel insurance, because medical insurance is nearly always one of the covers provided by such policies). So, risk awareness and people's attitudes to risk are two important determinants of the demand for insurance.

Knowing this helps insurance companies in developing effective marketing strategies. If somebody does not believe in insurance you will not be able to sell him a policy even if you almost give it away for nothing. If a person's attitude to risk is such that he does not want to buy insurance, all the usual marketing instruments like price competition, 'free gifts' and the like will be ineffective. So, heightening people's risk awareness and trying to influence their attitude to risk and insurance is the basis of any effective marketing strategy.

A2 INCOME AND WEALTH

While a person's attitude to risk may be the most important factor affecting his or her demand for insurance, there are nevertheless a few other factors we have to consider. A risk-averse attitude makes a person want to buy insurance, but if he has just enough money to buy enough food and other basic necessities he will hardly feel able to buy insurance. Insurance is not necessary for sur-

vival, so if a person is on a low income then food, clothing, heating and other necessities come first. Only if one's income exceeds a certain level will one consider spending money on insurance, and the higher a person's income, the more likely he is to spend on insurance.

The reasons for this are twofold: first the affordability aspect as discussed above, and secondly the fact that people with higher incomes are likely to have more insurable goods. Normally, a person with a high income will have more personal possessions (maybe a house, more expensive furniture, and so on) than a person on a lower income, and he may want insurance cover for those goods.

This link between income and the demand for insurance is also relevant in the light of the increase in living standards. The country is getting richer all the time. Many goods and services, like holidays abroad or motor cars, which were the province of the rich only one generation ago are now within the reach of average wage earners. As people's incomes increase in real terms they will spend more on insurance. In fact, the amount of money spent on insurance has grown faster than national income in most developed countries.

A3 THE PRICE OF INSURANCE

Even if a person would like to buy insurance and has a sufficient income to do so, he will not pay just whatever price is asked for it. A person with a given degree of risk aversion is willing to pay up to a certain price for insurance; if the premium demanded by insurance companies exceeds this level the individual will prefer not to insure. So the price of insurance is another factor which affects people's decisions about whether or not to take out insurance. This is particularly relevant in a market where customers have a choice between a large number of competing companies.

In such a market the price not only determines whether an individual wants to buy insurance or not; it also determines which company he or she will go to. After all, why should you pay £30 for a policy from company A if an equally reputable company B offers the same policy for £25? There are of course some policyholders who do not bother to shop around, but an insurance company that charges more than its competitors do is likely to lose some of those policyholders who do compare prices. Also, business placed by brokers is likely to go to those companies which offer the lowest premium rates, so not charging more than competitors is particularly important for those companies which attract a lot of their business through brokers.

Another reason why the price of insurance affects demand is the fact that insurance is not the only way of handling risk.

? Spend a moment jotting down other ways that you can think of in which a risk may be handled, before reading the ideas given in the text below.

If somebody finds the premium too high he can always retain the risk, merely hoping that nothing will go wrong.

Another option is to take out a policy with a large deductible (or excess). Large organisations (like companies) have several other such **self-insurance** options open to them. They can, for example, set up internal insurance funds or **captive** insurance companies. A captive is an insurance company insuring the risks of its parent company; such risks can either be retained by the captive or reinsured in the reinsurance market. There is a whole new area of study, risk management, which aims at working out the best way of handling risk in a given situation. Many large organisations (insurance and others) now have risk management departments or subsidiaries which try to work out the best way of handling the risks their organisation faces, and some insurance brokers now advise clients not only on insurance, but also on alternative methods of handling their risks. So, insurance is one way of handling risks, but there are many others. The price of insurance is one of the factors which will determine whether a company wants to insure or whether it prefers to manage its risks in some other way. The more expensive it is to insure, the more attractive from a customer's point of view are the other ways of handling risk.

Talking about the price of insurance leads to the problem of inflation. Does inflation affect the demand for insurance, and if so, how? If inflation makes people poorer, they are likely to buy less insurance because their real income has fallen. In Britain, however, wages have risen faster than prices most of the time, and if inflation does not affect a person's real income there is no logical reason why inflation should increase or reduce that person's demand for insurance in real (i.e. inflation-adjusted) terms. To keep one's insurance cover the same in real terms, sums insured have of course to be increased in line with inflation. This is often done automatically by **index-linking** sums insured.

A4 TAX

Sometimes governments use tax incentives to encourage people to take out certain types of insurance, for example by making premiums tax-deductible. In Britain this is the case for contributions to pension funds, and for companies insurance premiums are 'allowable expenses' for corporation tax purposes. Such tax relief makes insurance cheaper, and hence more desirable from the policyholder's point of view.

In life assurance, the taxation of the life fund may affect the demand. Many people use life assurance as a means of saving. If the taxation of life assurance funds is different from the taxation of alternative forms of savings such as unit trusts or building society accounts, many savers will favour that method of saving which enjoys the most favourable tax treatment.

In his 1989 budget speech, the Chancellor of the Exchequer announced some major changes in the taxation of life assurance, to be phased in in the early 1990s. He said,

The tax regime of life assurance is unique. The present system dates back to the First World War and has developed over the years in a piecemeal way, leading to a state of affairs in which the incidence of tax is extremely uneven, with some life offices paying no tax at all. There is clearly a powerful case for reform, with a view to securing a tax regime which is more equitable both within the industry and as between life assurance and most other forms of savings.

A5 COMPULSORY INSURANCE

So far we have assumed that individuals or companies are free to decide whether or not they want to take out insurance. This may be true in most cases, but there are a few exceptions. If you want to drive a car you must have motor insurance, and if you want to employ other people you must take out employer's liability insurance. One could argue that National Insurance, the professional indemnity cover required by some professional bodies of their members, and the deposit protection funds for banks and other deposit taking institutions are other forms of compulsory insurance.

If a certain type of insurance is made compulsory, the demand for that type of insurance should increase. If motor insurance were not compulsory, some drivers would probably choose not to be insured. Of course, there will be some people who drive without insurance even though motor insurance is compulsory, but the number of drivers prepared to break the law is likely to be smaller than the number who would not insure if that option was available to them legally.

(**Note:** The examples given in this section relate to the situation in the United Kingdom. In other countries, rules may be different.)

A6 LIFE ASSURANCE

Finally, on the demand for insurance, a few words more about life assurance. The demand for life assurance is a more complex issue than the demand for general insurance, since life assurance is not only a risk transfer mechanism but also a method of saving (see A4). As far as the risk transfer aspect is concerned, the demand for life assurance is affected by all the factors discussed in the previous sections. As far as the savings element is concerned, the demand depends on factors like people's desire to save (which can vary considerably over time, and between regions), alternative methods of saving, tax implications, and so on.

B
THE SUPPLY OF INSURANCE

The supply of insurance can vary in the same way as the supply of any other good. Those factors which affect its supply are discussed below.

B1 REASONS FOR VIRTUALLY UNLIMITED SUPPLY IN SOME LINES OF BUSINESS

Insurance companies are in business in order to make a profit, and providing insurance cover and other insurance services is the ultimate source of their profits. There may be other sources of revenue (like investment income), but if a company did not write any business it would have no money to invest and hence there would be no investment income; more about this in section 13D2 (insurance company accounts). If, essentially, insurance companies make money by underwriting other people's risks, it seems logical to assume that they will try to attract as much business as they possibly can. In other words, it seems logical to assume that they will sell as many insurance services as they can find buyers for.

In many lines of business, this is in fact the case. Usually, writing more business means more profit at the end of the day. Many companies reward staff who generate additional sales, either by direct monetary rewards like bonuses or by improved promotion prospects. An increased volume of business also means a wider spread of risks, which should make it possible to assess risks more accurately: if, theoretically, you insure only one house, it is impossible to predict what fire damage there will be; if you insure 100,000 houses you can predict the likely damage pretty accurately. In many lines of business, companies really use all the methods they can think of in order to drum up more custom, some going as far as using subscribers' lists to magazines and similar material as sources of addresses to which they then send advertising material. Indeed, Sedgwick said in their annual report 1988, 'The supply of those willing to underwrite business far outstrips demand for their products, leading to conditions where premium rates have been falling since early 1987.'

In addition to attracting more business from outside, insurance companies can influence the amount of risk they have on their books by deciding how much of the risk they want to keep for their own account and how much they want to reinsure. The less business is reinsured, the more is kept for the account of the primary insurer. For example, in the section dealing with US business the Commercial Union said in its 1988 annual report: 'Premium income also benefited from a decision to retain more of our good quality commercial property insurance portfolio which was previously ceded to external reinsurers.' Commenting on the same topic, Sedgwick said in their 1988 annual report: 'Insurance companies and Lloyd's underwriters have been changing their pattern of buying reinsurance, retaining more risk for their own account, reducing the volume of proportional reinsurance exchanges and relying on excess of loss protection.' So, an insurance company can 'supply' more insurance itself if it decides to pass on less of its business to reinsurers (who, basically, provide insurers with cover against large levels of claims).

B2 LIMITATIONS ON SUPPLY

The story so far seems to indicate that insurers want to supply as large an amount of insurance services as they possibly can. In many areas of insurance this is indeed so. However, there are a few exceptions or limitations to companies' desire to maximise business.

To start with reinsurance; it is all very well to increase one's own supply of insurance services by ceding less business to reinsurers, but buying less reinsurance means one's own operations become more risky. This will also affect the company's solvency margin, which may affect the total amount of business one can write in the first place (more about solvency margins later in the book).

Furthermore, companies may be unwilling to accept business which they feel is not likely to give them a reasonable profit, or which constitutes unpredictable levels of risk. In some areas of **commercial** insurance, claims can occur a very long time after an event has taken place. For example, the negative consequences of exposure to asbestos and certain other harmful substances may only start manifesting themselves many years after a worker has first been exposed to such materials, and in 1990 a study claimed that expo-

sure to nuclear radiation may increase the risk of leukaemia not only for the people exposed to such radiation, but also for their children. In areas where such long-term effects exist, the frequency and severity of claims are very difficult to predict, and consequently some insurance companies will not be very keen to accept such business: it will be difficult for customers to obtain insurance cover for such risks.

Nor should it be assumed that the supply of **personal** insurance is unlimited. There are various risks of a more or less extreme nature where insurers will either not provide cover at all or do so only at unusually high premium rates. Examples include household contents or buildings insurance in certain areas where theft or subsidence are unusually likely, or covering a risk of non-standard construction; motor insurance where the proposer has a poor driving record or high-risk vehicle, or lives in a high-risk location; and substandard personal accident and health insurance risks.

Another area where companies may be reluctant to provide cover is where they feel they cannot get what they consider to be a reasonable price. For example, to return to the Commercial Union's 1988 annual report: 'Elsewhere (in the USA) there was a reduction in underlying exposure levels as we allowed business to lapse which could not be renewed at satisfactory premium levels and we refused to write new business at inadequate prices.'

Such inadequate prices may come about as a result of market forces, one company having a very large share of the market, or government price controls. If too many insurers want to sell insurance services, supply will exceed demand and prices will drop. Sooner or later, some companies will then decide it is no longer worth their while to do business in such a market, and withdraw. If one company has a very large share of one particular market (take for example the Norwich Union's present major share of the UK motorcycle insurance market), that company has a wide spread of risks and can set premiums accordingly. Other companies lack that spread of risks and are therefore not able to do business in that market profitably at the prices charged by the market leader. Consequently, other insurers may not be very interested in offering business in that market.

A third way in which inadequate price levels can come about is by government price controls. For example, motor insurance premiums are subject to price controls in the US state of Massachusetts and in the Canadian province of Ontario, and, after the acceptance of 'Proposition 103' in 1989, government price controls on a wider scale may be on the horizon for the Californian insurance market.

Government price controls are something of a two-edged sword, in insurance as well as in other markets. (If you cannot remember the drawbacks of such controls in the economy generally, refer back to section 2E.) They are usually introduced with the intention of protecting consumers; in insurance that means that maximum premiums are fixed by law. However, if insurance compa-nies feel they cannot earn what they consider to be a reasonable profit, they will withdraw from the market in question; and the cheap insurance you cannot get does not do you any good. Following the acceptance of 'Proposition 103' in California, for instance, the CU said: 'Our expo-sure to personal business lines in this market will be eliminated as quickly as possible.' (CU annual report 1988)

In the UK, the government does not normally attempt to interfere with prices in the insurance market. After all, if a policyholder feels one com-pany charges too high a price, he is free to go to another company. The British Government believes that in the insurance market competition among insurers provides sufficient protection for policyholders as far as prices are concerned.

3
SELF-ASSESSMENT QUESTIONS

1. List and explain three factors which affect a person's demand for insurance.

    (i) *Attitude to risk — Some wish to have all | Some circumstances*

    (ii) *Price — above a certain price people will stop paying*

    (iii) *Income — Ability to pay | Value of goods*

2. Why is a person's attitude to risk particularly important in determining his or her demand for insurance?

    If people do not know about potential risks they can't have them

3. How and why will an increase in a person's income affect his demand for insurance?

    (a) *Can pay for it*

    (b) *Possessions tend to be worth more.*

4. Suppose an insurance company increases its premium rates. List three ways in which a large corporate policyholder can react to this.

    Move to another company

    later a higher excess

    reduce cover

5. How does the fact that motor insurance is compulsory affect the demand for that type of insurance?

    Maintain it — as comp less likely that people will not be

6. In what ways can tax considerations affect the demand for insurance?

    Can increase life Assur

7. Why are insurance companies eager to increase their exposure to some markets, but reluctant to accept business in others?

   _____

   _____

   _____

8. What can make a market unprofitable from an insurance company's point of view?

   _____

   _____

   _____

9. Give reasons for and against government price controls in insurance.

   _____

   _____

   _____

10. Are government price controls on insurance common in the UK? Why (not)?

    _____

    _____

    _____

ANSWERS TO SELF-ASSESSMENT QUESTIONS APPEAR OVERLEAF

3
ANSWERS TO SELF-ASSESSMENT QUESTIONS

1. **Income.** If a person's income is very low, he will spend all of it on more necessary items like food, clothing and heating. Only when his income reaches a certain level will he be able to afford insurance.

    The price of insurance. A person of a given degree of risk aversion will be willing to pay only up to a certain price for insurance. If the price is higher than that, he will prefer not to insure.

    Attitude to risk. Some people are risk averse, and try to minimise their risks. Such people will be keen to buy insurance. A person who does not care about risk will not be interested in buying insurance.

2. A person who does not care about risk will have no desire to eliminate or reduce it. Such a person will therefore not be prepared to spend money on insurance, and all the usual marketing strategies used by insurance companies will be ineffective.

3. An increase in a person's income is likely to increase his demand for insurance. Not only is he better able to afford insurance for his existing goods, but he is likely to buy more goods, for which he may also want insurance.

4. The policyholder may pay the higher premium, may go to another insurance company, or may resort to self-insurance. This last category includes the use of internal insurance funds and captive companies.

5. The compulsory nature of motor insurance increases demand for it. If it were not compulsory, some drivers would probably choose not to buy it.

6. If premiums are tax-deductible, the cost of insurance is reduced. This should make it more attractive from the policyholder's point of view.

    If life funds are taxed differently from other forms of savings, the attractiveness of life assurance for the saver also varies.

7. Insurance companies want to increase their exposure to profitable markets, but are reluctant to accept business which is unlikely to be profitable or which is unduly risky.

8. An unprofitable market can result from unpredictable risks, or from premiums which are too low (whether because of intense competition or government price controls).

3

ANSWERS TO SELF-ASSESSMENT QUESTIONS

9. Government price controls may reduce premium levels and make the market more transparent, which is good for policyholders. On the other hand, if the government sets the price too low then companies will withdraw from the market, making cover difficult to obtain.

10. Such controls are not common in the UK. The current British Government believes that competition among insurance companies provides enough consumer protection as far as prices are concerned.

4
THE NATURE OF COMPETITION

LEARNING OBJECTIVES

After studying this chapter, you should be able to:

▷ say how competition affects a company, particularly with regard to pricing decisions;

▷ outline differences in the extent of competition in different sectors of the economy;

▷ define the main factors affecting the extent of competition in an industry;

▷ give details of the main forms of competition, with special emphasis on insurance;

▷ explain the roles which competition and government regulation play in the area of consumer protection;

INTRODUCTION

We saw in Chapter 2 that in a market economy prices are determined by the interaction of supply and demand.

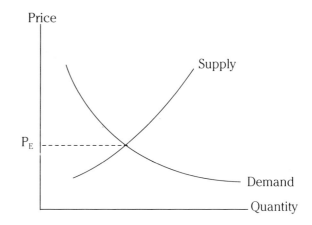

If the supply and demand curves are as shown in the diagram above, the equilibrium price will be P_E.

Q   Why, however, do firms accept this verdict of the market? Why do they not charge a price higher than PE?

A   To answer this question, just think of what would happen if a supermarket, or the insurance company you work for, increased its prices to some level above PE. Given that there is no price control on insurance, your company certainly has the **right** to increase its prices, but it does not have the **power** to force anybody to buy its products. So, if your company charged more than the market price, some people would buy their insurance elsewhere.

Your company is not the only insurance company in the market. There are many others, and it is the customers who decide with whom they will insure. This of course, does not apply only to

P.T.O

Why did producers charge what they like for their product?

insurance companies. The same is true of many other sectors of the economy. If you are not satisfied with the prices, the goods or the services provided by one supermarket, restaurant, bank, or car manufacturer, you can go to another one. In all these areas, a large number of companies **compete** for business, and customers can choose the company with which they want to deal, taking into account prices, the quality of the goods or services provided, and any other factor they consider relevant.

This does not mean, however, that all markets are subject to competition. The extent of competition differs considerably from one market to another; in some markets it is very intense, in others it may be non-existent.

? Spend a minute thinking of examples of each kind of market: where there is and is not competition. Two typical examples are given below.

If you find that a French car is cheaper than a British car of the same size and quality, you are free to buy that French car. If, on the other hand, you find out that electricity is cheaper in France than it is in Britain, you cannot plug yourself into the French power grid and tell your local electricity board to get lost. If you want to buy electricity, you can get it from only one supplier. There is nothing illegal about generating your own electricity, but this is not a practical alternative for most electricity consumers. So the extent of competition differs considerably, depending on what product we are talking about.

What causes these differences in the extent of competition, and in what ways do companies compete? These are the points we will look at in the following sections.

B
FACTORS AFFECTING THE EXTENT OF COMPETITION

The extent of competition is influenced by a number of factors. We will now look at these individually in depth.

B1 THE NUMBER OF FIRMS

One major factor affecting the extent of competition in an industry is the number of firms in that industry. If there is a large number of firms producing the same good or service, each customer can compare the prices and products on offer and buy from the supplier of his choice. We find this situation in many sectors of the British economy, among them insurance, banking, food and other retailing, restaurants, building services, hairdressers, car manufacturers and many others. If, on the other hand, there is only one supplier in a given market, customers have no choice as to the supplier; the only choice they have in such a situation is whether to buy the product or not. Electricity supplies, telephone services (with minor but growing exceptions) and some services provided by the Post Office can serve as examples.

To say that the number of firms in an industry affects the extent of competition is, strictly speaking, a bit of a simplification. For example, there are many electricity suppliers throughout the world, but that does not mean that they are in competition with one another. In most parts of the world you can buy electricity only from the one supplier who serves the area in which you live.

What really affects the extent of competition in an industry is the number of firms whose goods and services you can buy.

In some industries you can buy the products of producers located anywhere in the world. For example, anybody in Britain is free to buy Japanese cameras, Taiwanese textiles or German beer, so a British producer of cameras, textiles or beer faces competition from producers in those foreign countries. On the other hand, an electricity area board does not even face competition from a neighbouring electricity board a few miles away. Some services are also restricted to a fairly small geographical area, and providers of such services do not face competition from producers elsewhere. For example, you will hardly fly to India just to get a haircut, even if you know that a haircut is a lot cheaper in India than it is in Britain.

What is the situation in insurance, as far as this geographical aspect of competition is concerned? Well, it differs from one line of business to the next. British insurers providing household or private motor insurance, for example, face competition from other British companies offering these lines of business, but it is unlikely that an individual will want to insure his house with an insurer abroad. Marine insurance, aviation insurance and reinsurance, on the other hand, are truly international, and a British company providing such cover is exposed to competition not only from other British companies, but also from companies in many other countries. If Air Zimbabwe wants to insure its aeroplanes, or if the Zimbabwean company acting as primary insurer wants to reinsure this business, they can certainly get cover from a British insurer, but they can also get that cover from insurers in Switzerland or Japan.

B2 SUBSTITUTES

Another factor affecting the extent of competition in an industry is the availability or non-availability of **substitutes** for the product in question. If you want to travel by train from, say, London to Glasgow, then you have to go by British Rail. Since there is no other railway company linking these two cities, British Rail does not face any competition as far as rail travel is concerned. However, travelling by train is not the only way of travelling. If you want to go from London to Glasgow you can certainly go by train, but you can also travel by car, bus or aeroplane. This example shows that a company can face competition even if it is the only provider of a certain good or service, provided there are substitutes for the good or service in question; it is assumed here that travelling by bus or plane are reasonable substitutes for rail travel. The local electricity boards are the only suppliers of electricity in their service areas, so they face no competition from other electricity suppliers. However, they do face competition from suppliers of other forms of energy. There may be no acceptable alternative to electricity as far as lighting or powering certain types of machine is concerned, but when it comes to heating or cooking, electricity is in direct competition with oil, coal and gas.

Life assurance is an interesting example in this context. People buy life assurance for two rather different reasons: one is life cover, the other is saving. As far as the life cover is concerned, one life assurance company faces competition only from other life assurance companies, if we ignore the limited life cover available from some friendly societies. When it comes to saving, however, any one life office faces competition not only from other life offices but also from other forms of savings, like building society and bank accounts, unit trusts and government securities.

B3 CUSTOMERS' KNOWLEDGE AND ATTITUDES

If a prospective policyholder knows that company A charges £20 for a certain policy and company B charges £18 for the same cover, the customer will probably buy his policy from company B. Many people, however, do not shop around before buying insurance (or other products), but buy from a supplier with whose products they are familiar or who has been recommended to them by friends or relatives. If a customer does not know what is on offer with other companies, he obviously cannot make a rational choice as to which company to do business with.

? Try to analyse your own attitudes as a customer in the light of this. Do you develop loyalty to a supplier, or do you change readily in response to different prices and services?

In other words, factors like customer ignorance and customer loyalty to particular companies reduce the extent of competition, and a company which has a large number of loyal customers may be able to get away with charging higher premiums than its competitors.

Companies which want to inform potential customers that they offer better or cheaper products than their rivals can try to do so by advertising (see section C5). The presence of brokers should also increase market transparency: even if a customer does not know that company B charges less than company A for the same policy, his broker should know and advise him accordingly.

B4 EASE WITH WHICH FIRMS CAN ENTER THE MARKET

If you think you can sell apples more cheaply than the existing greengrocers in your area you are free to open a shop and sell apples at a lower price. However, even if you think you can profitably carry letters from, say, London to Glasgow by charging less than the Post Office does, you are not allowed to offer that service because the Post Office enjoys a virtual monopoly in the letter-carrying business. This example shows that some markets are far easier to enter than others, and the ease with which new businesses can enter a market affects the extent of competition in that market. Generally speaking, the easier it is to enter a market the more intense will be the competition in that market. If it is difficult to enter a market, those already in the market are sheltered from competition to a greater or lesser extent.

Why may it be difficult to enter a market? In some cases, there are legal barriers, as in the case of the Post Office's near monopoly in the letter-carrying business. In some countries (though not in Britain) a state-owned airline has a legally enshrined monopoly on air transport within that country, and no competitors are allowed. In India life assurance is a government monopoly, and in some countries only the central bank (the national equivalent of the Bank of England) is allowed to transact foreign exchange business.

Large capital requirements are another factor which makes it difficult to enter some markets. In Britain, the law does not prevent anybody from starting an airline or a steel mill, but very few people could do so because most people do not have the huge amount of capital which such a business requires. On the other hand, you do not need much capital to start a business as a greengrocer, newsagent or insurance broker, so these markets are far easier to enter as far as the need for capital is concerned.

A third kind of barrier which restricts access to certain markets is the qualifications which are required for some lines of business. To set up an insurance broking business, for example, you must have the qualifications required for registration as a broker. Likewise, you must be professionally qualified if you want to work as a doctor, dentist, optician or solicitor.

B5 COLLECTIVE AGREEMENTS

A further factor which may affect the extent of competition is a collective agreement among firms to charge the same prices, offer identical products, cut off supplies to firms which disobey collective agreements, and so on. If all companies charge the same price, customers can no longer get a lower price by going to another company. In many countries, such collective agreements are illegal. For example, the European Court of Justice ruled on 27 January 1987 that 'attempts by West German insurance companies to set common price rises for industrial fire cover were illegal' (The Times 28.1.87).

In Britain, there are several institutions set up to prevent collective agreements if these are thought to be against the public interest. Examples of such institutions are the Monopolies and Mergers Commission, the Restrictive Practices Court and the Office of Fair Trading.

Even when they are legal, collective agreements are difficult to enforce if there are companies which refuse to participate. If, for example, seven out of ten companies agree to raise prices, the main beneficiaries will be the three companies which do not take part in the agreement, since they will be able to increase their market share at the expense of their competitors. OPEC (the Organisation of Petroleum Exporting Countries) is a good example of a collective agreement which no longer works, partly because of increasing oil production by non-members (like Britain and Norway), and partly because even many member countries no longer adhere to OPEC resolutions.

B6 FOREIGN TRADE

Some people argue that the most effective consumer protection against monopolies, restrictive practices, collective agreements and the like is unrestricted foreign trade. If you are free to import, attempts by local manufacturers to raise prices or reduce competition are unlikely to be successful: if, as a result of such practices, domestically produced goods are more expensive than imported goods, consumers will buy foreign goods instead. The local producers then have the choice between losing their customers or revers-

collective agreements useless if free foreign trade

ing their price rises. Even if all domestic producers act in unison, or if there is only one local producer, the local producers have no market power if customers have the alternative of buying the product from overseas. So, free foreign trade increases competition considerably.

C
FORMS OF COMPETITION

In the previous section we looked at some of the factors which affect the extent of competition in a given market.

? For example, we studied the factors restricting access to particular markets. Jot down now the three major factors involved, and then compare your answers with section B4.

Let us now look at some of the forms which competition takes in those markets where it exists.

C1   PRICE

Probably the factor discussed more than any other in the context of competition is the price of the goods or services in question. If there are several producers in a market, consumers can decide which producer they want to buy from, and one of the factors which will influence their decision is the price charged by the various producers. Why pay producer A $5 if producer B offers the same product for $4.50? From a producer's point of view, this means he can try to attract more business by reducing his price to a level below that charged by his competitors. If we assume that the price compensates producers for the cost of production and gives them a profit, the producer who charges the lowest price is either the one who can produce at the lowest cost (in other words the most efficient producer), or the one who is prepared to work for the lowest profit.

Price competition is used in virtually all markets which are subject to competition; insurance and non-insurance alike. However, this does not necessarily mean that all producers charge the same price for the same good or service. A kilo of sugar will usually cost less in a supermarket than it does in a small corner shop, even though the product is exactly the same. Different insurance companies often quote different premium rates for the same kind of insurance (if you do not believe this, see for yourself by asking a number of companies what they charge for a given policy; you may be surprised by the differences). If price were the only factor determining where people buy, such differences would not be possible, since under such conditions everybody would buy from the supplier who charged the lowest price. The fact that price differences persist and high-price suppliers are able to retain customers shows that price is not the only factor determining where people buy, and consequently competition by means of price is not the only way in which companies can compete. Let us now look at some of the other forms of competition.

C2   'FREE GIFTS'

This is probably the form of competition most closely related to price competition. Instead of lowering the price of its product, a company gives customers a so-called free gift in addition to the main product: buy five bottles of this wine, and you get a mouse-trap free.

Such gifts used to be particularly popular in markets where companies were not supposed to reduce prices, for example because of collective agreements (see section B5). If you cannot reduce the price of your product you have to find some other way of attracting customers, and 'free gifts' were often used to circumvent collective agreements. Nowadays, however, such gifts are also used in markets where companies would be perfectly free to lower prices. Even some insurance companies have jumped on the band wagon, offering prospective policyholders 'free' calculators or other 'gifts' if they take out a policy.

Whether such 'gifts' (the cost of which have of course been incorporated into the price of the main product) are a good idea or a silly gimmick is probably a matter of personal opinion. Marketing people must be of the opinion that they are an effective way of attracting customers, otherwise they would not be used on such a large scale.

C3 LOCATION OF SHOPS AND SHOP OPENING HOURS

This is an important factor in retail trade. A given product will often be cheaper in a supermarket than in a small shop, but the supermarket may be two miles away whereas the small shop is right at your doorstep. Is it really worth travelling two miles just to save a few pence? Many small shops are able to retain customers in spite of higher prices, because they are more conveniently located or have longer or more convenient opening hours than their low-price competitors.

? Apply this point to insurance (or other services) which you have bought. Were the insurers easy to find and contact? Did you use a convenient intermediary? Did you shop around or merely use the service which was easiest to find?

C4 QUALITY OF THE GOODS OR SERVICES PROVIDED

If there is a (real or imagined) difference in the quality of different products, people will prefer the goods or services they consider to be of better quality, and may be prepared to pay a higher price for them. Once a producer has convinced buyers that his product is of better quality than that of his rivals, he can use the quality argument as a tool of competition in at least two different ways.

First, he can charge the same price as his competitors do, hoping to increase his sales at his rivals' expense; after all, why should a customer buy a lower quality product if he can get a higher quality one at the same price? Alternatively the manufacturer can use the (supposedly) better quality as a justification for charging a higher price: if customers believe that the products of manufacturer A are of better quality than the products of manufacturer B, some of them may buy manufacturer A's product even if it costs a bit more.

In manufacturing, the technical characteristics of the products and the after-sale service provided are important parts of the quality package. In retailing, the advice customers get from the shopkeeper is an important part of the quality of service. Some shops offer a wide variety of goods, but offer hardly any advice on the goods they sell. Other shops are more specialised, and the sales staff are experts on the goods they sell and can give customers detailed information and advice. Whether a customer needs such advice depends largely on the product involved and on his own knowledge about it. Nobody needs much advice when buying a salad bowl or a mouse-trap, but if you want to buy a personal computer you may need advice from a computer expert to choose the model best suited to your requirements, unless you are a computer expert yourself. Customers who want advice will obviously prefer shops where such advice can be provided.

Q How do you think that this 'quality question' arises with regard to insurance?

A In insurance, the quality question arises at two points: firstly the quality of the cover provided, and then the quality of service, for example in handling claims. A company which handles claims promptly and without much bureaucracy will be perceived by policyholders as offering a better service than a company which takes ages to settle a claim. So the types of policies, the extent of cover provided, and speed and generosity in handling claims are important quality aspects of insurance products and can be used as an instrument of competition.

In life assurance, bonuses* and surrender values are of particular importance. The financial press regularly publishes comparisons of the performance of policies issued by various life offices, and a company with a good track record of past bonuses, and a reputation for giving people who surrender their policies early a fair deal, is obviously in a better competitive position than is a company with the opposite reputation. This is particularly relevant now that the **Financial Services Act 1986** is in force. Under this Act, independent financial intermediaries must be seen to be giving

---

*Bonuses: some life-assurance policies are 'with-profits', allowing the policyholder to share in the profit made from investment by the assurance company. The share of the profit is paid when the policy matures or in the event of a claim, and is known as a bonus.

'best advice' to their clients; it would be difficult for such an intermediary to recommend the policy of a company with a lousy record and still to claim that he is giving his client the best possible advice.

C5   ADVERTISING

A very common tool of competition is advertising. The advertiser tries to attract people's attention, to inform them about the products he offers and, if possible, to persuade them that his products are better or cheaper than rival products.

If people are well informed about the products of company A, but hardly anyone knows that company B exists, then company A is obviously in a better position to sell its products. Whether advertising increases the price consumers have to pay is almost impossible to say. Of course advertising costs something, and the consumer is the one who ultimately pays for it. On the other hand, if an advertising campaign is successful it allows a firm to increase its sales and hence its production, and it is often possible to produce more efficiently on a larger scale. In this case the **'economies of scale'** may lower the cost per unit of output. For example, a manufacturer may get bulk discounts if he buys larger quantities of raw materials, and the larger volume of production may justify the purchase of more sophisticated machinery. In such cases the cost per unit of output falls, and this fall may more than compensate for the cost of advertising.

C6   COMMISSIONS PAID TO BROKERS

This is a point relevant to insurance, though not to many other industries. Many insurance companies attract a large part of their business through brokers. Therefore, instead of trying to persuade the ultimate buyers of insurance that its products are preferable to the products of its rivals, an insurance company can try to persuade brokers to recommend its products rather than those of its competitors. One way of doing that is to pay brokers a higher rate of commission than other insurance companies do.

In principle there is nothing wrong with this, unless it tempts less reputable brokers to recom-mend to clients not what is best for them, but what produces the fattest commission for the broker. An honest broker will of course recommend the product which is best for the client. After all, that is why the client uses the services of the broker, and knowingly to recommend a product which is not in the client's best interest is really a breach of trust by the broker. And, in the long term, honesty is often the best policy even if we leave moral arguments out altogether. A broker never knows how much a client knows, and if a client notices that the broker wants to sell him something which is clearly not the product best suited to his requirements, the client will hardly have much confidence in that broker when it comes to future deals. Dissatisfied customers are not a particularly good way of building a business!

D
CONSUMER PROTECTION: COMPETITION AND REGULATION

At the beginning of this chapter we asked why companies accepted the market's verdict about prices, instead of fixing prices at a higher level. What prevents companies from charging higher and higher prices?

One force which prevents companies from increasing prices beyond a certain level is competition, which we have discussed in some detail in this chapter. If one shop charges £2 for a given product, then some other shop may be able to charge a bit more if it is in a particularly good location or if customers prefer it for some other reason, but there is clearly an upper limit to the price other shops can charge. If a shop goes beyond that limit it will lose customers. However, where does this leave those sectors of the economy where there is no (or at least not much) competition, like electricity supplies, telephone services or the Post Office's letter-carrying business?

Well, these activities are normally subject to **government regulation** in one form or another. This does not mean that there is no government interference in competitive markets (think of the Insurance Companies Acts), but in areas where competition cannot protect the consumer the government tries to regulate the market in such a way that the monopolists cannot abuse their monopoly power to exploit consumers. Some of these markets are in fact in the hands of a government-owned enterprise, like the Post Office, and these organisations do not charge the highest price the market will bear, but a price based on the cost of providing the service plus what the government considers to be a reasonable profit margin. Private sector monopolies, like telephone services, are also subject to government regulation. In the UK, British Telecom must keep its price changes 4.5% below the inflation rate (more about the inflation rate in section 6A). That means that if we have 8.5% inflation British Telecom is allowed to increase its prices by 4%, and if we have 3.5% inflation it must reduce its prices by one per cent. The reason for the formula 'inflation rate minus 4.5%' is that, in the light of the rapid technological progress in this area, the government believes British Telecom can earn a reasonable amount of profit by limiting its price rises in this way. In North America, public utilities like telephone and electricity supply companies are also subject to government supervision, although there it is not prices but profits which are controlled. For example, Maritime Telegraph and Telephone, the company providing telephone and related services in the Canadian province of Nova Scotia, says in its 1988 annual report: 'A decision from the Board of Commissioners of Public Utilities for the province of Nova Scotia, in November 1988, set the allowed rate of return on common equity at 13.5%.' ('Common equity' is the amount which shareholders have invested in the company; more about this in Part III, the Financial Environment.) In deciding what prices to charge, the telephone company must take into account that it is not allowed to earn more than this specified amount of profit.

So, competition and government regulation are the two main forms of consumer protection in the market place. You can find more about consumer protection in the insurance industry in section 18F, at the end of this book. If a consumer or the government feels that somebody is exploiting monopoly power at the public's expense they can refer the matter to one of the bodies set up for investigating such misdemeanours, like the Office of Fair Trading, the Monopolies and Mergers Commission or the Restrictive Practices Court.

E

ABI CODES OF PRACTICE

To provide guidelines for the conduct of business between insurance companies, insurance intermediaries and policyholders (current or prospective), the Association of British Insurers* has laid down various codes of practice, some of which are reproduced at the end of this chapter.

---

*The ABI is the main trade association for insurers in the United Kingdom. It exists to protect and promote the interests of its members in a wide variety of ways.

ASSOCIATION OF BRITISH INSURERS

STATEMENT OF GENERAL INSURANCE PRACTICE

The following Statement of normal insurance practice applies to general insurances of policyholders resident in the UK and insured in their private capacity only.

1. **PROPOSAL FORMS**

    (a) The declaration at the foot of the proposal form should be restricted to completion according to the proposer's knowledge and belief.

    (b) Neither the proposal form nor the policy shall contain any provision converting the statements as to past or present fact in the proposal form into warranties. But insurers may require specific warranties about matters which are material to the risk.

    (c) If not included in the declaration, prominently displayed on the proposal form should be a statement:-

        (i) drawing the attention of the proposer to the consequences of the failure to disclose all material facts, explained as those facts an insurer would regard as likely to influence the acceptance and assessment of the proposal;

        (ii) warning that if the proposer is in any doubt about facts considered material, he should disclose them.

    (d) Those matters which insurers have found generally to be material will be the subject of clear questions in proposal forms.

    (e) So far as is practicable, insurers will avoid asking questions which would require expert knowledge beyond that which the proposer could reasonably be expected to possess or obtain or which would require a value judgement on the part of the proposer.

    (f) Unless the prospectus or the proposal form contains full details of the standard cover offered, and whether or not it contains an outline of that cover, the proposal form shall include a prominent statement that a specimen copy of the policy form is available on request.

    (g) Proposal forms shall contain a prominent warning that the proposer should keep a record (including copies of letters) of all information supplied to the insurer for the purpose of entering into the contract.

    (h) The proposal form shall contain a prominent statement that a copy of the completed form:-

        (i) is automatically provided for retention at the time of completion; or

        (ii) will be supplied as part of the insurer's normal practice; or

        (iii) will be supplied on request within a period of three months after its completion.

    (i) An insurer shall not raise an issue under the proposal form, unless the policyholder is provided with a copy of the completed form.

2. **CLAIMS**

    (a) Under the conditions regarding notification of a claim, the policyholder shall not be asked to do more than report a claim and subsequent developments as soon as reasonably possible except in the case of legal processes and claims which a third party requires the policyholder to notify within a fixed time where immediate advice may be required.

    (b) An insurer will not repudiate liability to indemnify a policyholder:-

        (i) on grounds of non-disclosure of a material fact which a policyholder could not reasonably be expected to have disclosed;

        (ii) on grounds of misrepresentation unless it is a deliberate or negligent misrepresentation of a material fact;

> (iii) on grounds of a breach of warranty or condition where the circumstances of the loss are unconnected with the breach unless fraud is involved.
>
> Paragraph 2 (b) above does not apply to Marine and Aviation policies.

(c) Liability under the policy having been established and the amount payable by the insurer agreed, payment will be made without avoidable delay.

3. RENEWALS

(a) Renewal notices shall contain a warning about the duty of disclosure including the necessity to advise changes affecting the policy which have occurred since the policy inception or last renewal date, whichever was the later.

(b) Renewal notices shall contain a warning that the proposer should keep a record (including copies of letters) of all information supplied to the insurer for the purpose of renewal of the contract.

4. COMMENCEMENT

Any changes to insurance documents will be made as and when they need to be reprinted, but the Statement will apply in the meantime.

5. POLICY DOCUMENTS

Insurers will continue to develop clearer and more explicit proposal forms and policy documents whilst bearing in mind the legal nature of insurance contracts.

6. DISPUTES

The provisions of the Statement shall be taken into account in arbitration and any other referral procedures which may apply in the event of disputes between policyholders and insurers relating to matters dealt with in the Statement.

7. EEC

This Statement will need reconsideration when the Draft EEC Directive on Insurance Contract Law is adopted and implemented in the United Kingdom.

Reference: J/636/001

January 1986

ASSOCIATION OF BRITISH INSURERS
ALDERMARY HOUSE, QUEEN STREET, LONDON EC4N 1TT   TEL: 01-248 4477

ASSOCIATION OF BRITISH INSURERS

STATEMENT OF LONG-TERM INSURANCE PRACTICE

The following Statement of normal insurance practice applies to policies of long-term insurance effected in the UK in a private capacity by individuals resident in the UK.

1. **PROPOSAL FORMS**

   (a) If the proposal form calls for the disclosure of material facts a statement should be included in the declaration, or prominently displayed elsewhere on the form or in the document of which it forms part:-

       (i) drawing attention to the consequences of failure to disclose all material facts and explaining that these are facts that an insurer would regard as likely to influence the assessment and acceptance of a proposal;

       (ii) warning that if the signatory is in any doubt about whether certain facts are material, these facts should be disclosed.

   (b) Neither the proposal nor the policy shall contain any provision converting the statements as to past or present fact in the proposal form into warranties except where the warranty relates to a statement of fact concerning the life to be assured under a life of another policy. Insurers, may, however, require specific warranties about matters which are material to the risk.

   (c) Those matters which insurers have commonly found to be material should be the subject of clear questions in proposal forms.

   (d) Insurers should avoid asking questions which would require knowledge beyond that which the signatory could reasonably be expected to possess.

   (e) The proposal form or a supporting document should include a statement that a copy of the policy form or of the policy conditions is available on request.

   (f) The proposal form or a supporting document should include a statement that a copy of the completed proposal form is available on request.

2. **POLICIES AND ACCOMPANYING DOCUMENTS**

   (a) Insurers will continue to develop clearer and more explicit proposal forms and policy documents whilst bearing in mind the legal nature of insurance contracts.

   (b) Life assurance policies or accompanying documents should indicate:-

       (i) the circumstances in which interest would accrue after the assurance has matured; and

       (ii) whether or not there are rights to surrender values in the contract and, if so, what those rights are.

   (Note: The appropriate sales literature should endeavour to impress on proposers that a whole life or endowment assurance is intended to be a long-term contract and that surrender values, especially in the early years, are frequently less than the total premiums paid.)

3. **CLAIMS**

   (a) An insurer will not unreasonably reject a claim. In particular, an insurer will not reject a claim or invalidate a policy on grounds of non-disclosure or misrepresentation of a fact unless:

       (i) it is a material fact; and

       (ii) it is a fact within the knowledge of the proposer; and

       (iii) it is a fact which the proposer could reasonably be expected to disclose.

   (It should be noted that fraud or deception will, and reckless or negligent non-disclosure or misrepresentation of a material fact may, constitute grounds for rejection of a claim.)

(b)   Except where fraud is involved, an insurer will not reject a claim or invalidate a policy on grounds of a breach of a warranty unless the circumstances of the claim are connected with the breach and unless:

       (i)   the warranty relates to a statement of fact concerning the life to be assured under a life of another policy and that statement would have constituted grounds for rejection of a claim by the insurer under 3 (a) above if it had been made by the life to be assured under an own life policy or

       (ii)   the warranty was created in relation to specific matters material to the risk and it was drawn to the proposer's attention at or before the making of the contract.

(c)   Under any conditions regarding a time limit for notification of a claim, the claimant will not be asked to do more than report a claim and subsequent developments as soon as reasonably possible.

(d)   Payment of claims will be made without avoidable delay once the insured event has been proved and the entitlement of the claimant to receive payment has been established.

(e)   When the payment of a claim is delayed more than two months, the insurer will pay interest on the cash sum due, or make an equivalent adjustment to the sum, unless the amount of such interest would be trivial. The two month period will run from the date of the happening of the insured event (i.e. death or maturity) or, in the case of a unit linked policy, from the date on which the unit linking ceased, if later. Interest will be calculated at a relevant market rate from the end of the two month period until the actual date of payment.

4.   DISPUTES

The provisions of the Statement shall be taken into account in arbitration and any other referral procedures which may apply in the event of disputes between policyholders and insurers relating to matters dealt with in the Statement.

5.   COMMENCEMENT

Any changes to insurance documents will be made as and when they need to be reprinted, but the Statement will apply in the meantime.

Note Regarding Industrial Assurance Policyholders

Policies effected by industrial assurance policyholders are included amongst the policies to which the above Statement of Long-Term Insurance Practice applies. Those policyholders also enjoy the additional protection conferred upon them by the Industrial Assurance Acts 1923 to 1969 and Regulations issued thereunder. These Acts give the Industrial Assurance Commissioner wide powers to cover inter alia the following aspects:-

(a)   Completion of proposal forms.

(b)   Issue and maintenance of Premium Receipt Books.

(c)   Notification in Premium Receipt Books of certain statutory rights of a policyholder including rights to:-

       (i)   an arrears notice before forfeiture,

       (ii)   free policies and surrender values for certain categories of policies,

       (iii)   relief from forfeiture of benefit under a policy on health grounds unless the proposer has made an untrue statement of knowledge and belief as to the assured's health.

       (iv)   reference to the Commissioner as arbitrator in disputes between the policyholder and the company or society.

The offices transacting industrial assurance business have further agreed that any premium (or deposit) paid on completion of the proposal form will be returned to the proposer if, on issue, the policy document is rejected by him or her.

J/636/001

January 1986 (2nd Edition)

ASSOCIATION OF BRITISH INSURERS

ALDERMARY HOUSE, QUEEN STREET, LONDON EC4N 1TT   TEL: 01-248 4477

ASSOCIATION OF BRITISH INSURERS

GENERAL INSURANCE BUSINESS - CODE OF PRACTICE FOR ALL INTERMEDIARIES (INCLUDING EMPLOYEES OF INSURANCE COMPANIES) OTHER THAN REGISTERED INSURANCE BROKERS (INTRODUCED JANUARY 1989)

This Code applies to general business as defined in the Insurance Companies Act 1982, but does not apply to reinsurance business. As a condition of membership of the Association of British Insurers, members undertake to enforce this Code and to use their best endeavours to ensure that all those involved in selling their policies observe its provisions.

It shall be an overriding obligation of an intermediary at all times to conduct business with the utmost good faith and integrity.

In the case of complaints from policyholders (either direct or indirect, for example through a trading standards officer or citizens advice bureau), the insurance company concerned shall require an intermediary to co-operate so that the facts can be established. An intermediary shall inform the policyholder complaining that he can take his problem direct to the insurance company concerned.

A. GENERAL SALES PRINCIPLES

1. The intermediary shall:-

    (i)   where appropriate, make a prior appointment to call. Unsolicited or unarranged calls shall be made at an hour likely to be suitable to the prospective policyholder;

    (ii) when he makes contact with the prospective policyholder, identify himself and explain as soon as possible that the arrangements he wishes to discuss could include insurance. He shall make it known that he is:-

        (a) an employee of an insurance company, for whose conduct the company accepts responsibility; or

        (b) an agent of one company, for whose conduct the company accepts responsibility; or

        (c) an agent of two or up to six companies, for whose conduct the companies accept responsibility; or

        (d) an independent intermediary seeking to act on behalf of the prospective policyholder, for whose conduct the company/companies do not accept responsibility;

    (iii) ensure as far as possible that the policy proposed is suitable to the needs and resources of the prospective policyholder;

    (iv) give advice only on those insurance matters in which he is knowledgeable and seek or recommend other specialist advice when necessary; and

    (v)   treat all information supplied by the prospective policyholder as completely confidential to himself and to the company or companies to which the business is being offered.

2. The intermediary shall not:-

    (i)   inform the prospective policyholder that his name has been given by another person, unless he is prepared to disclose that person's name if requested to do so by the prospective policyholder and has that person's consent to make that disclosure;

    (ii) make inaccurate or unfair criticisms of any insurer; or

    (iii) make comparisons with other types of policy unless he makes clear the differing characteristics of each policy.

B. EXPLANATION OF THE CONTRACT

The intermediary shall:-

    (i)   identify the insurance company;

    (ii) explain all the essential provisions of the cover afforded by the policy, or policies, which he is recommending, so as to ensure as far as possible that the prospective policyholder understands what he is buying;

    (iii) draw attention to any restrictions and exclusions applying to the policy;

    (iv) if necessary, obtain from the insurance company specialist advice in relation to items (ii) and (iii) above;

    (v) not impose any charge in addition to the premium required by the insurance company without disclosing the amount and purpose of such charge; and

    (vi) if he is an independent intermediary, disclose his commission on request.

C. DISCLOSURE OF UNDERWRITING INFORMATION

The intermediary shall, in obtaining the completion of the proposal form or any other material:-

    (i) avoid influencing the prospective policyholder and make it clear that all the answers or statements are the latter's own responsibility; and

    (ii) ensure that the consequences of non-disclosure and inaccuracies are pointed out to the prospective policyholder by drawing his attention to the relevant statement in the proposal form and by explaining them himself to the prospective policyholder.

D. ACCOUNTS AND FINANCIAL ASPECTS

The intermediary shall, if authorised to collect monies in accordance with the terms of his agency appointment:-

    (i) keep a proper account of all financial transactions with a prospective policyholder which involve the transmission of money in respect of insurance;

    (ii) acknowledge receipt (which, unless the intermediary has been otherwise authorised by the insurance company, shall be on his own behalf) of all money received in connection with an insurance policy and shall distinguish the premium from any other payment included in the money; and

    (iii) remit any such monies so collected in strict conformity with his agency appointment.

E. DOCUMENTATION

The intermediary shall not withhold from the policyholder any written evidence or documentation relating to the contract of insurance.

F. EXISTING POLICYHOLDERS

The intermediary shall abide by the principles set out in this Code to the extent that they are relevant to his dealings with existing policyholders.

G. CLAIMS

If the policyholder advises the intermediary of an incident which might give rise to a claim, the intermediary shall inform the company without delay, and in any event within three working days, and thereafter give prompt advice to the policyholder of the company's requirements concerning the claim, including the provision as soon as possible of information required to establish the nature and extent of the loss. Information received from the policyholder shall be passed to the company without delay.

H. PROFESSIONAL INDEMNITY COVER FOR INDEPENDENT INTERMEDIARIES

The intermediary shall obtain, and maintain in force, professional indemnity insurance in accordance with the requirements of the Association of British Insurers as set out in the Annex, which may be updated from time to time.

I. LETTERS OF APPOINTMENT

This Code of Practice shall be incorporated verbatim or by reference in all Letters of Appointment of non-registered intermediaries and no policy of the company shall be sold by such intermediaries except within the terms of such a Letter of Appointment.

ANNEX

**CODE OF PRACTICE FOR THE SELLING OF GENERAL INSURANCE
PROFESSIONAL INDEMNITY COVER REQUIRED
FOR NON-REGISTERED INDEPENDENT INTERMEDIARIES**

As from 1st January 1989 (new agents) and by 1st July 1989 (existing agents) all non-registered independent intermediaries must take out and maintain in force professional indemnity cover in accordance with the requirements set out below.

The insurance may be taken out with any authorised UK or EEC insurer who has agreed to:-

(a) issue cover in accordance with the requirements set out below;

(b) provide the intermediary with an annual certificate as evidence that the cover meets the ABI requirements, this certificate to contain the name and address including postcode of the intermediary, the policy number, the period of the policy, the limit of indemnity, the self-insured excess and the name of the insurer;

(c) send a duplicate certificate to ABI at the time the certificate is issued to the intermediary;

(d) inform ABI, by means of monthly lists, of any cases of non-renewal, cancellation of the cover mid-term or of the cover becoming inadequate.

[handwritten margin note: What an insurer offering Prof. indemnity to I.S.S. must agree to d]

The requirements are as follows:-

A. **LIMITS OF INDEMNITY**

The policy shall at inception and at each renewal date, which shall not be more than 12 months from inception or the last renewal date, provide a minimum limit of indemnity of either:-

(a) a sum equal to three times the annual general business commission of the business for the last accounting period ending prior to inception or renewal of the policy, or a sum of £250,000, whichever sum is the greater.

In no case shall the minimum limit of indemnity be required to exceed £5m, and a minimum sum of £250,000 shall apply at all times to each and every claim or series of claims arising out of the same occurrence.

or

(b) a sum equal to three times the annual general business commission of the business for the last accounting period ending prior to inception or renewal of the policy, or a sum of £500,000 whichever sum shall be the greater.

In no case shall the minimum limit of indemnity be required to exceed £5m.

B. **MAXIMUM SELF-INSURED EXCESS**

The maximum self-insured excess permitted in normal circumstances shall be 1% of the minimum limit of indemnity required by Paragraph A(a) or A(b) above as the case may be. Subject to the agreement of the professional indemnity insurer, the self-insured excess may be increased to a maximum of 2% of such minimum limit of indemnity.

C. SCOPE OF POLICY COVER

The policy shall indemnify the insured:-

(a) against losses arising from claims made against the insured:

    (i) for breach of duty in connection with the business by reason of any negligent act, error or omission; and

    (ii) in respect of libel or slander or in Scotland defamation, committed in the conduct of the business by the insured, any employee or former employee of the insured, and where the business is or was carried on in partnership any partner or former partner of the insured; and

    (iii) by reason of any dishonest or fraudulent act or omission committed or made in the conduct of the business by any employee (other than a director of a body corporate) or former employee (other than a director of a body corporate) of the insured;

    and

(b) against claims arising in connection with the business in respect of:-

    (i) any loss of money or other property whatsoever belonging to the insured or for which the insured is legally liable in consequence of any dishonest or fraudulent act or omission of any employee (other than a director of a body corporate) or former employee (other than a director of a body corporate) of the insured; and

    (ii) legal liability incurred by reason of loss of documents and costs and expenses incurred in replacing or restoring such documents.

D. GENERAL BUSINESS ONLY

The above requirements relate only to the intermediary's general insurance business.

Association of British Insurers
November 1988

ASSOCIATION OF BRITISH INSURERS
ALDERMARY HOUSE, QUEEN STREET, LONDON EC4N 1TT   TEL: 01-248 4477

ASSOCIATION OF BRITISH INSURERS

LIFE INSURANCE (NON-INVESTMENT BUSINESS) SELLING CODE OF PRACTICE

INTRODUCTION

The term "life insurance" used in this code covers only those types of long term insurance contracts and permanent health insurance which are not "investments" within the terms of Schedule 1 to the Financial Services Act 1986.

Part I of the code applies to "intermediaries", i.e. all those persons selling life insurance who are not subject to rules regulating the selling of life insurance in respect of the business in question.

Part II of the code applies to "introducers", i.e. those who merely introduce a prospective policyholder to a life office but take no part in the subsequent selling process.

Members of the Association have undertaken, as a condition of membership, to enforce the code and to use their best endeavours to ensure that all those involved in selling their policies observe its provisions.

In the case of complaints from policyholders received either directly or indirectly, e.g. through a trading standards officer or Citizens Advice Bureau, that an intermediary has acted in breach of the code, the intermediary shall be required to co-operate with the life office concerned in establishing the facts. The complainant shall be informed that he can refer the complaint to the relevant life office.

PART I - CODE FOR INTERMEDIARIES

It shall be an overriding obligation of an intermediary at all times to conduct business with the utmost good faith and integrity.

A. GENERAL SALES PRINCIPLES

1. The intermediary shall -

(i) where appropriate make a prior appointment to call. Unsolicited or unarranged calls shall be made at an hour likely to be suitable to the prospective policyholder;

(ii) when he makes contact with the prospective policyholder, identify himself and explain as soon as possible that the arrangements he wishes to discuss could include the life insurance policies of one or a number of offices, as the case may be;

(iii) ensure as far as possible that the policy proposed is suitable to the needs and not beyond the resources of the prospective policyholder;

(iv) give advice only on those matters in which he is competent to deal and seek or recommend other specialist advice if this seems appropriate;

(v) treat all information supplied by the prospective policyholder as completely confidential to himself and to the life office or offices to which the business is being offered;

(vi) in making comparisons with other types of policy, make clear the different characteristics of each policy.

2. The intermediary shall not -

(i)   inform the prospective policyholder that his name has been given by another person unless he is prepared to disclose that person's name if requested to do so by the prospective policyholder and has that person's consent to make that disclosure;

(ii)   make inaccurate or unfair criticisms of any insurers;

(iii)   attempt to persuade a prospective policyholder to cancel any existing policies unless these are clearly unsuited to his needs.

B. EXPLANATION OF THE CONTRACT

The intermediary shall -

(i)   explain all the essential provisions of the contract, or contracts, which he is recommending so as to ensure as far as possible that the prospective policyholder understands what he is committing himself to;

(ii)   draw attention to any restrictions applying to the policy;

(iii)   draw attention to the long term nature of the policy and, where appropriate, to the consequent effects of early discontinuance and surrender;

(iv)   in the case of change to a policy qualifying for tax relief on the premiums, draw attention to the fact that the relief may be lost as a result of the change.

C. DISCLOSURE OF UNDERWRITING INFORMATION

The intermediary shall in obtaining the completion of the proposal form or any other material -

(i)   avoid influencing the proposer and make clear that all the answers or statements are the latter's own responsibility;

(ii)   ensure that the consequences of non-disclosure and inaccuracies are pointed out to the proposer by drawing his attention to the relevant statement in the proposal form and by explaining them himself to the proposer.

D. ACCOUNTS AND FINANCIAL ASPECTS

The intermediary shall -

(i)   keep a proper account of all financial transactions with a prospective policyholder which involve the transmission of money in respect of insurance;

(ii)   acknowledge receipt (which unless the intermediary has been otherwise authorised by the office shall be on his own behalf) of all money received in connection with an insurance policy and shall distinguish the premium from any other payment included in the money;

(iii)   forward without delay any money received for life insurance.

PART II - CODE FOR INTRODUCERS

1. The introducer shall -

(i)   give advice only on those matters in which he is competent and seek assistance from the life office when necessary;

(ii)   at the earliest opportunity call upon a qualified representative from the life office whose contract he wishes to be presented to the prospective policyholder, to explain the contract to the prospective policyholder.

2. The introducer shall not -

(i)   solicit life insurance business outside the terms of his appointment;

(ii)   attempt to influence the prospective policyholder with regard to the completion of the proposal form.

Association of British Insurers, Aldermary House, Queen Street, London EC4N 1TT. Tel: 01-248 4477   11th August 1988.

4
SELF-ASSESSMENT QUESTIONS

1. Why does your company not double its premium rates?

   - People would go to another company
   - or just wouldn't insure

2. What causes differences in the extent of competition in various sectors of the economy?

   No of firms
   quality of good
   price

3. In what way does the number of firms in a market affect the extent of competition in that market?

   greater the number more competition
   the lower the less competition when
   sub goods available

4. Westland is the only manufacturer of helicopters in the UK. Does this mean there is no competition in the market for helicopters?

   foreign competition
   if price is less high people will
   buy planes/cars - or nothing

5. Why is it easier to set up an insurance broking business than it is to set up an insurance company?

   Because of ① legal requirement
   ② capital req to start ③ Qualifications

6. How does foreign trade affect competition?

   Increases it

4
SELF-ASSESSMENT QUESTIONS

7. Why do some people buy groceries in small shops which charge higher prices than supermarkets do?

   Convenience

   Very while quality is better

8. Do all insurance companies charge the same price for the same product?

   No — some offer free gifts and

   all claim their policy is the best.

9. List a few methods by which (a) general insurance companies; and (b) life assurance companies, compete?

   (a) *Price*   (b) *Gifts*

   3/4 *Gifts*   *Quality of policy*

   Ads   *Ads*

10. To what extent are building societies in competition with life assurance companies?

    Most life policies are for saving

    reasons — so people will look at

    Building Society interest rates

11. What ethical problems may arise if insurance companies use brokers' commissions as a way to attract more business?

    Unscrupulous brokers could place

    business with an insurer as their

    earning will be greater even though

    the policy may not be what the client requires

12. What is the aim of the ABI's codes of practice?

    to maintain the highest quality

    1/4 *of service possible*

10/75

12   84.5%

ANSWERS TO SELF-ASSESSMENT QUESTIONS APPEAR OVERLEAF

4
ANSWERS TO SELF-ASSESSMENT QUESTIONS

1. If your company doubled its premium rates, it would lose many customers.

2. The extent of competition is influenced by the number of producers in the market, what substitutes are available, consumers' knowledge and attitudes, and many other factors. These factors differ from product to product. If you want to buy electricity, you can get it only from one supplier, but if you want household insurance then you have a choice between a large number of insurance companies. There is thus more competition in insurance than there is in electricity distribution.

3. If there is only one firm, customers either buy from that firm or go without the product. This gives the monopolist considerable market power. If there are many suppliers, customers can choose where to buy.

4. The fact that Westland is the only manufacturer of helicopters in the UK does not mean that there is no competition in that market. There are helicopter manufacturers in many other countries, and you are free to import helicopters.

5. Setting up an insurance company requires a lot more capital than starting a broking business.

6. If you are free to import, you have a wider choice than you would have if you could buy only from local producers. Free foreign trade therefore increases competition.

7. Small shops may be in more convenient locations, have longer opening hours, offer a more personal service, or have some other advantage which compensates for higher prices.

8. No: prices sometimes differ substantially even if the insurance cover is the same.

9. (a) Methods include premium rates, advertising, speed of handling claims, and brokers' commissions.

    (b) The same methods as in (a) apply, and also such things as bonuses and surrender values of policies.

10. Life assurance policies provide life cover and can be used as a means of saving. Depositing money in a building society is an alternative way of saving. Building societies are therefore in competition with life assurance companies as far as saving is concerned.

11. In such a situation, less reputable brokers may place business with the insurance company which pays the highest commission to the broker, rather than the one which is in the best interest of the client.

12. The codes aim to provide guidelines for the conduct of business between companies, intermediaries and policyholders.

4

ASSIGNMENT 1

You should work this assignment after studying Chapters 1 to 4. Answer any three questions, and allow yourself one and a half hours to complete it.

1. The UK has often been described as a mixed economy. Explain what the term 'mixed economy' means.

2. Explain how prices come about in an uncontrolled market.

3. Discuss the consequences of the legislative imposition of (a) maximum prices; (b) minimum prices. Give an example in each case.

4. In what ways can competition and government regulation be regarded as methods of protecting consumers?

① Plan.

(i) Into Two main types of economy
Market = run by force of supply
+ demand
Planned — decisions made by govt.

(ii) Mixed economy is integration of
each type of the above

(iii) eg of how Both econ
Contains aspects of both
Market → Many individuals selling
up to
Planned → BR/Brit Steel

(iv) Summary

② (1) Define Uncontrolled econ
Market
② Supply
③ Demand
④ Interaction of S+D
⑤ Summary

③ Max →Cause Shortage
Black market
Min → over production

④

5

NATIONAL INCOME AND RELATED CONCEPTS

LEARNING OBJECTIVES

After studying this chapter, you should be able to:

▷ say what causes differences between living standards in different countries;

▷ explain the concept of gross domestic product (GDP);

▷ illustrate the circular flow of income;

▷ explain the relevance of factors of production, with special emphasis on capital, savings and investment;

▷ give details of the role of insurance in the production process.

A
WHAT MAKES A COUNTRY RICH OR POOR?

There are huge differences between the levels of income, wealth and development of various countries. Not only the figures for income per capita (whose accuracy and comparability one may well question in some cases), but also the more tangible variables like the number of physicians per 10,000 inhabitants, illiteracy rates, life expectancy and calorie intakes differ enormously between rich and poor countries. The following table gives a glimpse of some often-used development indicators.

NATIONAL INCOME AND RELATED CONCEPTS

	Income per capita 1987($)	Daily calorie intake per capita	Physicians per 10,000 inhabitants	Life expect-ancy at birth (years)	Infant mortality per 1,000	Illiteracy rate (%)	Telephones per 100 inhabitants
Developed countries:							
UK	7,181	3,148	14.71	75	11	0.9	52
USA	11,216	3,682	20.00	75	11	1.0	76
Japan	11,925	2,695	13.51	78	8	1.0	54
Soviet Union	4,200	3,332	37.04	70	29	1.0	10
Intermediate countries:							
Brazil	1,384	2,657	7.69	65	80	24	8
Turkey	708	3,218	6.54	65	125	30	7
Underdeveloped countries:							
Ethiopia	74	1,704	0.11	46	150	82	0.3
India	129	2,126	2.70	57	125	64	0.4

Sources: IMF International Financial Statistics 1988
World Bank : World Development Report 1988
Statistical Abstract of the United States 1987

Why is it that many countries in Africa, Asia and Latin America cannot offer their inhabitants the amounts of income and food, and the medical and educational services, which are taken for granted in most places in Europe, North America and Japan? **Why are some countries rich whereas others are poor?**

Let us look at a recent and, unfortunately, recurring example: the Ethiopian famine. Why is it that Ethiopia is in such a catastrophic state that it is incapable of satisfying the most basic need of its inhabitants; namely, enough food? Some may say that it is due to droughts, soil erosion, civil wars and the like. There is, of course, some truth in all these points. If these things had not occurred, Ethiopia would have been able to produce more food, and if more food had been produced Ethiopians would have had more to eat. Food production is certainly important, but it is only part of the story. Does the United Arab Emirates produce enough food to feed its people? It does not and probably never will, because most of it is desert. So, like Ethiopia, the UAE does not produce enough food to feed its population, but it is certainly not suffering from famine; on the contrary, it is one of the richest countries in the world.

In the case of these two countries the reason for the difference in their levels of income is easy to see: true, the UAE does not produce enough food to feed its people, but it produces huge quantities of oil which it can export, and with the export revenue it can buy the necessary food and many other things as well. Ethiopia is in a less favourable position: it does not produce enough food, and it does not produce much else either which could be exchanged for food. This simple example indicates what makes a country rich or poor: the level of production *per capita*.

In a stone-age village the link between production and living standards is easy to see. If the inhabitants of such a village catch 100 kilos of fish, then 100 kilos of fish is what they can eat. If next week they catch 120 kilos they can eat more, and if in the following week the catch is down to 70 kilos they will just have to eat less, unless they have saved some fish in the more prosperous weeks before. If, in a different village, the inhabitants catch more fish per person, they will have a higher standard of living than the people in the first village: the level of output (*per capita*) determines the standard of living.

Net Income = Value of Goods + Services Prod.
Net Spending = Net Income

B
GROSS DOMESTIC PRODUCT

In a modern economy the link between production and living standards may not be as easy to see as in the hypothetical stone-age villages mentioned in the previous section, but it nevertheless applies. In a modern economy, where most commercial transactions involve the use of money, national income is equal to the value of all the goods and services produced in the economy, and since one person's income is some other person's spending, income or the value of output must also be equal to the total expenditure in the economy. The following table shows how income, the value of output, and spending add up to the same total in the British economy.

You should note that there are several 'national income' concepts. One of them is gross domestic product, which is the one we are concentrating on at this stage. Some of the other national income concepts, together with the differences between them, will be outlined in section D.

Table 5.1: Britain's gross domestic product 1987 (£ millions)

Value of output

Agriculture, forestry and fishing	5,901
Energy and water supply	24,184
Manufacturing	85,552
Construction	21,524
Services	215,076
Gross domestic product	352,237

Income

Income from employment	226,343
Income from self-employment	32,959
Rent	24,798
Profits etc.	68,137
Gross domestic product	352,237

Expenditure

Private consumption	211,777
Government consumption	80,379
Capital formation	65,827
Exports	102,902
subtract : Imports	112,030
Errors and omissions	3,382
Gross domestic product	352,237

Source : UK National Accounts, 1988 edition

C
THE CIRCULAR FLOW OF INCOME

The identity of the value of output, income and expenditure can also be illustrated in a diagram showing the 'circular flow of income'. For simplicity, let us ignore foreign trade and the government. Our simplified economy consists of 'households' who work in and receive an income from a 'factory', and the households spend their entire income on goods and services produced by that factory. We then get the following flows of money and goods and services:

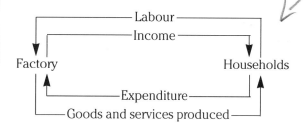

This diagram illustrates that measuring income, output and expenditure are really different ways of measuring the same thing, which is why they all add up to the same total. Needless to say, this 'economy' is a highly simplified one. The model can be made more realistic by incorporating household savings, the government and foreign trade, but this would just make things more complicated; the conclusion (i.e. the identity of income, expenditure and the value of output) would be exactly the same.

D
OTHER NATIONAL INCOME CONCEPTS

In section B we concentrated on gross domestic product, or GDP. There are a number of similar concepts, the main one being gross national product, or GNP. What is the difference between them?

Britain's gross domestic product is the value of all the goods and services produced in Britain during a given period of time (usually a year). Britain's gross national product is the total of all incomes accruing to British residents. These two concepts

GDP

GNP

would be identical (think of the identity of income, expenditure, and the value of output) if it were not for some cross-border transactions. If a British resident owns American company shares, the dividends he receives are certainly part of his income; that means, these dividends are income accruing to a resident of the UK, and so they are part of Britain's gross national product. However, those dividends do not stem from any production carried out in the UK; consequently they are not part of Britain's gross domestic product.

In numerical terms, the difference between GNP and GDP is fairly small, and the same is true of all the other variants of national income. Some national income concepts allow for depreciation on machinery and other assets whereas others do not; some use prices before VAT whereas others include VAT, and so forth. The main thing is not to be confused by a large number of details. It is important that you understand the basic idea underlying all these national income concepts, as explained in sections A, B and C; the differences between the various concepts and definitions are of secondary importance.

E
COMPONENTS OF GDP

Let us now explain the entries in the GDP tables in section B in some more detail.

E1 CALCULATING GDP FROM OUTPUT

The figures in the output section of table 5/1 indicate the value of output in the various sectors of the economy. You may be surprised by the relatively low figure for agriculture, forestry and fishing, and the rather high one for services. This, however, is a fairly typical pattern which can be observed in most of the developed countries.

Until the 18th century the majority of the population worked on the farms, and this was necessary in those days in order to produce enough food. Since then, however, the development of more scientific and commercial attitudes in farming has led to vast improvements in agricultural productivity (in this context, 'productivity' means output

per worker). For example, Jethro Tull, who lived from 1674 to 1740, conducted experiments to find the best level at which to sow seed, 'realising that carefully planned sowing as opposed to the traditional broadcast method was much more productive.'[1] Robert Bakewell (1725-1795) 'was the greatest early exponent of the scientific breeding of lifestock. He used turnips as winter food, and this made possible fatter and better stock and the consequent increase in manure improved the land. His most important contribution was to develop the technique of carefully controlled selective breeding'.[1]

These are just two examples to show how a rational approach can increase productivity on the farms, and of course agricultural research did not stop with Tull and Bakewell. Over the years, more and more methods were discovered to increase farm productivity, and the end result of this process is that in developed countries nowadays enough food can be produced even if only a small percentage of the population works in agriculture (between 2% and 8% in most West European countries). The rest of the population is therefore free to produce other things.

Q Do you know where the labourers no longer needed in agriculture turned for alternative employment?

A At first the manufacturing sector provided the main employment alternative (think of the Industrial Revolution), but later on the emphasis shifted more and more to services.

E1A The role of services

People sometimes wonder whether it is not somehow 'bad for the country' if more and more people work in the services sector. Well, the main point of the answer to that question is that nobody has suffered any shortages of agricultural or manufactured products as a result. Just as progress in agriculture makes it possible to produce enough food even if only about 5% of the population work in farming, so progress in manufacturing processes allows the same quantity of manufactured goods to be produced by fewer and fewer people. The services sector quite reasonably absorbs the people who are no longer needed in agriculture

[handwritten margin note: Improved technology has enabled developed countries to move the bulk of their workforces from agriculture & manufacturing to service industries]

or manufacturing. There is no way back to the days when 50% of the world's ships were built on the Clyde; unless British workers are to agree to work for Brazilian or Korean wage levels.

Furthermore, a modern economy cannot function without a large number of people providing a wide range of services. British industry, for instance, relies on imported raw materials. The label in a pair of jeans may say 'Made in Britain', but what does that mean? The cotton from which those jeans were made certainly did not grow in Britain, and the ton of metal required for producing a 'British-made' car was not mined in Britain either. On the other hand, a considerable part of the output of British industry is exported. This exporting and importing is only possible if there are reliable transport services, and these create income and employment not only for lorry drivers, seamen and airline captains, but also for freight forwarders and other intermediaries who organise transport, bankers who finance foreign trade and arrange money transfers from one country to another, insurers who provide marine and other insurance, and so on.

[handwritten margin note: Production includes services as well as tangible goods]

A further explanation may be useful at this point. In everyday language the use of the word **'production'** is often confined to the production of tangible goods, like potatoes or motor cars. In this sense of the word a farmer or factory worker produces but a bus driver does not. In economics we do not make this distinction. In the economic sense of the word a farmer certainly produces, but so does a bus driver; the only difference between the two is that the former produces tangible goods whereas the latter produces a service. About 60% of Britain's income and employment now results from the production of services. These services cover a very wide range of activities: medical services, transport, teaching, banking, insurance, wholesale and retail trade, the police, entertainment (such as singers and actors), administration, and many others.

From an international point of view, services are also important as a source of 'invisible earnings' for the British balance of payments. This will be explained in more detail in Chapter 8.

E1B Multiple counting

Finally, in this comment on the output section of the GDP table, it is worth pointing out that the figures have been adjusted for multiple counting. If a farmer produces wheat, a miller transforms that wheat into flour and a baker buys that flour to make bread, it would of course not make sense to add up the wheat, the flour and the bread; if one did so, one would count the flour twice and the wheat three times. One can avoid such multiple counting either by considering only final products (in this example, the bread), or by including only the 'value added' at each stage. If the wheat is sold for £100, the flour for £140 and the bread for £200, the farmer has produced goods worth £100, the miller has added £40 to the value of those goods and the baker has added another £60 (total: £200, the same as the value of the final product). The GDP statistics are based on this 'value added' principle. By the way, this 'value added' concept is also the basis for value added tax, or VAT.

E2 CALCULATING GDP FROM INCOME

The income section of the GDP statistics is fairly self-explanatory. Most people's main source of money is the wage or salary they earn: their income from employment. This is reflected in the GDP statistics, which show that income from employment accounts for nearly two thirds of Britain's GDP. Income from self-employment accounts for another ten per cent or so, and the rest is made up of rent, profits and a few other items. Note that transfer incomes (e.g. social security benefits) are not included in the GDP statistics. This is because these items do not add anything to the country's output or income; all they do is to redistribute the existing income.

For the reasons explained earlier (see section B) the various categories of income must add up to the same total as the value of output.

E3 CALCULATING GDP FROM EXPENDITURE

In the expenditure column, the biggest single item is private consumption. This includes all the food, clothing, transport, entertainment and the like on which you and I spend much of our incomes. Government consumption includes all those government purchases of goods and services which are not 'capital formation' (see below) or transfer payments like social security benefits; for reasons explained in section E2 such payments do not affect GDP at all. Examples of government consumption would include the salaries of civil servants, soldiers, teachers and other public sector employees, medicines used by the National Health Service, and stationery used in public administration.

E3A   Capital formation

This is expenditure on items like machinery, the infrastructure (roads, hospitals, ports ...) and housing. We could also call this item **investment in real (or physical) capital.** Such investment is very important for the future well-being of the country. If we do not invest enough in machinery, for example, this will adversely affect the amount of goods and services we can produce in the future. The figure shown in the national income statistics includes expenditure on capital formation by both the public and the private sectors. Note that the capital formation figure does not include investments in financial assets, like company shares or building society deposits. The reason for this is that you do not create any income by investing in financial assets. This does not mean that investing in financial assets is useless: often financial instruments are used to finance investment in physical assets. For example, if British Airways want to buy new aeroplanes, they can raise the money they need to buy those planes by selling more shares. By buying some of those shares, you provide British Airways with money without which they could not buy those planes. Your purchase of British Airways shares is an investment in financial assets; British Airways' purchase of aeroplanes is an investment in physical assets. The latter is recorded in the national income statistics under the 'capital formation' heading, but the former is not. In fact, if the financial investment was recorded as well as the physical investment, one would really count the same transaction twice since the former is used to finance the latter. The role of capital will be discussed in more detail in section G.

E3B   Exports and imports

One person's spending is another person's income. So, if non-residents spend money on British goods or services, they create income in this country. Therefore, exports have to be added if we want to work out the total income earned in Britain. This applies both to goods and to services. A non-resident who buys tangible goods which were made in Britain (such as a Trident aeroplane or Scotch whisky) certainly creates income in Britain, but so does a non-resident who buys British-made services (as with a foreign airline insuring its planes at Lloyd's or a foreign tourist who stays at a British hotel).

Talking about exports leads quite logically to the question: how are we to treat imports? Well, whenever you spend money you create an income for somebody, but if that somebody lives abroad, you create an income abroad and not in Britain. Spending on imports can therefore be treated in two different ways, both of which lead to the same result. One way is to ignore imports completely, which means we add up only those amounts of money which are spent on British goods and services. Alternatively we can add up all the money spent in Britain no matter whether the goods are of British or foreign origin, and then deduct those amounts which have been spent on imports. The latter is much easier in practice, and this is therefore the approach used in the national income statistics. Suppose you buy a pair of jeans. Those jeans may have been manufactured by a British textile factory from cotton which was imported from Egypt. It would be impossible now to add up only the money spent on British goods, because of the 'dual nationality' of those jeans (and the same is true of many other goods). Therefore, the national income statistics regard the total amount spent on the jeans as private consumption, and the amount the textile manufacturer has spent on the imported cotton is deducted under the imports heading. The difference is the amount of income created in Britain.

Q   Check your understanding of this treatment of imports with a simple example:

Kwikdrinx manufacture and sell drinking chocolate in the UK. To make a particular batch, they import cocoa worth £1,000, sugar worth £700, and metal worth £500. (The metal is used for making tins for the powdered chocolate, rather than for producing that distinctive Kwikdrinx taste.) The batch is sold, in the UK, for £5,000.

How much income is created in Britain through this process?

A The total is found by subtracting the amounts paid for the imported goods (£1,000 + £700 + £500 = £2,200) from the income received by Kwikdrinx (£5,000). The income created in the UK is £2,800.

Now we have discussed all the items in the national income statistics in section B logically, the three approaches must add up to the same total, since all spending other than transfer payments is for goods or services provided **(expenditure = value of output),** and one person's spending is another person's income **(expenditure = income).**

F

FACTORS OF PRODUCTION

In the previous sections we saw the importance of production for the material well-being of a country. Saying that what makes a country rich or poor is how much it produces *per capita* leads straight to another question: **why is it that some countries produce more than others?**

Going back to our comparison of the UAE and Ethiopia, the answer is easy. The UAE can produce oil because there happens to be oil on its territory, whereas Ethiopia is not so lucky. Some countries have been more generously endowed by nature than others, and this affects their ability to produce. We cannot just produce goods and services from thin air. To produce, we need so-called 'factors of production'. **Natural resources,** often just called 'land' for simplicity, are one of these factors. A country generously endowed with natural resources like fertile land and mineral reserves is obviously in a better position to produce than is a country which is poorer in natural resources.

However, the availability or non-availability of natural resources is by no means the whole story: if it were, Zaire should be one of the richest countries in the world and Switzerland one of the poorest, whereas in reality it is just about the other way round. Natural resources only produce an income (be it in cash or in kind) if one makes use of them, and some countries have brought about food shortages in areas where almost anything will grow. Besides, one can earn an income by producing things other than agricultural or mining products, for instance manufactured goods or services. To produce manufactured goods or services, the availability of natural resources on one's territory is normally not vital: think of Switzerland, Japan or Singapore, all of which are rather poor in natural resources. However, to produce manufactured goods or services (and even to use one's natural resources effectively) one needs other factors of production, such as **labour** and **capital.**

'Labour' does not just mean lots of people. The people must have the right skills to be useful in the production process. Of course, the labour market requires lots of different kinds of labour, such as people with managerial talent or technical skills in a wide variety of areas, as well as unskilled labour.

A country with an educated labour force which has a production-oriented attitude and the skills required by producers is obviously in a better position to produce than is a country whose labour force lacks those characteristics.

Another factor of production is **capital.** Capital in this sense does not mean money (money does not produce anything), but rather machinery, tools and other items used in the production process. Imagine you wanted to catch fish without using any capital. How would you have to go about it?

Well, if you really want to catch fish without using any capital, you have to stand at the bank of the river, watch out for fish and, when you see one, jump into the water, swim after the fish and try to catch it with your bare hands. You may catch some fish that way, but you will not catch very many, because the fish may not like the idea of being caught and in addition they may be more experienced swimmers and divers than you are. So, trying to produce without any capital is not likely to yield very much. A simple rod or net (i.e.

simple forms of capital) will allow you to increase your catch substantially, and a modern fishing fleet can help you to increase that output even further. The same thing can be said about any other economic activity.

The more capital you use in the production process, the more you can produce. Developing countries usually employ less capital in the production process than developed countries do.

G
CAPITAL, INVESTMENT AND SAVINGS

The relationship between these three things is important. We will now consider each in turn.

G1 CAPITAL

Given the importance of capital, let us look at this factor of production in some more detail. The availability of capital is of crucial importance to what we can produce, and often also to the quality of the goods and services we produce. For example, an excellent doctor in a developing country can often do less for his patients than a mediocre doctor in a developed country, because the latter will usually have access to the medicines and medical technology his patients need whereas the former often does not. By the same token, it does not help people that they want to build that road or port or bridge if they do not have the necessary tools or machinery to do so, or if the supply of cement is erratic because the local cement factory can only operate at half capacity due to frequent power cuts (a common problem in many developing countries). A worker in Europe, North America or Japan usually earns many times as much as his colleague in parts of Africa, Asia or Latin America, and the reason for this is, again, that the workers in the developing country often have to work with relatively primitive equipment: the consequence is that the workers in developed countries can achieve a far greater output per capita than their Third World colleagues. These few examples illustrate the importance of tools, machinery, power stations (and one could add transport facilities, housing, hospitals...) to the economic well-being of a country.

G2 INVESTMENT

However, these things do not just fall from heaven; they must be made, and the channelling of money or other resources into such capital formation is known as 'investment' (in physical assets). To have an adequate supply of such assets is very important for a country since its ability to produce depends on it; and one can only consume what has been produced beforehand.

Since machines and parts do not last for ever, a certain amount of resources must be set aside each year, at least to replace capital equipment which has become obsolete, otherwise people will sooner or later have nothing to work with. If the population of a country increases, it is not even enough just to replace obsolete pieces of capital equipment; in this case one has to increase the nation's capital stock at least in line with the increase in population, otherwise there will sooner or later be people who have no houses in which to live and no tools with which to work. Obviously, if one can increase certain items of the capital stock at a faster rate than the rate of population growth, so much the better.

Because of the importance of investment, most countries spend huge amounts of money on it. As the table in section B shows, Britain devotes about 20% of its GDP to 'capital formation'. In the USA and West Germany the percentage is similar, and Japan devotes nearly 30% of its GDP to capital investment each year.[2] The following table provides some more information on investment in Britain:

Table 5.2: Investment by type of asset, 1987

	£ million
Vehicles, ships and aircraft	6,724
Plant and machinery	25,095
Dwellings	14,136
Other building	16,131
Other items	3,741
Total	65,827

(of which private sector: 49,271)

Source: UK National Accounts, 1988 edition

 Q If investment in physical assets (capital formation) helps to raise a country's living standards, why do countries not just increase their capital formation?

A The reason is that capital formation has a price. We cannot spend all our incomes on food, clothing and entertainment and buy houses and machinery at the same time, and this is true for a country as a whole just as it is for an individual. In other words, if we want to invest, we must refrain from consuming, which is the same thing as saying: we must save. Hence our ability to invest is limited by what we are willing and able to save.

G3 SAVINGS

Who, then, saves all the money which is necessary to finance Britain's capital formation? Well, just about everybody can save.

Companies can save by not paying out all their profits to shareholders, and indeed a sizeable proportion of Britain's capital formation is financed in this way. This will be discussed in more detail in Part III of this course (The Financial Environment).

Then, **government can save,** for example by running budget surpluses as the British Government did from 1987 to 1990. And, last but not least, **many individuals save,** and their savings can be made available for capital investment. This channelling of funds from individual savers to investors is usually done through financial institutions. A saver can, for example, deposit his savings in a building society which then lends that money to a housebuyer. Alternatively, an individual can put his savings into a bank which lends most of the money deposited with it to industry and commerce. Yet another way in which an individual can save is by buying company shares or government securities: in this case he or she makes his or her savings available to companies or to the government and helps them to finance their capital expenditure.

Insurance companies also play a role in this process. A claim can only occur after a premium has been paid, and in the meantime the money can be invested. This investment is particularly important in life assurance, since there the length of time between receiving premiums and paying claims is longer, so the amounts which can be accumulated are larger. The investment policy differs from one insurance company to the next, depending on the structure of the company's liabilities and the views of its investment managers on the prospects of the various kinds of investment. However, most British insurance companies invest about 90% of their money in three kinds of assets: company shares, interest-bearing securities (issued by the government or large companies), and property. Investment in property is investment in physical assets, investment in company shares or interest-bearing securities is investment in financial assets.

By buying company securities, insurance companies make money available to the companies whose securities they buy and thereby help them to finance their capital investment (e.g. new machinery, oil platforms and so on, depending on the line of business the company is in). By buying government securities, insurance companies make money available to government (central or local) and thereby help government to finance its capital expenditure on items such as roads, schools or hospitals. And by investing in property (like factory halls, warehouses, office blocks and shopping centres), insurance companies provide premises in which other people can carry on their business. So, if an individual saves by paying premiums on a life policy, his money is made available for capital investment in a variety of ways.

Let us conclude this section with an example. In 1988, United Biscuits (makers of McVities' biscuits and at that time owners of the Wimpy and Pizzaland restaurants) spent £406.9 million on fixed assets and new businesses. The 'funds generated from operations'[3] amounted to £137.8 million (after tax and dividends paid to shareholders). Obviously, the £137.8 million generated by the business is not enough to pay for capital investments of £406.9 million, so where did the difference come from? The company's source and application of funds statement3 provides the answer: £110 million was made by selling new shares, £96.7 million came from bank loans, and the rest was provided mainly by running down cash balances the company had accumulated in previous years.[4]

H
THE ROLE OF INSURANCE IN THE PRODUCTION PROCESS

Earlier on in this chapter we have seen the importance of production for the material well-being of society (see section A). In what way does insurance contribute to the nation's output?

Obviously, insurance does not produce any tangible goods like food or machines. Insurance is one of the service industries, and as explained in section 3A1 the main service provided by the insurance industry is that of a risk transfer mechanism. The existence of such a mechanism not only provides peace of mind for many individuals (a service many people are prepared to pay for), but it also helps traders, manufacturers and others to increase or maintain their production. As explained in section 3A1, many small businesses would have to cease trading if a fire destroyed their premises, and this would lead to a reduction in output and employment. Insurance enables the owner of the business to rebuild the premises after the fire, so production can resume and the people who work in his business do not lose their jobs. Furthermore, some people might not be prepared to commit their savings to a business if there was no way of transferring some of the risks (like fire, employer's liability and others) to an insurance company. In this case the availability of insurance

increases investment in machinery, factories and other productive assets, thereby creating output, income and employment, In addition, insurance companies are a source of funds for other businesses, as explained in section G. By providing money for capital investment, insurance companies enable other businesses to increase their production.

I
SUMMARY

In this chapter we have seen that what makes a country rich or poor is the value of the goods and services it produces per capita. Britain is richer than Portugal, but poorer than Denmark, because Britain's output per capita is larger than Portugal's, but smaller than Denmark's.

In order to produce we need factors of production; these are often summarised under the headings land, labour and capital. Saving is a prerequisite for capital formation.

The insurance industry produces a wide range of services which help other sectors of the economy to increase their own production.

References

1 Bernard J. Smales: Economic History Made Simple, Heineman, London 1981
2 Source: IMF International Financial Statistics
3 This will be explained in more detail in Chapter 13.
4 Source of the figures : United Biscuits' annual report 1988.

1. Why are wages usually higher in the USA than they are in Britain?

    _____

    _____

    _____

2. Why are some countries poorer than others?

    _____

    _____

    _____

3. Why is national income the same as the value of all goods and services produced?

    _____

    _____

    _____

4. What is meant by 'capital formation'?

    _____

    _____

    _____

5. What is meant by 'government consumption'?

    _____

    _____

    _____

6. Why are social security benefits not included in Britain's GDP?

    _____

    _____

    _____

7. What is the importance of investment in physical assets?

    _____

    _____

8.   What prevents countries from increasing investment?

   _____

   _____

   _____

9.   Explain the term 'factors of production'.

   _____

   _____

   _____

10.   In what ways does insurance contribute to Britain's GDP?

   _____

   _____

   _____

ANSWERS TO SELF-ASSESSMENT QUESTIONS APPEAR OVERLEAF

5

ANSWERS TO SELF-ASSESSMENT QUESTIONS

1. Wages are usually higher in the USA because the productivity of labour (i.e. the output per worker) is higher in that country.

2. How rich or poor a country is depends on its output *per capita*. This differs substantially from country to country.

3. Your income is the amount of money which other people spend on the goods and/or services that you produce. The same is true of every other person in the country. Therefore, total income = value of output.

4. Capital formation is investment in physical assets, like machines, roads and ports.

5. Government consumption is its spending on items other than capital formation, and income redistribution. Examples include medicines used in NHS hospitals, teachers' and civil servants' salaries, and stationery used in public administration.

6. Social security benefits do not increase or reduce a country's national income. They just redistribute the existing national income.

7. The more we invest in physical assets (like machinery), the more we can produce and the higher will be our national income.

8. You cannot spend all your income on consumer goods and buy machines at the same time: investment requires saving. The amount a country can invest is therefore limited by the amount of savings available.

9. Production does not come about automatically. It requires the input of human labour, capital and natural resources. These are known as 'factors of production'.

10. Insurance helps a country to increase output by providing a risk transfer mechanism (for example, financing the rebuilding of a factory destroyed by fire), and by being a source of capital. In addition, insurance is a source of invisible earnings for the balance of payments.

6

TWO ECONOMIC PROBLEMS: INFLATION AND UNEMPLOYMENT

A   Inflation

B   Unemployment

C   Why is it so difficult to combat inflation and unemployment?

LEARNING OBJECTIVES

After studying this chapter, you should be able to:

▷ detail some periods of rising and falling prices in the past;

▷ state the differences between inflation rates in various countries;

▷ explain how inflation can be measured, with particular reference to the Retail Prices Index;

▷ outline the main consequences of inflation;

▷ explain the main causes of inflation, and remedies to combat inflation;

▷ state the extent of unemployment in different parts of the country at the moment;

▷ give an account of the difficulties in measuring unemployment;

▷ explain the main causes of unemployment, and remedies to combat unemployment;

▷ say why it is difficult to combat inflation and unemployment.

A INFLATION

Rising prices and costs present a major problem for governments, companies and individuals. We will now look at a number of aspects of this problem.

A1   HISTORICAL INTRODUCTION

You will know from your own experience that a pound (or other monetary unit) buys less now than it did one, five or ten years ago. Prices of most goods and services have risen in the meantime; we have had **inflation.** This does not mean, however, that it is some immutable law of nature that prices should rise; during the course of history there have been periods of falling prices just as there have been periods of rising prices. In Britain, for example, prices fell in the second half of the nineteenth century, and again during the recession of the 1930s. Japan, Switzerland, West Germany and Holland experienced falling prices for two years or so in the mid-1980s. Most of the period after the Second World War has, however, been an inflationary one, both in Britain and elsewhere.

Inflation is not a new phenomenon. There are references to rising prices in the Bible (e.g. 2nd book of Kings, chapter 6, verse 25). King Henry VIII in the 16th century reduced the silver and gold content of English coins so that he could produce more coins from a given quantity of precious metal, and this increase in the money supply led to inflation. Massive imports of gold and silver from the newly-discovered American continent pushed prices up in Spain in the 16th century, and during the French Revolution an uncontrolled issue of paper money produced rising prices at first and a collapse of the French currency later. One of the worst inflations ever recorded occurred in Germany between 1921 and 1923; in November 1923 the mark-dollar exchange rate reached the remarkably astronomical figure of

4,200,000,000,000 marks to the dollar! After that, the old currency was declared worthless, and a new mark was introduced whose exchange rate was fixed at 4.20 marks to the dollar.

In the 1980s, the countries with the lowest inflation rates were usually Switzerland, Japan, Germany (East and West), Singapore, Austria and Holland. Typical high-inflation countries are Israel, Iceland, Poland, Yugoslavia and many South American countries; in 1989 a 'joke' circulated in Brazil which claimed that the Brazilian inflation rate was 0.1% - per hour! The following table shows for a number of countries how the cost of a basket of commodities costing 100 local currency units in 1960 has developed since then.

	UK	USA	West Germany	Japan	Iceland
1960	100	100	100	100	100
65	119	108	115	134	168
70	149	131	129	175	300
75	275	182	174	300	921
80	538	279	212	413	5,263
85	761	364	256	474	28,537
88	860	399	259	480	51,081

Source: IMF International Financial Statistics

A2 HOW CAN WE MEASURE INFLATION?

At least once a month you can read in the newspapers that 'the inflation rate is now so-and-so many per cent.' What does that figure mean, and how is it arrived at? The first part of the question is easy to answer. If the government says that the inflation rate is now, for example, 8%, it means that prices are now, on average, 8% higher than they were a year ago. This leads us to the second part of the question, which is: how do they arrive at that figure?

If all goods and services went up in price by the same percentage, measuring inflation would be easy. If all prices were now 5% higher than twelve months ago, it is obvious that the inflation rate would be 5%. However, things are usually more complicated than that. Normally, the prices of different goods go up by different amounts, and some goods may indeed become cheaper while others are going up in price. During the last few years, for example, quartz watches and electronic calculators have fallen in price while most other prices have risen. If one wants to find 'the inflation rate' when in fact different prices have changed in different ways, one must somehow average out those various price changes, and this can be done by using a statistical technique known as a 'price index'.

A price index is based on a so-called **basket of commodities.** The British Government has found out what the average British household spends its money on, and those goods and services form the basket of commodities underlying the **Retail Prices Index** (**RPI** for short). This is the index usually used to measure inflation in Britain. In addition to the composition of the basket of commodities, the government must decide a 'base period' for the index. This can be any period, and the present Retail Prices Index has January 1987 as its base. At that time the index was (by definition) 100.

Every month, the government collects the prices of the goods and services that make up the Retail Prices Index, and basically the computation of the index figure then boils down to the following formula:

$$\text{Retail Prices Index now} = \frac{\text{cost of basket of commodities now}}{\text{cost of basket of commodities in Jan 1987}} \times 100$$

So, if the goods and services contained in the basket of commodities cost £300 in January 1987, and the same combination of goods and services costs £360 now, then the Retail Prices Index is now

$$\frac{360}{300} \times 100 = 120.$$

The Retail Prices Index is published every month, and the latest figure can be found every day in the major newspapers.

The Retail Prices Index indicates by how much prices have changed since the base period. If the index is now 120, then prices have risen by 20% since January 1987, since at that time the RPI was 100. The 'inflation rate', which is the percentage by which prices have changed during the last twelve months, can be found by using the following formula:

Inflation rate (percentage) =

$$\frac{\text{RPI now} - \text{RPI 12 months ago}}{\text{RPI 12 months ago}} \times 100$$

Q So, if the RPI is now 120 and 12 months ago it was 112, what is the inflation rate?

A $\dfrac{120 - 112}{112} \times 100 = 7.14\%$

As stated earlier, the inflation rate is the percentage by which the RPI has changed during the last twelve months, and in this example prices have risen by 7.14% during that period.

The Employment Gazette, the Economist and other publications regularly show the current inflation rates for Britain and various other countries.

A3 CONSEQUENCES OF INFLATION

In most countries inflation is considered to be undesirable. Why is that so? Well, inflation has several consequences which are pleasant for some people but unpleasant for others. The main problems of inflation are that it leads to an arbitrary and often unfair redistribution of income and wealth, and that it creates problems regarding foreign trade and exchange rates. These problems are discussed in more detail below.

A3A Distribution of wealth

Inflation may lead to an unfair redistribution of income and wealth. People whose incomes are fixed in money terms suffer, because a given sum of money buys less than it used to if prices have risen in the meantime. For example, if you buy £1,000 of a 10% UK government security repayable in 20 years' time, you will get £100 interest each year for the next 20 years, and in 20 years' time you will get your £1,000 back. These amounts are fixed in money terms, and if prices rise the money you will get will buy less than it does today. You **will** get your £1,000 in 20 years' time, but you will not get any more even if £1,000 only buys an ounce of peanuts by that time.

Some pension schemes and annuities provide pensions or annuities fixed in money terms, and the people who get those benefits can buy less and less for their income as prices rise. However, wages and social security benefits have normally risen faster than prices, so that wage earners and people receiving social security benefits have generally not suffered from inflation.

Just as people who **receive** fixed amounts of money suffer from inflation, so people who **owe** fixed amounts of money benefit from it. Many housebuyers have had the experience that their mortgage repayment swallowed, say forty per cent of their take-home pay at first, whereas a few years later the same mortgage repayment represents a much smaller percentage of their income. And if they sell their house, the house is likely to have gone up in value (expressed in money terms), so that they are left with a nice lump sum of money after they have paid off the mortgage.

So, inflation makes some people richer and others poorer, and the way in which income and wealth are redistributed as a result of inflation is often haphazard and unfair.

A3B Foreign trade

In addition to the way in which it redistributes income and wealth, **inflation may lead to problems in foreign trade**. If all countries had the same rate of inflation, inflation would not matter as far as foreign trade is concerned, but this is rarely the case (see the table in section A1). If different countries have different inflation rates, high-inflation countries price their goods out of the market unless they devalue their currencies (more about exchange rates, devaluations and so on in Chapter 8 on the balance of payments).

The main reason why the pound has fallen considerably in relation to the US dollar or the German mark during the last 20 years* is that inflation in Britain has been higher than in the USA or in West Germany (see table in section A1). If a high-inflation country refuses to devalue its currency, its goods will be more expensive than similar goods made in low-inflation countries. The effect of this

---

*In 1970, £1 was US$2.40 or DM 9.60

will be that people will not buy the goods made in the high-inflation country, and if producers cannot sell all their output they will sooner or later reduce production and dismiss part of their work force. So, high-inflation countries must choose between suffering cutbacks in production and employment or devaluing their currencies.

A4   CAUSES OF INFLATION; HOW CAN WE COMBAT INFLATION?

If we have inflation and are unhappy about it, the logical thing is to ask what we can do to get rid of it. However, just as a doctor can only help a patient once he knows the cause of the symptoms, so an economist can only provide remedies for inflation if he knows what has caused prices to rise. So what causes inflation?

A4A   Demand inflation

Basically, there are two possible causes. One is an **excessive level of demand**. We saw in Chapter 2 that in a market economy prices are determined by supply and demand. If demand rises and supply does not or cannot rise in line with demand, prices are pushed up. This type of inflation is known as **demand inflation**. The inflation Britain experienced between 1988 and 1990 was almost certainly of this kind. In the years leading up to that period there was a strong demand for loans. Lending by banks and other financial institutions increased sharply. People borrowed as if there were no tomorrow, and spent the money. The British economy did not have the productive capacity to satisfy all this additional demand, so prices and imports rose.

What can be done about this kind of inflation? Well, if inflation is caused by an excessive level of demand, the logical way to reduce inflation is by reducing the level of demand. This can be done, for example, by increasing taxes (if you have to pay more taxes you cannot spend as much as before), by reducing the government's expenditure (in Britain the government's expenditure accounts for about 37% of total spending), or by making it more difficult or more expensive to borrow. These measures will be discussed in more detail in the chapter on monetary and fiscal policy (Chapter 7).

A4B   Cost inflation

The other possible cause of inflation is **increased costs of production**. If costs of production go up, producers will try to pass these cost increases on to consumers in order to maintain profit margins. This type of inflation is called **cost inflation**.

The high rates of inflation which many countries experienced in the 1970s were caused, at least initially, by the trebling of the price of oil which took place early in the decade. Manufacturers passed the higher energy costs on to consumers by increasing prices, and then trade unions demanded wage increases to compensate for the higher prices. These wage increases added another inflationary push to the economy in that producers then tried to pass the higher labour costs on to consumers in the form of yet higher prices (which promptly led to another round of wage demands). This is the infamous **'wage-price spiral'**.

What can a government do to combat this type of inflation? The answer depends largely on what the costs are which push prices up. The main costs of production in most manufacturing industries are raw material costs and labour costs. If the cost of a raw material (like oil) over whose price the government has no control goes up, the answer to the question as to what the government can do about it is simply, 'not a lot'! Generally speaking, the British Government will have no control over prices which are determined by the interaction of supply and demand worldwide, and this applies to all the main raw materials like oil, metals, wool and cotton. However, costs which are determined within Britain are, at least potentially, under the control of the British Government. The main cost item in this category is labour costs.

If wages go up by more than the output per worker, labour costs per unit of output rise. For example, if last year a worker earned £200 per week and he produced 100 garden gnomes during that time, the labour cost per gnome was £2. If this year he can produce 105 gnomes due to some improvement in the method of production, the labour cost per gnome will be

$$\frac{£200}{105} = £1.90$$

if the wage is still £200 per week. If the wage is £210, the labour cost per gnome is £2, the same as in the previous year; if, however, the wage is now £220 per week, the labour cost per gnome will be

$$\frac{£220}{105} = £2.10$$

In other words, if labour costs rise by more than five per cent (this being the increase in the output per worker, or productivity, in this example), labour costs per unit of output will rise, and manufacturers will try to pass that cost increase on to consumers in order to maintain profit margins.

Government has three options on how to deal with such a situation.

(i) It can adopt a monetary, fiscal and exchange rate policy (more about these in Chapters 7 and 8) which makes it difficult for firms to increase prices. In this case, wage rises exceeding the increase in productivity reduce profit margins (costs rise, prices do not); some firms will make losses instead of profits, and some will go out of business. This leads to higher unemployment. Governments using this approach hope that unions will moderate their wage claims once they realise that high wage demands lead to more unemployment. The British Government used this approach to 'squeeze inflation out of the system' in the early 1980s. Inflation actually fell from 18% in 1980 to little more than 2% in 1986, but the number of registered unemployed (see section B of this chapter) increased from about 1.8 million to nearly 3.3 million during the same period.

(ii) Government can adopt a monetary, fiscal and exchange rate policy which makes it easy for firms to raise prices. In this case prices rise, but profit margins are maintained and bankruptcies are largely avoided: the government tolerates inflation in order to safeguard employment. This type of policy was often used in Britain in the 1960s and 1970s.

(iii) Incomes policy. The government tries to bring wages under control, by recommending that wages should not rise by more than a certain percentage per year. If an incomes policy succeeds in keeping wage rises in line with productivity increases, unit labour costs (that is labour costs per unit of output) remain stable, and this is consistent with stable prices.

This third approach may seem the best one to overcome wage-cost inflation. However, in a country with strong unions an incomes policy will only work if it gets sufficient support from the unions. More often than not British unions have been against an incomes policy, since it interferes with what they see as their right to free collective bargaining.

B
UNEMPLOYMENT

Another major cause of social concern and unrest in modern times is unemployment. We will look now at some of the problems involved in dealing with unemployment.

B1 HOW MANY PEOPLE ARE OUT OF WORK?

In April 1989 the official UK unemployment figure was 1.89 million people. This is the number of people who were **claiming unemployment benefit** in the UK at that time. Whether this figure is an adequate indicator of the problem is difficult to say. On the one hand, some people who would like to have a job do not claim benefit because they do not qualify (for example, housewives), or because they feel there is little chance of getting a job and they therefore opt to stay on in full-time education or to retire early. On the other hand, some people may claim benefit without being interested in getting a job or without being prepared to retrain or to move to another part of the country where jobs may be easier to get. In a few (criminal) cases, people who actually work may be claiming benefit. So, the 'true' unemployment figure may be higher or lower than the number of people claiming unemployment benefit; defining unemployment is therefore more difficult than it may seem at first sight.

B1A The unemployment rate

Unemployment is often measured by the 'unemployment rate' rather than by the number of people who are claiming unemployment benefit. This is particularly useful for inter-regional or international comparisons. If, for example, the number of people claiming benefit in London is the same as that in Scotland, this does not mean that the magnitude of the problem is the same in these two parts of the country; in fact, it would mean that the problem is about twice as bad in Scotland as it is in London because Scotland has only about half as many inhabitants as London has. Half the population and the same number of unemployed means that the proportion of the population affected by unemployment is twice as high in Scotland as it is in London.

In the UK, the unemployment rate is defined as the **number of people who are claiming unemployment benefit, expressed as a percentage of the workforce**; in this context, 'workforce' means the number of people who are economically active (either employed or self-employed) plus those who are claiming benefit. For example, in April 1989 1.89 million people were claiming benefit and the workforce was 28.5 million. Consequently, the unemployment rate for that month was

$$\frac{1.89 \text{ million}}{28.5 \text{ million}} \times 100 = 6.6\%^{[1]}$$

The following table shows unemployment rates in different parts of the world in April 1989.

UK regions

South East England	4.0 %
East Anglia	3.5 %
South West England	4.9 %
West Midlands	6.5 %
East Midlands	5.9 %
Yorks/Humberside	7.8 %
North West England	9.1 %
North of England	10.3 %
Wales	8.6 %
Scotland	9.8 %
Northern Ireland	15.6 %
UK total	6.6 %

Some other countries

Australia	7.5 %	Italy	16.5 %
Austria	6.6 %	Japan	2.4 %
Belgium	14.0 %	Luxembourg	1.6 %
Canada	8.6 %	Netherlands	14.1 %
Denmark	9.4 %	Norway	5.3 %
Finland	4.8 %	Portugal	7.8 %
France	10.0%	Spain	18.7 %
W. Germany	7.2 %	Sweden	1.3 %
Greece	7.3 %	Switzerland	0.7 %
Irish Rep.	18.0 %	USA	5.0 %

Source : Employment Gazette, June 1989

B2 CAUSES AND CURES OF UNEMPLOYMENT

Many factors can result in unemployment. Not all are easily remedied. We will look in the following sections at some of the most significant causes of unemployment.

B2A Lack of demand

If the British car industry can produce one million cars by employing all the available car workers, but it can sell only 800,000 cars, it will sooner or later reduce output to 800,000; and to produce that number it does not need all the car workers.

Remedies: If lack of demand is the cause of unemployment, the obvious remedy is to increase demand. This can be done, for example, by reducing taxes. If people pay less taxes, they have more money to spend. Another way of increasing demand is to make borrowing cheap and easy. The former is a fiscal policy measure; the latter is an example of a monetary policy measure (fiscal and monetary policy will be discussed in more detail in Chapter 7). Furthermore, one can try to increase the demand for British goods by not allowing competing foreign goods into the country, or by making foreign goods more expensive by means of import duties or currency devaluations. Let us assume a British car costs $6,000 and a French car of the same size and quality costs 56,000 francs. Which one will you buy if you have no nationalistic preferences? Well, we cannot answer the question yet, because the answer depends on the exchange rate. If one pound is worth ten francs, the French car costs £5,600 and is cheaper than the British one; consequently, you will buy the French car if you have no nationalistic preferences. If, however, the value of the pound is reduced to 8 francs, the cost of the French car, expressed in sterling, will go up to £7,000 (the sterling equivalent of 56,000 francs at the exchange rate of 8 francs to the pound). Now the British car is the cheaper one, so some people who would have bought the French car at the old exchange rate will now buy the British one: the devaluation of the pound has increased the demand for British goods, and this should increase employment in the UK (more about the balance of payments and exchange rates in Chapter 8).

B2B   Structural unemployment

Not all unemployment is caused by a lack of overall demand. Sometimes the skills of the workforce do not coincide with the skills required by employers, and the fact that there is an urgent demand for electronics specialists does not help an unemployed shipyard worker whose skills are no longer in demand. This type of unemployment is called structural unemployment.

Structural unemployment occurs frequently when the structure of the economy changes. In this case people lose their jobs in the declining industries (like steel,shipbuilding or coalmining), and may not have the skills required by the more prosperous new industries (like electronics or financial services).

Remedy: Given that the cause of structural unemployment is a mismatch between the skills the workforce has and the skills employers need, the logical remedy is to do away with that mismatch. This can be done by retraining and by informing school leavers about job prospects in the various sectors of the economy.

B2C   Regional unemployment

In most countries which are a bit bigger than Liechtenstein or Monaco there are regional differences in the level of unemployment. In the UK, unemployment is usually lowest in East Anglia

and the South East of England, and highest in Northern Ireland (see the table in section Bl). Regional differences in unemployment rates arise mainly for the following two reasons.

Firstly, not all regions are equally attractive to investors. If you set up a lemonade factory on the outskirts of London, you have ten million potential consumers on your doorstep; if you set up the same factory in Stornoway on the Isle of Lewis you hardly have ten thousand people nearby. Proximity of markets, availability of raw materials and access to suitable transport facilities are some of the factors which affect the desirability of a given location for the purpose of setting up factories or other production facilities.

The other important factor causing regional differences in unemployment rates is the fact that some parts of the country suffer more than others from the decline of industries like coalmining or shipbuilding. If a region relies heavily on an industry which is now in decline, unemployment in that region will be higher than in regions which are not affected by the decline in that industry. Many of the present unemployment troublespots in Britain are places where people used to depend on what are now declining industries.

Remedies: The main cures for regional unemployment are to persuade people to leave high unemployment areas and to move to areas where jobs are easier to find (if they can afford to do so), and/or incentives for companies to invest in high-unemployment areas.

B2D   Demographic factors

A baby boom now will lead to an increase in the number of first-time job-seekers in sixteen to twenty years' time, but that does not mean that additional jobs will just come about automatically at that time. Likewise, a fall in the birth rate now will lead to a fall in the number of school leavers in about 18 years' time. These examples show that changes in birth rates can increase or reduce unemployment at some time in the future because the number of jobs available does not automatically go up or down in line with the number of job seekers. Other demographic factors which affect the number of job seekers are the age structure of the population in general (a higher percentage of elderly people means fewer job seekers), and the percentage of people who want a job; 50 years ago it was rare for a married woman to have a paid job, but nowadays it is quite common, so the percentage of people who want a job changes over time.

B2E Seasonal unemployment

Some industries operate mainly in one particular season of the year; agriculture and tourism can serve as examples. These industries provide more employment during their busy season than they do during the rest of the year. In the UK, unemployment is usually higher in winter than it is during the summer.

B2F Frictional unemployment

This is really a catch-all for all other causes of unemployment, and includes things like unemployment due to lack of information about vacancies, unemployment between leaving one job and taking up another, and so on.

Irrespective of the economic situation, there will always be some unemployment. Job centres can do a lot to provide information about vacancies, but it will never be possible to inform every unemployed person about every suitable vacancy. There will always be some people who are unemployed for a few weeks between leaving one job and taking up another. And then there will always be some people who are unemployable because of severe physical or mental handicaps, lack of reliability, or other factors. Therefore, unemployment will hardly ever be zero, even in ideal economic circumstances.

B2G Unemployment in developing countries

The causes of unemployment which we have discussed above are those which are common in developed countries. You should appreciate that in countries which are still developing different considerations apply. For example, many people may be unemployed even though there is a great demand for all kinds of goods.

A major cause of unemployment in such countries is the lack of factors of production other than unskilled labour. There is often a lack of capital (such as machinery), of suitable skills among the workforce, of managerial or technical capability, or of usable land.

Clearly, although these elements differ significantly from those which cause unemployment in developed countries, they are no less serious in their effects, and no easier to combat.

C

WHY IS IT SO DIFFICULT TO COMBAT INFLATION AND UNEMPLOYMENT?

We have now looked at the various causes of inflation and unemployment, and suggested remedies for most of them. If there are all these remedies, why do we still have inflation and unemployment?

One reason is that some policy measures which reduce inflation will increase unemployment, and vice versa. For instance, reducing demand will reduce inflation, but increase unemployment. Devaluing the pound may persuade some people to buy British instead of foreign goods (which should increase employment in Britain), but such a measure will also increase the cost of goods we have to import, such as foodstuffs or raw materials which cannot be produced in Britain, thereby leading to higher inflation. And import controls may not lead to any increase in the demand for British goods if foreign countries retaliate by not allowing British goods into their markets any more.

Another reason why inflation and unemployment are difficult to combat is that they are partly the result of people's attitudes and behaviour, which are difficult to change. An unemployed shipyard worker who refuses to do any work other than shipbuilding probably condemns himself to being unemployed for the rest of his life. If there are a lot of people who refuse to leave unemployment troublespots in order to find work in more prosperous parts of the country, the chances of reducing unemployment are bleak. And if a nation insists on living beyond its means, it condemns itself to inflation. In Britain, for instance, output per capita has, in the long term, risen by about 2% per year. Attempts to increase living standards at a faster rate than output, be it by reckless borrowing or by wage claims, will sooner or later lead to inflation because demand will exceed supply.

Reference

1   Source : Employment Gazette, June 1989

6

SELF-ASSESSMENT QUESTIONS

1. Has Britain always had inflation?

   _____

   _____

   _____

2. What is the Retail Prices Index?

   _____

   _____

   _____

3. What does the term 'inflation rate' mean?

   _____

   _____

   _____

4. Why is inflation considered to be undesirable in most countries?

   _____

   _____

   _____

5. Explain the difference between demand inflation and cost inflation.

   _____

   _____

   _____

6. What does the term 'unemployment rate' mean?

   _____

   _____

   _____

7. What is the national unemployment rate at the moment? Is this higher or lower than last year?

   _____

   _____

8.   Which are the areas of (a) highest; (b) lowest unemployment rates in the UK?

_____

_____

_____

9.   Why is unemployment higher in Newcastle than it is in London? Why is it rather low in Shetland?

_____

_____

_____

10.   How would you expect the current fall in the number of school leavers to affect the extent of unemployment among young people?

_____

_____

_____

11.   Why does the government not give a job to every unemployed person and, if necessary, print money to pay the wages?

_____

_____

_____

ANSWERS TO SELF-ASSESSMENT QUESTIONS APPEAR OVERLEAF

6

ANSWERS TO SELF-ASSESSMENT QUESTIONS

1. No: prices fell for some time during Queen Victoria's reign, and again in the 1930s.

2. The Retail Prices Index is a tool used to measure inflation. It is based on a 'basket of commodities' which is made up of the goods and services that an average household buys. Every month, the government works out the cost of that basket. The RPI is worked out by dividing the cost of the basket now by its cost in the 'base period' (January 1987).

3. The inflation rate is the percentage change in the Retail Prices Index during the past twelve months.

4. Inflation is considered undesirable because it leads to an unfair redistribution of income and wealth, causes cash flow problems for companies and leads to problems in the areas of foreign trade and exchange rates.

5. Demand inflation: prices rise because of an excessive level of demand (demand exceeds the productive capacity of the economy).

    Cost inflation: prices rise because costs of production (like wages or raw material prices) have risen and manufacturers try to pass on those price rises to consumers in order to maintain their profit margins.

6. The unemployment rate is the number of people claiming unemployment benefit, expressed as a percentage of the economically active population.

7. The answer to this question changes over time. You should try to find it from newspapers or other current material.

8. In the UK, unemployment is usually highest in Northern Ireland and lowest in the South East of England or in East Anglia.

9. Newcastle suffers from the decline in the coal industry, whereas London benefits from the relative prosperity in financial and other services. Shetland benefits from the oil industry.

10. The fall in the numbers leaving school, and so seeking work, has reduced youth unemployment considerably.

11. Such a policy would increase inflation.

6

ASSIGNMENT 2

You should work this assignment after studying Chapters 5 and 6. Answer any three questions, and allow yourself one and a half hours to complete it.

1. Gross domestic product (or other concepts of national income) can be calculated in three different ways. What are these three ways, and why do they all lead to the same total?

2. The control of inflation is a central theme of UK economic policy. Explain why inflation is considered to be a problem, and describe its main causes.

3. Describe the main causes of unemployment. Why is unemployment considerably higher in Scotland than it is in the south of England?

4. There are enormous differences between the levels of material well-being of different countries. Explain the reasons for these differences, from an economic point of view.

7
MONETARY AND FISCAL POLICY

A   Controlling demand by monetary and fiscal policy

B   Monetary policy

C   Fiscal policy

D   How do monetary and fiscal policies affect the insurance industry?

LEARNING OBJECTIVES

After studying this chapter, you should be able to:

▷ outline the role of monetary and fiscal policies in controlling demand;

▷ define the attitude of the present British government towards monetary policy as opposed to fiscal policy;

▷ give various definitions of the money supply;

▷ explain the role of interest rates in controlling the money supply;

▷ explain the use of interest rates in managing exchange rates;

▷ define the role of government in a western-type economy;

▷ list the main income and expenditure items of the British government;

▷ explain how government finances can be used as a tool of economic policy;

▷ outline how monetary and fiscal policy affect the insurance industry.

A
CONTROLLING DEMAND BY MONETARY AND FISCAL POLICY

We have already seen on several occasions in this course that a mismatch between supply and demand causes problems. Just to recap: suppose the government decides to spend more money on something, and prints the money to finance this additional expenditure. What will happen next? Well, the people who get the newly printed money will spend at least part of it, and that's where the trouble starts. One can easily print more money, but one cannot print the machines, farmland, skilled workers and so on (the factors of production) which one needs to produce the additional goods and services which people want to buy with their newly printed money.

If demand rises by more than the productive capacity of the economy, there are only two ways out.

(i) **The additional demand is not satisfied.** In this case the excess demand leads to rising prices (inflation) in an uncontrolled economy, and to shortages and black markets if government price controls prevent prices from rising (see section 2E).

(ii) **The additional demand is satisfied by importing the additional goods and services people now want to buy.** This may help us to avoid inflation since there is no excess demand (the additional demand having been satisfied by the imported goods), but if we import more without at the same time increasing our exports, we will get into trouble with our balance of payments (more about this in Chapter 8).

So, if demand grows at a faster rate than the productive capacity of the economy, we get either inflation or balance of payments problems (assuming there are no government price controls). If demand grows at a slower rate than the productive capacity of the economy we also get problems, namely demand-deficient unemployment (see section 6B2A). This example shows that if we want to avoid these problems, we have to make sure that demand grows at roughly the same rate as the productive capacity of the economy.

How can we bring this about? In modern capitalist economies, the main tools used by the authorities to influence demand are monetary and fiscal policy. The term **'monetary policy'** refers to all those measures which aim at influencing or controlling the amount of money in circulation (the so-called money supply), or the price of money. By 'price of money', economists traditionally meant interest rates; the rate of interest being the price you have to pay for the temporary use of other people's money (a loan). Nowadays the 'price of money' is often taken to be the exchange rate, this being the price of one sort of money (e.g. pounds) in terms of some other sort of money (e.g. dollars). The Chancellor of the Exchequer said in his 1989 budget speech, "The exchange rate is of particular importance in the conduct of monetary policy."

'Fiscal policy' refers to the use of the government's expenditure and revenue for economic policy purposes (for instance to control demand). Given that the government's revenue and expenditure account for a large percentage of the total revenue and expenditure in an economy (about 40 % in the UK), they have a strong influence on the economy and government can use its revenue and expenditure as instruments of economic policy. Stanlake, in his textbook 'Introductory Economics'[1], defines fiscal policy as the 'deliberate manipulation of government income and expenditure so as to achieve desired economic or social objectives.'

A1 WHAT KIND OF MEASURES TO USE

Should we use monetary or fiscal measures if we want to influence demand? This is largely a matter of personal choice and political opinion, and the popularity of each kind of policy has varied over time. From the depression of the 1930s right through to the early 1970s fiscal policy reigned supreme, but since then monetary policy has had the upper hand. The popularity of fiscal policy earlier in this century was largely due to the theories of the English economist Lord John Maynard

Keynes, whereas the predominance of monetary policy nowadays is, at least partly, the result of the work of the American economist Milton Friedman.

At the present time, many governments consider the fight against inflation to be the main task of economic policy, and monetary policy the main instrument to achieve this aim. Fiscal policy is accorded a much more limited role. For example, the Swiss National Bank says in its 1988 annual report, 'The aim of the National Bank's monetary policy is the long-term stability of prices in Switzerland.' The Reserve Bank of New Zealand Act 1989 says, 'The primary function of the (Reserve) Bank is to formulate and implement monetary policy directed to the economic objective of achieving and maintaining stability in the general level of prices.' (The Swiss National Bank and the Reserve Bank of New Zealand are, respectively, the Swiss and New Zealand equivalents of the Bank of England. The quotation regarding the Reserve Bank of New Zealand has been taken from the Bank of New Zealand's publication 'New Zealand Economic Indicators', June 1989.) The Chancellor of the Exchequer gave a clear indication of the attitude of the British Government in these matters when he said in his 1989 budget speech:

> **Inflation is a disease of money, and monetary policy is its cure. Monetary policy plays and must always play the central role in the battle against inflation. The role of fiscal policy is to bring public accounts into balance and keep them there, and thus underpin the process of re-establishing sound money.**

B
MONETARY POLICY

Now that we know what monetary and fiscal policy are about, let us look at each of them in some more detail, beginning with monetary policy.

B1 WHAT IS MONEY?

Suppose you want to know how much money you

have. How do you find out? Probably you will start by getting your purse out and counting the cash that is in it. No doubt, the cash (notes and coin) in your purse is part of the money you have, but is it all? If you find yourself in a shop with $5 cash in your pocket but you want to buy something that costs $8, will you have to go home to get more cash before you can buy that item? Not necessarily. If you have your cheque book with you, you may well be able to pay by cheque. So, money you have in a current account with a bank is almost as 'spendable' as is cash in your pocket; consequently, should you not also include your current account balance when working out how much money you have? And if you include your current account balance, how about savings accounts, deposit accounts, building society accounts, National Savings Certificates.....? This shows that there is no such thing as the definition of the money supply. The Governor of the Bank of Canada said in his Bank's 1982 annual report, 'A financial system generates a variety of liquid financial assets that possess money-like characteristics in some degree. These can be combined in different ways giving alternative definitions of the money supply.'

For the purposes of monetary policy, the authorities will adopt those monetary aggregates which have shown a close relationship with the variables which the authorities want to control, such as inflation. How, then, do the UK authorities define the money supply?

B2 DEFINITIONS OF THE MONEY SUPPLY

At the present time, three measures of the money supply are published regularly by the Bank of England. These monetary aggregates are known as M0, M4 and M5. The 'gap' between M0 and M4 exists because the monetary aggregates in between (i.e., M1, M2, and M3) have become obsolete for one reason or another. For example, M1 and M3 included deposits with banks, but not with building societies. Such a distinction may have made sense in the past, but over the last couple of years the difference between banks and building societies has become more and more blurred, and some building societies have even officially re-constituted themselves as banks (the first one to do so was the Abbey National in 1989).

Consequently, the Bank of England no longer considers it meaningful to include bank deposits in a definition of the money supply and to leave building society deposits out, and as a result of this concepts like M1 and M3 have been overtaken by events (they were compiled and published for the last time in June 1989).

As the table below shows, M0, or the money supply narrowly defined, includes notes and coin in circulation with the public, notes and coin held in the tills of banks and other financial institutions, and those institutions' deposits with the Bank of England. M4 and M5 measure the amount of money held by members of the public. M4 includes notes and coin in circulation with the public, and private sector bank and building society deposits. M5 is an even wider monetary aggregate; it includes all of M4, plus private sector holdings of National Savings investments (National Savings Bank accounts, National Savings Certificates...) as well as certain money market instruments.

Definitions of the money supply (amounts in £millions)

	End 1988	End 1987
M0 :		
Notes and coin in circulation with the public	14,765	13,592
Notes and coin held by financial institutions		
Deposits of banks etc with the Bank of England	3,275	3,041
	18,040	16,633
M4 :		
Notes and coin in circulation with the public	14,765	13,592
Private sector deposits with banks	189,125	146,876
Private sector deposits with building societies (net)	153,597	143,473
	357,487	303,941
M5 :		
M4	357,487	303,941
Private sector holdings of National Savings investments	11,567	10,682
Private sector holdings of money market instruments	3,611	4,777
	372,665	319,400

Source : CSO Financial Statistics, June 1989

You may be surprised to see that the amount of money in circulation (no matter whether you take M0, M4 or M5) changes over time, which normally means that it increases as time goes by. Where does this additional money come from, and who is in the business of 'manufacturing money'? To answer this question we must look separately at M0 on the one hand, and M4 and M5 on the other.

B3 CONTROLLING THE MONEY SUPPLY M0

Only the Bank of England can increase the amount of M0 (some other people may try occasionally, but they end up in prison if they get caught). To increase M0 the Bank of England has to buy something. Theoretically, this 'something' can be anything, but in practice the Bank of England will usually buy bills of exchange if it wants to increase M0. A bill of exchange is a short-term (usually three months) security used normally to finance trade transactions. In other countries the practice may be different. In Switzerland, for instance, the National Bank buys or sells foreign currencies in order to control the money supply, and in the USA the Federal Reserve (the US equivalent of the Bank of England) buys or sells government securities. But why do Bank of England purchases of, for example, bills of exchange increase M0? The answer is easy. Suppose the Bank of England agrees to buy a bill of exchange from you. In that case you give a bill of exchange to the Bank of England, and in exchange you get Bank of England notes; that is, money. The money you

To increase money supply (M0) Bank of E. buys something it pays money for it thus increasing money supply — to reduce money they sell something

get from the Bank of England for your bill was not in circulation before this transaction, so the fact that the Bank of England bought your bill has increased the amount of money (M0) in circulation: Bank of England purchases of bills of exchange increase M0. Bank of England sales of bills of course have the opposite effect: they reduce M0.

Almost every day you can read in the 'Money Markets' section of the Financial Times that the Bank of England has bought or sold so and so many million pounds' worth of bills of exchange to compensate for shortages or surpluses of cash in the money markets.

B4 CONTROLLING THE MONEY SUPPLY M4 AND M5

Now that we know how changes in M0 come about, let us turn to the other monetary aggregates, namely M4 and M5. These measures of the money supply consist largely of deposits with banks and building societies, and consequently the main factors at work behind changes here are the activities of banks and building societies, rather than those of the Bank of England. How does all this work, and how is it that banks and building societies are able to influence the money supply ?

Let us assume somebody opens a new current account with a bank, by depositing £100 in Bank of England notes. What will the bank do with that £100? Well, it will have to keep some of that money as a cash reserve in case this or some other customer wants his money back, but it need not keep the entire £100 since the probability of all customers wanting all their money back at the same time is remote. The portion of the money which the bank does not need as a cash reserve can be lent out. If we assume that the bank wants to keep half of the £100 as a cash reserve, it can lend out the other £50. Suppose now that somebody borrows that £50 from the bank, and withdraws that money in cash. What is the money supply (M4 or M5) now?

The original depositor of the £100 still has his £100 deposit, and bank deposits are part of M4. In addition, the person who has borrowed the £50 from the bank has £50 cash, and cash (notes and coin

in circulation with the public) is also part of M4. So, M4 is now £100 + £50 = £150. The £50 held in the bank's till does not affect M4 since M4 includes only notes and coin in circulation with the public, not cash held by financial institutions.

What will happen next? Well, people hardly borrow and pay interest on the amount borrowed just for the fun of hoarding cash; they usually borrow in order to spend the money. Let us assume the person who has borrowed the £50 spends this money in a shop. Shopkeepers usually pay the day's takings into their bank account at the end of the day, for security and other reasons. Ignoring any other money the shopkeeper may get, he now pays the £50 into his bank account.

What will the bank do with these £50? Well, it will do the same thing as the previous bank did after getting its £100 deposit: it will keep part of the money as a cash reserve, and lend out the rest. If this bank also maintains a 50% cash ratio, it will keep 50% of the £50 (i.e. £25) as a cash reserve and lend out the other £25.

What will the money supply be after that £25 has been lent (for simplicity assume again that the borrower has withdrawn the amount borrowed in cash)? The original depositor still has his £100 deposit, the shopkeeper has a £50 deposit, and the latest borrower has £25 cash; so the money supply (M4) is now £175.

We can conclude from this that every loan creates additional purchasing power, and that is the same thing as saying that every loan increases the money supply.

How does this process go on? If, as we have assumed so far, each bank keeps a cash reserve amounting to 50% of its deposit liabilities (in other words, 50% of the amount customers have deposited with it) and lends out the other 50%, the money supply develops as follows:

$$100 + 50 + 25 + 12.5 + 6.25 + 3.125 + ...$$

The six items listed on the line above add up to 196.875, but the process does not stop there. Mathematically speaking, we are talking about an infinite geometric series, and one can show that the sum of the series above is exactly 200.

If money is deposited in a bank the bank will lend part of that money out again (say 50%). As M4 includes deposit A/Cs and money in circulation M4 has kept 50%

You may now wonder whether the 50% reserve ratio is not just an arbitrary figure. Could we not just as well have assumed any other percentage? We could indeed, and if the reserve ratio had been different we would have ended up with a different money supply. If banks keep less in reserve they can lend more, and since every bank loan increases the money supply a lower reserve ratio leads to a larger money supply.

If the reserve ratio is 1/3, the money supply develops as follows:

$$100 + 66.67 + 44.44 + 29.64 + 19.77 + 13.19 + ... = 300$$

A reserve ratio of 25% leads to the following money supply:

$$100 + 75 + 56.25 + 42.19 + 31.64 + 23.73 + 17.80 + ... = 400$$

Q If the reserve ratio is 25%, why is the first addition to the original money supply (of 100) 75 and not 25?

A The bank with which the first customer deposits his £100 will keep £25 as a cash reserve and lend out the remaining £75. It is the £75 lent, not the £25 kept in reserve, which increases the money supply.

Let us recap. We started with a money supply of £100. Bank lending has increased this to £200, £300 or £400, depending on the reserve ratio. This example shows that lending by banks and other financial institutions is a major force behind changes in the broader versions of the money supply (M4 and M5): in fact, the major force, as the following statistic demonstrates.

Counterparts to changes in M4 during 1988 (£ millions):

Lending to the private sector by banks, building societies and other financial institutions	+81,951
Public sector contribution	-4,564
External and foreign currency transactions	-11,784
Banks' non-deposit liabilities	-12,252
Other factors	+ 195
Change in M4 during 1988	+ 53,546

Source : CSO Financial Statistics, June 1989

As we saw in section B1, M4 increased by £53,546 million during 1988. The 'counterparts' show how that increase has come about. Bank and other lending to the private sector added £81,951 million to M4. The activities of the public sector (largely the government) led to a reduction of M4 by £4,564 million. The reason for this is that the British government now has a budget surplus, part of which is used to pay off debts incurred in previous years (more about this in the fiscal policy section C below); just as lending increases the money supply, so the repayment of loans reduces it. External and foreign currency transactions led to a reduction of M4 by £11,784 million; the reason for this is that Britain had a balance of payments deficit in 1988, and this can be viewed as money flowing out of the country and thereby reducing

the amount of money in circulation in Britain. The only other numerically important factor among the 'counterparts' is the banks' non-deposit liabilities, which produced a reduction of the money supply by £12,252 million. This item relates to transactions like share issues by banks. If a bank issues more shares, most buyers will pay for their new shares by writing a cheque which is debited to their current account; in other words, the purchase of newly issued bank shares reduces people's bank deposits, and hence the money supply.

Given that lending to the private sector is the main force behind changes in the money supply (M4 or M5), it follows that if the authorities (government and Bank of England) want to control the money supply they have to control that lending.

Q How can they do that?

A Banks and other financial institutions can only lend if people are prepared to borrow. Therefore, the money supply can be controlled by encouraging or discouraging borrowing. Higher interest rates discourage borrowing; lower interest rates encourage it.

Why should interest rates affect people's desire to borrow? Suppose you want to buy a house and need a $40,000 mortgage to do so. If the mortgage rate is 10% the interest cost of such a mortgage is $4,000 per year; if the mortgage rate is 15%, the interest cost of the same mortgage is $6,000 p.a. There are people who can afford to pay $4,000 but not $6,000 in interest per year, and these people may borrow if the interest rate is 10% but they can no longer afford to borrow if the interest rate goes up to 15%. The increase in interest rates has thus reduced the demand for loans, and if people do not want to borrow banks and other institutions cannot lend. Indeed, interest rates are now the main tool of monetary policy in the UK. As the Chancellor said in his 1989 budget speech, "Short-term interest rates remain the essential instrument of monetary policy," and his successor in 1990 said, "..monetary policy and interest rates... provide the key to progress on inflation."

If the authorities want to slow down the expansion of the money supply, they increase interest rates. At the higher rates of interest people will not borrow so much, and less bank lending means a slower growth rate of the money supply (see counterparts to changes in M4 earlier on in this section). Obviously, if the authorities want a faster expansion of the money supply, they will lower interest rates, thereby encouraging borrowing. The authorities can manipulate interest rates by the Bank of England's operations in the money markets (see section B2). The Bank of England can, so to speak, dictate at what rates of interest it is prepared to buy or sell bills of exchange; these interest rates affect the cost of money to the banks, and spread from there through the entire financial system.

B5   EXCHANGE RATE TARGETS

Until the middle of 1985 the Bank of England attempted to control the money supply (at that time, the now defunct M3 was the most popular monetary aggregate). After that, the emphasis shifted to the exchange rate of the pound. To understand this shift in emphasis one has to recall the main aim of the present government as far as monetary policy is concerned: it wants to use monetary policy as a tool to bring down inflation. Some economists believe that the best way to ensure low inflation rates is a tight control of the money supply (allowing the money supply, however defined, to grow no faster than the productive capacity of the economy); others believe that low inflation can best be achieved by linking the pound to a foreign low-inflation currency, which for practical reasons would have to be either the West German mark or the ecu (European Currency Unit). Evidence from other countries, as well as theoretical considerations, indicates that if the exchange rate of the pound in relation to the other West European currencies is kept stable, Britain will, in the long term, have roughly the same rate of inflation as those other West European countries. Since in the last 20 years Britain's inflation rate has nearly always been above the West European average, such a policy would mean a reduction of the inflation rate in Britain. In the light of these views, it will be interesting to watch the effect of Britain's entry into the EC exchange rate mechanism.

Well, how can we control the exchange rate of the pound if we decide that that is what we want to do? (Whether we want to control the money supply or the exchange rate is a political question). Interest rates are again the answer. If the exchange rate of the pound is already at the desired level there is, of course, no need for any intervention. If, however, the exchange rate of the pound is not where they want it to be, then the authorities can use interest rates to bring it to the desired level. Higher British interest rates make the pound more attractive as an investment currency. If British interest rates go up, people from many countries will want to invest their money in Britain in order to benefit from those higher interest rates. To invest money here, however, they first have to buy sterling, and this increased demand for pounds on the foreign exchange markets increases the value (the exchange rate) of the pound.

Lower interest rates have the opposite effect. If British interest rates fall, Britain becomes less attractive as a place for investing your money.

People will start selling pounds, and these sales of sterling will push the value of the pound down. In short: **higher interest rates increase the value of the pound, lower interest rates reduce the value of the pound.** As explained earlier, the Bank of England can influence interest rates through its operations in the money markets (see the end of section B4).

C

FISCAL POLICY

Fiscal policy is determined by a number of disparate factors, which we will now consider.

C1 THE ROLE OF GOVERNMENT IN A WESTERN-TYPE ECONOMY

We have seen earlier in this chapter that monetary and fiscal policy are the two main instruments of economic policy. Before we look at the details of the government's revenue and expenditure, let us discuss a more general point: what is the role of government in a western-type economy? Why does the government spend money at all? After all, Britain is predominantly a market economy and not an economy based on government control.

? Before reading on, make a note of the kinds of item on which the government has to spend money. Why is it that such items have to be paid for by the government?

Well, even if Britain is predominantly a market economy, there are numerous areas where it is felt that the market could not operate satisfactorily. For instance, the shipping industry needs lighthouses along the coast. Could such a service be provided by the private sector? Clearly not, because there is no way of running a 'Lighthouse plc' as a profitable enterprise. Once a lighthouse is there, every skipper benefits from its presence, and it is impossible to restrict the benefit to those who are willing to pay for it. Why should a skipper pay for the services of a lighthouse if he gets the benefit anyway, whether he pays for it or not?

A shopkeeper can make his goods available to those people who are willing and able to pay for them, and refuse them to people who are not prepared to pay for them. You cannot do that with lighthouses, street lighting and many other services. If it is not possible to restrict a good or service to those who are prepared to pay for it, it is not possible to make a profit by providing that good or service, and consequently there is no incentive for the private sector to provide it. If we want that good or service, the government will have to provide it, because only the government can force everybody to pay towards it (by means, for example, of taxes).

Going one step further, there are some areas where it would be **possible** to provide a service only to those willing and able to pay for it and to refuse it to others, but where it is thought **undesirable** to do so. For instance, society is quite prepared to say, "If you can't afford a television set, do without one." However, society in general is not prepared to say, "Don't go to hospital if you have no money." Most people in Britain believe that everybody should have access to medical services irrespective of his ability to pay. Since we are not prepared to deny medical services to those who need them but cannot pay for them, we need a government presence in this area of the economy. Much the same can be said of education. This does not mean that there is or that there should be a government monopoly in these areas. There are private schools and hospitals, and they may restrict their services to people willing and able to pay for them; but there are also schools and hospitals run by the government, and access to them does not depend on a person's ability to pay.

So, goods and services which we do not want to restrict to those people who are willing and able to pay for them cannot be provided satisfactorily by the private sector alone; the government has to provide them.

Whether government involvement is desirable in other areas of the economy is a matter of political opinion. Should the government own railway companies or airlines, or should these activities be left to the private sector? There is no objective answer to this question, and different countries have adopted different solutions. For example,

The govt must supply some service because
① it is not possible to restrict service to only those paying - Street lights
② it is not desirable to restrict service to only those paying - hospitals

there are no government-owned airlines in the UK or the USA, but in France, Ireland and many other countries the main airline is state-owned. Japan and West Germany have adopted a half-way solution, in that the major airline is a private sector company whose shares are quoted on the stock-market, but the government is a major share-holder.

Beyond the provision of goods and services, the government's involvement in the economy also extends to the redistribution of income and wealth.

In every society there are people who, for a variety of reasons, are not able to earn what the government considers to be a reasonable minimum income. To help those people, most developed countries have a welfare or social security system which guarantees a certain minimum income to everybody. If somebody does not earn the specified minimum amount, the government makes up the difference; the whole scheme is financed by taxes and National Insurance contributions which have to be paid by those who earn more than a certain amount. So, the social security system is a mechanism which redistributes income from people who earn more than a certain amount to people who earn less than a certain amount.

A third use to which government finances may be put is to regulate demand.

If the government wants to increase total demand in the economy, it can do so by increasing its own spending or by reducing taxes; lower taxes mean individuals (taxpayers) have more money to spend. The opposite measures can be used to reduce demand.

C2 REVENUE AND EXPENDITURE OF THE BRITISH GOVERNMENT

The British Government spends money on social security, the health service, education, defence, public administration and many other things. Government spending is financed mainly by taxation; in addition there are charges for some government services. For example, you have to pay something if you want a passport or if you want to attend college. Before 1987, the government's expenditure usually exceeded its revenue, and the

difference was known as the public sector borrowing requirement (PSBR for short). From 1987 to 1990, the government ran budget surpluses, and the surplus was used to pay off debt accumulated in the past (hence the expression 'public sector debt repayment', or PSDR).

The following table lists the main items of government revenue and expenditure in 1989-90 and in 1984-85.

Government revenue and expenditure (£ billions)			
REVENUE	1989-90	1984-85	
Income tax	46.9	32.7	
Corporation tax	22.4	8.2	
Value added tax (VAT)	30.0	18.4	
Rates	20.6	12.8	
National Insurance contributions	34.0	23.6	
Other revenues	52.5	44.2	
		206.4	139.9
EXPENDITURE			
Social security	51.0	35.2	
Health	23.2	13.4	
Defence	20.1	17.1	
Education and science	19.6	11.5	
Interest	17.1	16.5	
Other expenditure	68.3	55.8	
		199.3	149.5
		7.1	-9.6
Privatisation proceeds		5.0	0
Central government debt repayment		12.1	-9.6
Public corporations' debt repayment		1.7	-0.9
Public sector debt repayment		13.8	-10.5

Note: The negative public sector debt repayment in 1984-85 means a public sector borrowing requirement in that year.

Source : Budget Report 1989-90 and 1984-85

The figures above show that the government's financial position has moved from a deficit (or PSBR) of £10,500 million in 1984-85 to a surplus (or PSDR) of £13,800 million in 1989-90. What has caused this favourable development?

The period in question was one of rapid economic growth. The government's revenue rose by 48%, which is roughly in line with the increase in national income during that period (+46%). The fact that the government's revenue should rise roughly in line with national income is not surprising; after all, higher personal incomes mean individuals have to pay more income tax, higher company profits mean more corporation tax, and if people spend their higher incomes in the shops the government gets more VAT. Government spending, on the other hand, was only allowed to rise roughly in line with prices; during the five-year period in question, government spending rose by 33% and the Retail Prices Index rose by 30%. So, government revenue rose in line with incomes and government spending rose in line with prices. Since incomes rose faster than prices, the government's revenue rose faster than the government's expenditure. This combination of things allowed the government to turn its deficit into a surplus.

C3   GOVERNMENT FINANCE AS A TOOL OF ECONOMIC POLICY

The present British Government uses its revenue in order to finance its expenditure on goods and services and to finance the income redistribution (social security) system. It does not use its finances to control demand to any great extent. Previous British governments, and governments in some other countries even now, have viewed this situation differently and have used their finances as a tool of demand management. How does this work?

Government finances can be used as a tool of demand management in the following ways:

▶ Government can increase or reduce total demand in the economy by increasing or reducing its own spending. Since government spending accounts for about 40% of all spending, changes in government spending have an important effect on total spending.

▶ Government can increase or reduce its spending on particular goods, services, regions, etc.

▶ Government can increase or reduce other people's ability to spend, by reducing or increasing taxes; either taxes in general, like income tax or

VAT, or taxes on particular goods and services, like the taxes on petrol or tobacco.

▶ Government can affect the economy by the amount and source of its borrowing, or the amount and disposal of its surplus. If the government borrows from banks it increases the money supply, since any bank lending adds to the money supply (see section B4); using a surplus to repay earlier bank loans reduces the money supply. Government borrowing from, or repayments to, private individuals within the country, on the other hand, has no effect on the money supply. If you invest £50 in National Savings Certificates, the government has £50 more and you have £50 less, so the amount of money (M4) is unchanged. If the government borrows from overseas, the money supply will increase since additional money is brought into the country from abroad. Usually the British Government has not borrowed much abroad, but overseas borrowing has been an important source of revenue for the government of the Irish Republic.

The final point above shows that fiscal policy can seldom be seen in isolation. A given fiscal stance will have an impact on the conduct of monetary policy, no matter whether that impact is intended or not. This is what the Chancellor meant when he said in his 1989 budget speech, "The role of fiscal policy is to bring public accounts into balance and keep them there, and thus underpin the process of re-establishing sound money."

D

HOW DO MONETARY AND FISCAL POLICIES AFFECT THE INSURANCE INDUSTRY?

Now that we know the main aims and instruments of monetary and fiscal policy, let us find out in what ways these policies affect the insurance industry. These effects can be summarised under the following headings:

(i)   Total demand in the economy.

(ii)   Interest rates.

(iii) Exchange rates.

(iv) Taxation.

D1   TOTAL DEMAND IN THE ECONOMY

As we have seen in section A, monetary and fiscal policy can be used to increase or reduce total demand in the economy. If monetary or fiscal policy is successful in bringing about the desired change in demand, then this will almost certainly have repercussions on the demand for insurance.

Q   Why will an increase in total demand have an influence on the demand for insurance?

A   If people buy more houses, cars or furniture, and if businesses invest more in machinery, they will want insurance cover for at least some of those additional assets, so an expansionary monetary or fiscal policy will increase the demand for insurance, and a contractionary policy will have the opposite effect.

D2   INTEREST RATES

As explained earlier, interest rates are one of the main tools of monetary policy, and fiscal policy often affects interest rates through the public sector's borrowing requirements or debt repayment. Changes in interest rates affect insurance companies' investment income. Claims can only occur after premiums have been received, and in the meantime the money can be invested. The higher the rates of interest, the more investment income can be earned on a given amount of money. Since this makes insurance operations more profitable, some companies may react by increasing their underwriting capacity. Since the demand for insurance does not automatically increase just because companies want to do more business, such an increase in underwriting capacity may lead to increased competition among insurers and a downward pressure on premium rates. Indeed, such 'soft markets' have often occurred after increases in interest rates.

D3   EXCHANGE RATES

As explained in section B5, monetary and fiscal policy can affect exchange rates. Since many of the large insurance organisations derive a considerable part of their income from overseas, their earnings will be affected by any changes in exchange rates. This will be discussed in more detail in the balance of payments chapter (section 8H).

D4   TAXATION

Taxation is the main source of government revenue and is therefore an important tool of fiscal policy. Changes in taxation affect the insurance industry in a number of ways.

Changes in the rate of corporation tax affect the amount of tax which insurance companies and incorporated brokers have to pay on their profits, just as the rates of income tax affect the amount of income tax which unincorporated brokers have to pay. Furthermore, the structure of the taxation system affects the demand for insurance. This has already been discussed in section 3A4.

Examples of tax changes which have affected the life assurance industry can be found in the **Finance Act 1989.** From 1 January 1990, income and realised capital gains allocated to policyholders have been taxed at the basic rate of income tax rather than at corporation tax and capital gains tax rates. Income allocated to shareholders continues to be taxed at corporation tax rates. Expenses of acquiring new business can no longer be offset against income immediately, but have to be spread forward over a seven year period (with some transitional relief for the period up to 1994). Life assurance policy duty has been abolished with effect from 1 January 1990, and from the same date life assurance companies which also do pensions business can no longer set the expenses of their pensions business against their life assurance profits.

Reference
1 G F Stanlake: Introductory Economics (1989, Longman).

7

SELF-ASSESSMENT QUESTIONS

1. Why is there a need to control demand?

    If demand rises faster than supply
    It leads to inflation
    Can also lead to rise in imports

2. Why are there several definitions of the money supply?

    as money is not only cash in your
    pocket but also deposits in banks
    loans ect.

3. What are the main differences between M0, M4 and M5?

    M0 is physical money
    M4/5 inc Savings deposits - unusable
    money

4. Why does bank lending increase the money supply?

    No effect on M0
    M4 up as the money in form of deposit
    is still there but the cash is being
    used again

5. Why does the government believe an increase in interest rates will slow down the expansion of the money supply?

    people will be reluctant to
    borrow money

6. Why do interest rates affect exchange rates?

    Higher Int means people wish to
    invest in UK but they must buy £ first
    so value of £ ↑ and vice versa

7. Which are the main income and expenditure items of the British Government?

    → Goods + Services
    → Income redist

8. What led to the elimination of the PSBR?

   PSBR

   What caused them to pay of back?

9. In what way can the government affect total demand?

   buy buying more stock

   Taxation

   Int

10. What links are there between monetary and fiscal policy?

11. What main role does the present British Government assign to monetary policy?

    reducing inflation

12. In what ways does fiscal policy affect the insurance industry?

    demand   Int rates

    Tax

    Exchange

8 2/3

12

ANSWERS TO SELF-ASSESSMENT QUESTIONS APPEAR OVERLEAF

7

ANSWERS TO SELF-ASSESSMENT QUESTIONS

1. Too low a level of demand leads to unemployment; too high a level leads to inflation and balance of payments deficits. To avoid these problems, the government tries to make sure that demand is at the right level.

2. In a modern economy there is a variety of liquid assets: cash, bank deposits, building society deposits, treasury bills and others. These can be combined in various ways to produce different definitions of the money supply.

3. M0 includes only Bank of England money (i.e. cash and deposits with the Bank of England). M4 includes cash, and bank and building society deposits held by the private sector. M5 includes M4 and private sector holdings of National Savings and money market investments.

4. Bank lending increases people's purchasing power; it makes more money available for spending. This is the same thing as saying that it increases the money supply.

5. The main force behind the expansion of the money supply is bank lending. Banks can lend only if people are willing to borrow. Higher interest rates will discourage borrowing.

6. If Britain increases its interest rates, sterling becomes more attractive as an investment currency. Investors then buy pounds in order to benefit from the high British interest rates. The additional demand for sterling increases the price of sterling in the foreign exchange markets (i.e. the exchange rate). Lower British interest rates have the opposite effect.

7. **Main income items:** income tax, VAT, corporation tax, National Insurance contributions.

   Main expenditure items: health, social security, education, defence.

8. Government revenues rose in line with national income, whereas government spending rose only in line with prices. Since national income rose faster than prices, government revenue overtook government spending.

9. The government can affect demand either by changing its own demand (by increasing or reducing its own spending) or by affecting other people's ability to spend (by increasing or reducing taxes).

10. The main link is the way in which deficits are financed, or surpluses used. For example, government borrowing from banks increases the money supply, whereas repaying such loans reduces it.

11. Monetary policy is viewed as a way to bring inflation down, and keep it down.

12. Fiscal policy affects total demand in the economy, which in turn affects the demand for insurance. The tax treatment of life funds affects the attractiveness of life assurance as an investment. Changes in corporation tax rates affect insurance companies' profits after tax.

7

ASSIGNMENT 3

You should work this assignment after studying Chapter 7. Answer any three questions, and allow yourself one and a half hours to complete it.

1. Explain why and how the government attempts to control the money supply.

2. Why does lending by commercial banks affect the money supply?

3. What is the role of government in a western-type economy?

4. Explain what is meant by 'fiscal policy'. In what ways can the government use fiscal policy to regulate demand in the economy?

8

THE BALANCE OF PAYMENTS: EXCHANGE RATES

A   What is the 'balance of payments'?

B   Balance of payments statistics

C   The effect of current account surpluses and deficits

D   The desirability of current account surpluses and deficits

E   Causes of current account surpluses and deficits

F   Balance of payments policy

G   Exchange rates

H   Alternative methods of presenting balance of payments statistics

I   Insurance and the balance of payments

LEARNING OBJECTIVES

After studying this chapter, you should be able to:

▷ define the term 'balance of payments';

▷ define other main terms found in British balance of payments statistics;

▷ give details of alternative presentations of balance of payments statistics;

▷ explain the effects of current account surpluses and deficits on the economy;

▷ explain the causes of current account surpluses and deficits;

▷ give details of the main policy instruments (monetary and fiscal policy, exchange rates) which influence the balance of payments;

▷ define the difference between fixed and floating exchange rates;

▷ outline how the insurance industry affects the balance of payments;

▷ explain how the insurance industry is affected by the balance of payments and exchange rates.

A
WHAT IS THE 'BALANCE OF PAYMENTS'?

No country lives in isolation from the rest of the world. British industry, for instance, depends on imported raw materials. If we want to drink tea or coffee we have to import it because we cannot grow it in Britain for climatic reasons. On the other hand, Britain is a net exporter of oil, Rolls Royce sells nearly 80% of the aeroplane engines it makes to foreign airlines or aeroplane manufacturers, and Lloyd's gets more than 50% of its premium income from overseas. Japan and West Germany are net importers of raw materials and

net exporters of manufactured goods, whereas in Australia and Chile it is the other way round. Saudi Arabia exports huge quantities of oil, and imports manufactured and agricultural goods. Spain and some of the other countries around the Mediterranean earn large amounts of money from tourism, because the countries around the Mediterranean are popular holiday destinations among those North Europeans who are of the opinion that 15 degrees centigrade and drizzle is not the optimal summer weather.

[handwritten margin note: "Balance of Payments is the financial transaction between the residents of a country and the rest of the world"]

As a result of activities like those described above, thousands of financial transactions take place every day between people living in Britain and people living overseas. If a foreign airline wants to buy Rolls Royce engines it will of course have to pay for them, just as we have to pay the Brazilians if we want to drink their coffee.

All the financial transactions that take place between residents of a country on the one hand and non-residents on the other, make up that country's **balance of payments.**

B
BALANCE OF PAYMENTS STATISTICS

What are the main factors affecting the British balance of payments? Numerically, the most important sections of the British balance of payments are imports and exports of tangible goods, like oil, motor cars, timber and bananas. As table 1 in section B2 shows, Britain exported about £80,000 million worth of goods in 1988 and imported about £100,000 million worth. If exports exceed imports, the **balance of trade** (also known as the trade balance or **'visible balance'**) is said to be in surplus: in the opposite case it is in deficit, and if exports equal imports it is in equilibrium. Since imports exceeded exports by about £20,000 million in 1988, Britain's trade was in deficit in that year.

Visible trade
This is the export and import of tangible goods, and is an important part of the balance of payments, but inflows and outflows of money can also be caused in other ways. Just as one can import or export tangible goods, so one can import or export **services.** A British resident going to Spain for a holiday, or a foreign airline insuring its aeroplanes with a British insurer, certainly cause money to flow across national boundaries, even if no tangible goods like steel or bananas are shipped from one country to another. In 1988 the import and export of services produced a surplus of £3,428 million for the British balance of payments.[1]

Then there are what the official statistics call **'transfers'.** These transfers include items like cash gifts made by people living in one country to people living in another; inheritances across national boundaries; pensions paid to or received from other countries (the pensions the British government pays to retired Gurkha soldiers are an outflow of money from Britain, and an important source of revenue for Nepal); grants to developing countries; payments for Britain's diplomatic and military presence abroad, and so forth. Transfers caused a deficit of £3,579 million for the British balance of payments in 1988.[1]

The next items we have to look at are **interest, profit and dividend payments.** Of course, if a British resident receives a dividend from a British company then that does not affect the balance of payments, because it is a payment entirely within Britain. If, on the other hand, a British resident gets a dividend from, say, an American company, then that is an inflow of money into Britain from America, and so it affects the balance of payments of these two countries. In the same way, dividends paid by British companies to shareholders living outside Britain are outflows of money from Britain. Interest and profit remittances affect the balance of payments in the same way as dividends. Since British investments overseas exceed foreign investments in Britain, interest, profits and dividends usually produce a surplus for the British balance of payments. In 1988, that surplus amounted to £5,772 million.[1]

Invisibles
The three areas we have just discussed, namely services, transfers, and interest, profit and dividends, are known as the **'invisibles'.** These invisibles have always been the strength of the British balance of payments. Even though the government nearly always spends more money overseas than it receives from other countries, the private sector has always been able to achieve substantial surpluses (net inflows of money) in this area, and insurance is a major contributor. As table 1 in section B2 shows, the invisibles produced a surplus of £5,621 million in 1988.

Current account
The trade balance and the invisibles together are known as the **'current account',** and this is the most important part of the balance of payments. As table 1 shows, Britain had a current account deficit of nearly £15,000 million in 1988.

The British balance of payments

Table 1 : The current account (£ millions)

	1988	1987	1986	1985
Exports	80,157	79,422	72,678	77,988
Imports	100,714	89,584	81,394	80,334
Visible balance	- 20,57	- 10,162	- 8,716	- 2,346
Invisibles	+ 5,621	+ 7,658	+ 8,517	+ 5,683
Current balance	- 14,936	- 2,504	- 199	+ 3,337

Sources: CSO: Economic Trends, June 1989

CSO: The UK balance of payments, 1988 edition

BALANCE OF PAYMENT

Exports

(—) Imports

VISIBLE BALANCE

+/- Invisibles

Current Balance

(Surplus/deficit)

Table 2: Britain's Foreign Trade: Geographical Analysis

£ million

	1977	1978	1979	1980	1981	1982	1983	1984	1985	1986	1987
EXPORTS											
European Community (1)	12 414	14 059	18 084	21 467	21 938	24 267	27 957	32 962	37 902	34 751	39 021
Other Western Europe	3 852	3 632	4 766	5 581	5 054	5 282	6 021	7 072	7 547	7 157	7 788
North America	3 768	4 209	4 763	5 279	7 125	8 360	9 524	11 465	13 292	12 120	12 992
Other developed countries	2 072	2 297	2 472	2 656	2 922	3 245	3 153	3 704	3 801	3 644	4 085
Oil exporting countries	4 329	4 669	3 648	4 816	5 991	6 505	6 133	5 801	5 944	5 497	5 280
Rest of world	5 247	6 115	6 737	7 348	7 638	7 671	7 910	9 259	9 502	9 509	10 256
Total	31 682	34 981	40 470	47 147	50 668	55 330	60 698	70 263	77 988	72 678	79 422
IMPORTS											
European Community (1)	14 223	16 545	20 793	20 710	21 853	25 442	30 417	36 060	39 958	43 162	48 031
Other Western Europe	4 174	4 524	5 886	5 805	6 132	6 614	8 372	10 696	11 473	11 318	12 327
North America	4 584	4 949	5 818	6 819	6 838	7 480	8 462	10 411	10 936	9 418	10 140
Other developed countries	2 627	2 712	2 754	2 844	3 082	3 934	4 555	5 158	5 939	6 388	6 892
Oil exporting countries	3 420	3 030	2 945	3 885	3 441	3 235	2 585	2 672	2 612	1 856	1 606
Rest of world	4 978	4 814	5 672	5 731	5 972	6 407	7 382	9 846	9 416	9 252	10 588
Total	34 006	36 574	43 868	45 794	47 318	53 112	61 773	74 843	80 334	81 394	89 584
VISIBLE BALANCE											
European Community (1)	-1 809	-2 486	-2 709	757	85	-1 175	-2 460	-3 098	-2 056	-8 411	-9 010
Other Western Europe	-322	-892	-1 120	-224	-1 078	-1 332	-2 351	-3 624	-3 926	-4 161	-4 539
North America	-816	-740	-1 055	-1 540	287	880	1 062	1 054	2 356	2 702	2 852
Other developed countries	-555	-415	-282	-188	-160	-689	-1 402	-1 454	-2 138	-2 744	-2 807
Oil exporting countries	909	1 639	703	931	2 550	3 270	3 548	3 129	3 332	3 641	3 674
Rest of world	269	1 301	1 065	1 617	1 666	1 264	528	-587	86	257	-332
Total	-2 324	-1 593	-3 398	1 353	3 350	2 218	-1 075	-4 580	-2 346	-8 716	-10 162

(1) Figures for all years relate to the eleven countries.

Source: CSO, The UK Balance of Payments, 1988 edition

Table 3: Britain's Foreign Trade: Commodity Analysis

£ million

	1977	1978	1979	1980	1981	1982	1983	1984	1985	1986	1987
EXPORTS											
Food,beverages and tobacco	2 184	2 869	2 908	3 233	3 615	3 940	4 230	4 677	4 937	5 445	5 534
Basic materials	996	1 066	1 320	1 495	1 351	1 387	1 653	2 069	2 199	2 109	2 252
Oil	1 970	2 224	4 144	6 118	9 092	10 671	12 486	14 833	16 114	8 202	8 445
Other mineral fuels and lubricants	113	140	166	296	509	551	602	457	662	462	302
Semi-manufactured goods	9 959	10 696	12 461	13 866	13 017	13 979	15 864	18 135	19 920	20 839	22 444
Finished manu-factured goods	15 608	17 026	18 488	21 009	21 880	23 334	24 283	28 420	32 319	33 616	38 213
Commodities and transactions not classified according to kind	852	960	983	1 130	1 204	1 468	1 580	1 672	1 837	2 005	2 232
Total	31 682	34 981	40 470	47 147	50 668	55 330	60 698	70 263	77 988	72 678	79 422
IMPORTS											
Food,beverages and tobacco	5 396	5 581	5 877	5 557	5 918	6 525	7 154	8 138	8 444	9 218	9 333
Basic materials	3 532	3 294	3 694	3 499	3 411	3 428	4 194	4 975	4 908	4 500	4 974
Oil	4 744	4 211	4 881	5 810	5 986	6 032	5 514	7 901	8 013	4 146	4 261
Other mineral fuels and lubricants	154	291	517	742	879	1 072	1 257	2 004	2 203	1 831	1 542
Semi-manufactured goods	8 449	9 534	11 846	12 515	11 605	12 980	15 755	18 330	19 849	21 451	24 023
Finished manu-factured goods	11 244	13 134	16 413	16 910	18 717	22 054	26 753	32 279	35 515	38 714	44 124
Commodities and transactions not classified according to kind	486	527	640	761	801	1 021	1 146	1 216	1 402	1 534	1 327
Total	34 006	36 574	43 868	45 794	47 318	53 112	61 773	74 843	80 334	81 394	89 584

VISIBLE BALANCE

Food,beverages and tobacco	-3 212	-2 712	-2 969	-2 324	-2 303	-2 585	-2 924	-3 461	-3 507	-3 773	-3 799
Basic materials	-2 536	-2 228	-2 374	-2 004	-2 060	-2 041	-2 541	-2 906	-2 709	-2 391	-2 722
Oil	-2 774	-1 987	-737	308	3 106	4 639	6 972	6 932	8 101	4 056	4 184
Other mineral fuels and lubricants	-41	-151	-351	-446	-370	-521	-655	-1 547	-1 541	-1 369	-1 240
Semi-manufactured goods	1 510	1 162	615	1 351	1 412	999	109	-195	71	-612	-1 579
Finished manu-factured goods	4 364	3 892	2 075	4 099	3 163	1 280	-2 470	-3 859	-3 196	-5 098	-5 911
Commodities and transactions not classified according to kind	366	433	343	369	403	447	434	456	435	471	905
Total	-2 324	-1 593	-3 398	1 353	3 350	2 218	-1 075	-4 580	-2 346	-8 715	-10 162

Source: CSO, The UK Balance of Payments, 1988 edition

Surplus ?:
① if goods exported are paid for in currency not that of the exporting nation then its foreign assets are increased
② if goods are paid for in £ -foreign liabilities reduced

C

THE EFFECT OF CURRENT ACCOUNT SURPLUSES AND DEFICITS

In the previous section, we saw that Britain had a current account surplus in 1985, and deficits in 1987 and 1988. In 1988 the USA also had a current account deficit whereas Japan and West Germany had surpluses. What is the relevance of such deficits and surpluses? In what way do they affect the countries concerned?

C1 SURPLUSES

To answer these questions, let us simplify the matter. Let us assume that during a given period of time there is only one transaction affecting the British balance of payments: a German oil importer buys 1,000 barrels of oil at the Sullom Voe oil terminal, at a time when the price of oil is $17 per barrel (oil prices are usually quoted in dollars). What is Britain's current account balance in this case?

Well, Britain has a current account surplus of $17,000. But how will this surplus affect the British economy?

The German buyer will of course have to pay for his oil. Using the figures from the example above, he owes the British exporter $17,000. He could pay, for example, by giving the British exporter a cheque for $17,000. In this case, the British exporter has $17,000 more than he had before he sold the oil. If he wants to keep the dollars, he can pay his cheque into an American bank account or invest the money in US government securities. If he prefers sterling, he can sell his US dollar cheque to somebody else (normally, but not necessarily, through a bank). But no matter whether the exporter keeps the dollars or sells them for sterling, **somebody** in Britain now has $17,000 more than was the case before the Germans bought their oil: **the $17,000 current account surplus has increased Britain's foreign assets by $17,000.**

What will happen if the Germans pay in sterling and not in dollars? If, on the day of the transaction, the exchange rate is $1.70 to the pound, $17,000 = £10,000, so the German oil importer could pay his debt by giving the British exporter £10,000. In this case Britain does not acquire any foreign assets as a result of her current account surplus, so what benefit does she get?

Well, pounds held by non-residents of Britain are technically a debt Britain has towards those non-residents. If non-resident holders of sterling use their pounds to buy British goods or services, they run down their sterling balances. Going back to our oil example, after the German oil importer has given the British exporter £10,000, non-residents have £10,000 less than they had before this transaction, and that means that Britain's debt to those non-residents has gone down by that amount.

We can say, therefore, that **a current account surplus either increases Britain's foreign assets, or reduces Britain's foreign liabilities.**

C2 DEFICITS

Q From the principles explained in section C1, you should now be able to work out the effect of a current account deficit. Again, let us simplify the matter by assuming that there is only one transaction affecting the British balance of payments: a British coffee importer buys ten tons of coffee from Brazil, at a total price of $15,300. Work out what the effect will be on Britain's balance of payments if the importer pays in (a) dollars, and (b) sterling (if £1 = $1.70).

A (a) If payment is made in dollars, Britain's holdings of dollars, and therefore her foreign assets, are reduced by $15,300.

(b) The sterling equivalent of $15,300 is £9,000. If the British coffee importer pays his supplier £9,000, then that is an amount paid to a non-resident of Britain: Britain's liabilities to non-residents go up by that amount.

Therefore, **a current account deficit either reduces Britain's foreign assets, or increases Britain's foreign liabilities.**

In fact, another way of paying the $15,300 would be to borrow that amount, maybe in America or in Japan (given Japan's huge current account surplus). In this case, we also pay for our current account deficit by increasing our foreign liabilities; we owe non-residents the $15,300 we have borrowed from them.

D
THE DESIRABILITY OF CURRENT ACCOUNT SURPLUSES AND DEFICITS

We have seen that a current account surplus increases a country's foreign assets or reduces its foreign liabilities, whereas a deficit has the opposite effect. What does this mean for the desirability of current account surpluses and deficits?

D1 DEFICITS

The easiest way of answering this question is by starting with the deficit, asking ourselves whether Britain (or any other country) could sustain current account deficits forever. The answer, clearly, is that it cannot. As we have seen earlier, a deficit either reduces Britain's foreign assets or it increases Britain's foreign liabilities. Our foreign assets are limited, so if we run current account deficits for a prolonged period we will sooner or later run out of foreign assets with which to pay for our deficit. Could we not go on running deficits by increasing our foreign liabilities? Perhaps we can do that for a while, but certainly not for ever. Britain can increase its foreign liabilities either by borrowing overseas, or by persuading non-residents to accept payment in sterling. However, non-residents will be prepared neither to lend Britain unlimited sums of money nor to hold unlimited amounts of sterling. So, if we run current account deficits year after year, we will sooner or later get into trouble. The over-indebtedness of countries like Brazil or Argentina can serve as examples. **Consistent current account deficits are clearly undesirable.**

D2 SURPLUSES

What does that mean for the desirability of current account surpluses? A current account surplus increases our foreign assets or reduces our foreign liabilities. If we have a large amount of foreign debt, we will be keen to achieve current account surpluses so that we can pay off those debts; in fact debt-ridden countries like Argentina, Brazil, Mexico or Poland have to do this. If we have no foreign debt, however, further current account surpluses lead to an increase in our foreign assets. Having some foreign assets is certainly desirable, if only to pay for any current account deficits that may arise in the future. However, this does not mean that it makes sense to run current account surpluses year after year.

Firstly, having a current account surplus means we have a lower living standard than we could afford; we could, for instance, increase imports and thus have more goods and services to enjoy. Secondly, a current account surplus means an inflow of money from abroad; this may lead to an increase in the money supply, which could be inflationary. And thirdly, it is impossible for all countries to have current account surpluses. If one country has a surplus, then at least one other country must have a deficit. This is particularly easy to see if, for simplicity, we assume there are only two countries in the world; in this case, the surplus of one of the two countries is equal to the deficit of the other. In the real world there are of course more than two countries, but this does not change the fact that, for the world as a whole, surpluses and deficits must cancel each other out. The world as a whole cannot have a current account surplus (unless we start interplanetary trading...), so if some countries have surpluses others must have deficits. Given that deficits are undesirable (as we have seen earlier on in this section), the deficit countries will sooner or later grumble about, and take measures against, the surplus countries. Japan has often been criticised for its surpluses in the past, and has been forced to accept 'voluntary' restrictions on its exports to the EC and the USA.

In the long run, therefore, a country should try to bring about a current account equilibrium. There is nothing wrong with having a deficit for a year or two and then a surplus for a year or two, but consistent current account surpluses or deficits cause problems for all countries concerned.

E
CAUSES OF CURRENT ACCOUNT SURPLUSES AND DEFICITS

Why is it that Britain had a current account surplus in 1985, but deficits in 1987 and 1988? Why, in 1988, did Britain and the USA have current account deficits whereas Japan and West Germany had surpluses? To answer questions like these, we have to compare the total income and the total expenditure of the country concerned: the solution is quite simple.

An individual who spends less than he earns, saves; an individual who spends more than he earns either has to run down existing savings, or he must borrow. In exactly the same way, a country which spends less than it earns has a current account surplus, whereas a country which spends more than it earns has a current account deficit.

The following table explains Britain's 1987 current account deficit on this basis:

Britain's income (£ millions) :

Value of output (see section 5B)	352,237	
Interest, profits and dividends from abroad	+ 5,523	
Transfers	− 3,503	354,257

Britain's expenditure (£ millions) :

Private consumption (see section 5B)	211,777	
Government consumption (see section 5B)	80,379	
Capital formation (see section 5B)	65,827	357,983
Statistical errors and omissions		+ 1,222
Balance on current account (cf. section B)		− 2,504

F
BALANCE OF PAYMENTS POLICY

We have seen in section D that a country should try to bring its current account into equilibrium in the long term. How can this be done? If the cur-

rent account is in equilibrium already, there is of course no need for anybody to intervene. But what can we do if this is not the case? What can we do to overcome unwanted current account surpluses or deficits? Let us start with the deficit, because that is the situation Britain is in at the time of writing.

F1   CORRECTING A DEFICIT

One possibility is to reduce Britain's total spending. We have seen in section E that a current account deficit arises if a country spends more than it earns. It follows that if we reduce our spending sufficiently, our current account deficit will disappear. How can we reduce spending? The main tools to increase or reduce total spending in the economy are monetary and fiscal policy, as discussed in Chapter 7. In fact, Britain's current account deficit in 1987 and 1988 can to a large extent be attributed to the rather euphoric (not to say reckless) borrowing that had gone on in the years leading up to that period.

Another way to reduce or even eliminate a deficit on the current account of the balance of payments is either to increase exports or to reduce imports; as we have seen in section B the current account balance is equal to exports minus imports plus invisibles.

? The 'invisibles' are an important concept, so remind yourself here of what they comprise. Note down the items you think are included in them, and then check your answer against section B.

If we can somehow increase exports or reduce imports sufficiently, the current account deficit will disappear. How can we do this?

Again, monetary and fiscal policy can help. If we use monetary or fiscal policy to reduce total spending in the economy, imports are likely to fall since imports are a fairly constant proportion of total spending.

Another important policy instrument is **exchange rates.** How do they affect imports and exports? Suppose a certain French car costs 60,000 francs. How much is that in sterling? The answer, of course, depends on the exchange rate. If £1 = 12 francs, the French car costs £5,000, but if £1 is 10 francs the same car costs £6,000. This example shows that a devaluation of the pound (a reduction in its value in terms of foreign currencies, e.g. from 12 to 10 francs) makes foreign goods more expensive in sterling terms, so the demand for such goods in Britain should fall. And if people do not buy so many imported goods any more, the deficit on the current account of the balance of payments will disappear (or at least it will be reduced).

A devaluation of the pound will not only affect imports; it will affect exports as well. Why is that so? Suppose a British car costs £6,000. A Frenchman who is considering buying that car is not really interested in the price in sterling; he wants to know the price in French francs (in the same way as a British buyer of a French car is interested in the price in sterling and not in francs). So, how many francs does that British car cost? Again, the answer depends on the exchange rate. If £1 is 12 francs the British car costs 72,000 francs. If the pound is worth 10 francs, it costs only 60,000 francs. So, a devaluation of the pound from 12 francs to 10 francs makes the British car cheaper in French franc terms (in sterling terms the price is still the same, but that is irrelevant for the French buyer). And if British goods become cheaper, the demand for them should increase: British exports should rise, and this, too, tends to eliminate or at least to reduce a current account deficit.

To sum up: **A devaluation of the pound makes foreign goods more expensive in Britain, and British goods cheaper abroad. That should discourage imports and encourage exports, which is just what we need to get rid of a current account deficit.**

F2   CORRECTING A SURPLUS

It is now easy to see what a country can do to get rid of an unwanted current account surplus. Since the current account is equal to income less expenditure (ignoring statistical discrepancies), a country can eliminate a current account surplus by increasing its expenditure, and this, as we know, can be achieved by fiscal or monetary measures (see Chapter 7).

The other way is to use exchange rates. Just as a devaluation of the pound discourages imports and encourages exports, so a revaluation of the pound (an increase in its value in foreign currency terms, e.g. from 10 to 12 francs) encourages imports and discourages exports.

Q Why is this?

A If £1 = 10 francs, a British car which costs £6,000 will cost a French buyer 60,000 francs. If the pound is revalued to 12 francs, the same car will cost 72,000 francs. So, a revaluation of the pound makes British goods more expensive abroad, and some people will no longer buy them at the higher prices: exports are discouraged. At the same time foreign goods become cheaper in sterling terms. A French car costing 60,000 francs cost £6,000 when the pound was worth 10 francs, but after the revaluation of sterling to 12 francs the same car costs £5,000: foreign goods become cheaper in Britain, so imports are encouraged. If a revaluation of the pound succeeds in increasing imports and reducing exports, the unwanted current account surplus will disappear.

G

EXCHANGE RATES

We have seen in section F that exchange rates can be used as an instrument in balance of payments policy. However, **how** can one increase or reduce the value of the pound in relation to other currencies, and how do exchange rates come about in the first place?

The exchange rate is a **price,** namely the price of one currency in terms of some other currency: for example £1 = US $1.70; US $1 = 140 Japanese yen; 1 Swiss franc = 4 French francs, and so on. Before the First World War, exchange rates were defined in terms of gold, but that is no longer relevant nowadays. Exchange rates can be **fixed** or floating. Let us now look at these two possibilities in more detail.

[handwritten: To keep Exchange rate at the same level the demand + supply for say £ + $ must be equal, if demand + supply do not equal]

G1 FIXED EXCHANGE RATES

In a system of fixed exchange rates, exchange rates are fixed by the government or the central bank (the Bank of England or its equivalent). In some cases no fluctuations are allowed at all, in others exchange rates are allowed to fluctuate within narrow limits. For example, until 1980 the Irish pound had the same value as the UK pound; there were no fluctuations at all between those two currencies. On the other hand, the pound to dollar rate was a bit more flexible even at the time of 'fixed' exchange rates. For example, from 1949 to 1967 the exchange rate of the pound was fixed at US $2.80; this was the so-called 'central rate', and the pound was allowed to fluctuate between $2.78 and $2.82. At the moment there are fixed exchange rates (with fluctuations only within narrow limits) within the Exchange Rate Mechanism (ERM) of the European Monetary System (EMS) of which all EC countries except Greece and Portugal are members.

If supply and demand in the foreign exchange markets balance at the fixed rate of exchange, all is well and there is no need for any intervention. If, however, supply and demand are not equal at that rate of exchange, the central bank or some other authority has to intervene to keep the exchange rate at the desired level or within the desired band. The following example shows how this works.

Let us assume that the British Government wants to keep the pound at a fixed exchange rate to the US dollar; say 2 dollars to the pound. We then have three possibilities as far as the balance between the supply and demand for dollars is concerned:

(i) Supply equals demand.

If there is a demand for $100 (say, from people who need dollars to pay for imports), and the supply is also $100 (perhaps from export revenues), then the foreign exchange markets can handle the situation without any outside help (in Britain the foreign exchange market consists mainly of the leading banks). Ignoring commissions and the like, we get the following currency flows:

(ii) Supply exceeds demand.

If exports exceed imports (and there is no supply or demand from other sources, like invisibles), the supply of dollars exceeds the demand for dollars. If our exports total $100 but we only want to import goods worth $80, we get the following situation:

In this case there is a surplus of dollars, and a shortage of pounds, in the foreign exchange markets. If the authorities do not do anything about this, the dollar will fall and the pound will rise in value. If the authorities do not want such a change in the value of the currencies involved (for example they want to maintain the exchange rate of $2 = £1), they must make sure that demand equals supply at that rate of exchange. This can be done by the Bank of England buying the surplus dollars:

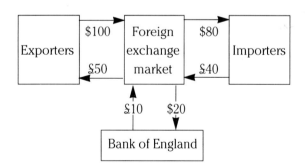

In this case supply and demand are again in balance. The supply of dollars is $100 (from exporters), and the demand for dollars is also $100 ($80 is bought by importers, and the Bank of England buys $20). The $20 bought by the Bank of England add to the Bank's foreign exchange reserves; that is to say, the

Bank of England now has $20 more than it had before this transaction. Note that the dollar purchase by the Bank of England has increased the money supply: by buying $20 the Bank of England has put £10 into circulation which was not in circulation before this transaction. In fact, Bank of England purchases of dollars affect the money supply in the same way as Bank of England purchases of bills of exchange (see section 7B2).

(iii) Supply falls short of demand.

Suppose exports earn $100, but we want to import goods worth $120. We then get the following situation:

Again, supply is not equal to demand; this time there is a shortage of dollars and a glut of pounds. If nothing is done about this, the pound will fall in relation to the dollar. To prevent this from happening (we are still assuming the authorities want to maintain a fixed exchange rate of $2 to the pound) the authorities must step in by supplying additional dollars:

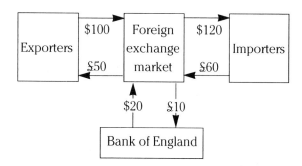

Q This situation cannot go on for ever. Why not?

A Intervention of this kind reduces the Bank of England's dollar reserves, and if the Bank of England just goes on selling dollars it will sooner or later have none left.

As stated earlier, in a system of fixed exchange rates the authorities try to maintain exchange rates at a certain level ($2 to the pound, in the example above). Temporary disparities between supply and demand can be tackled by Bank of England intervention, as shown above. However, such intervention cannot be used indefinitely; constant Bank of England purchases of dollars increase the money supply in Britain, which leads to more inflation, and constant sales of dollars deplete the country's foreign exchange reserves. So, if surpluses or deficits persist, measures other than intervention in the foreign exchange markets will have to be used. These can either be fiscal or monetary measures to increase or reduce total demand (a reduction in total demand will also reduce the demand for imports), or changes in the exchange rate. Even in times of 'fixed' exchange rates, occasional revaluations or devaluations are unavoidable if the existing exchange rates lead to persistent balance of payments surpluses or deficits. Since, in a system of fixed exchange rates, rates are decided by the government (or the central bank), a change in the exchange rate comes about by the government (or central bank) fixing it at a different level. In our example where we assumed a fixed exchange rate of $2 to the pound, the authorities could devalue the pound to, say, $1.80 if the $2 exchange rate leads to persistent balance of payments deficits, or they could revalue the pound to, say $2.20 if the $2 exchange rate leads to persistent surpluses. Or, to give a real example, in 1967 the British Government decided that the exchange rate of $2.80 to the pound which had been in force since 1949 was no longer tenable because it led to constant current account deficits; so the government decided that from a certain day in November 1967 onwards, a pound was no longer worth $2.80, but only $2.40.

G2 FLOATING EXCHANGE RATES

In a system of floating exchange rates, exchange rates are determined by supply and demand and not by government decision. If the demand for pounds in the foreign exchange markets exceeds the supply of pounds, the pound will rise in value; in the opposite case its value will drop. In such a system the exchange rate is affected by all the factors affecting the supply of, and the demand for, a particular currency. The main such factors are:

*Why demand for currency
may rise or fall*

► **The current account of the balance of payments**

A current account surplus tends to strengthen a currency; if exports exceed imports, the demand for the currency of the country in question exceeds the supply of that currency, so its price (or value, or exchange rate) will rise. The other side of the coin is that a current account deficit tends to weaken a currency.

► **Differences in inflation rates between various countries**

High inflation currencies will fall, low inflation currencies will rise in value. The reason for this is that if country A has a higher rate of inflation than country B, A's products will sooner or later be more expensive than similar products made in B. Consequently, people will buy the products of country B and not those of country A. For the foreign exchange markets that means an increased demand for the currency of country B and a reduced demand for the currency of country A: if you no longer buy country A's products you do not need any of that country's currency, but if you want to buy things made in country B you do need that country's money. As a result of this, the value of the currency of country B (the low-inflation country in our example) will rise in terms of the currency of country A. As explained earlier (see section 6A3 of this course), the main reason for the long-term decline in the value of the pound in relation to currencies like the US dollar, the German mark and the Japanese yen is the fact that inflation has usually been higher in Britain than in the USA, Germany or Japan during the last 40 years.

► **Interest rate differentials**

If one country has higher interest rates than other countries, some people will want to invest their savings in the high-interest country. To be able to do that, they first have to buy some of the high-interest country's currency: the higher rates of interest have increased the demand for the high-interest currency, and as a result its price (exchange rate) will go up.

► **Confidence**

If people have more confidence in the economic prospects of country A than those of country B, they may want to invest their savings in country A. This will increase the demand for

(and hence the value of) country A's currency.

► **Speculation**

If people expect a currency to go up in value, they may want to buy some of that currency now in order to sell it later at a profit. Whether speculation increases or reduces currency fluctuations is a moot point; one can find theoretical 'evidence' either way.

► **Government intervention**

We have seen at the beginning of this section that, in a system of floating exchange rates, exchange rates are determined by supply and demand. Sometimes governments try to influence exchange rates by manipulating the supply of, or the demand for, their currencies. This can be done either by the central bank buying or selling currencies in the foreign exchange markets (see section G1, cases (ii) and (iii)), or by increasing or reducing interest rates (see above).

If government tries to influence exchange rates in such a way, we can no longer regard this as a case of truly floating exchange rates. Such a system (floating in principle, but with government intervention) has been called 'dirty floating'. Britain operated such a system for much of the 1970s and 1980s, until she joined the ERM in October 1990.

H
ALTERNATIVE METHODS OF PRESENTING BALANCE OF PAYMENTS STATISTICS

We saw in section B that the British balance of payments is now presented as follows:

> exports
> less : imports
> = visible balance
> + invisibles
> = current account balance

We have seen in section C that a current account surplus increases the country's foreign assets or reduces its foreign liabilities, whereas a current account deficit has the opposite effect.

Some countries go one step further in their balance of payments statistics, to show whether the current account balance has affected the foreign assets or liabilities of the private sector, or those of the central bank. Britain also used this approach in the past.

This approach leads to the following presentation:

exports
less : imports

= visible balance
+ invisibles

= current account balance
– increase in private sector's foreign assets

= change in the central bank's foreign

currency reserves

Up to the current account balance the two presentations are identical.

If the country in question has a current account surplus of $1,000, then somebody in that country must have $1,000 more than he had before that surplus was achieved (assuming the surplus has led to an increase in the country's foreign assets rather than a decrease in its foreign liabilities). This 'somebody' can be a private individual, a bank, a company, or the central bank (see sections G1 and G2).

If the entire $1,000 is held by the private sector, the balance of payments statistic will read:

current account surplus	$1,000
increase in private sector foreign assets	$1,000
change in central bank's foreign currency reserves	0

If, on the other hand, the entire $1,000 is bought by the central bank, the statistic looks as follows:

current account surplus	$ 1,000
increase in private sector foreign assets	0
change in central bank's foreign currency reserves	$ 1,000

And then, of course, the situation may be somewhere in between, for example:

current account surplus	$ 1,000
increase in private sector foreign assets	$ 600
change in central bank's foreign currency reserves	$ 400

I

INSURANCE AND THE BALANCE OF PAYMENTS

The relationship between insurance and the balance of payments is complex. Let us now consider the factors which have a bearing on it.

I1   THE INTERNATIONAL NATURE OF THE BRITISH INSURANCE INDUSTRY

Many of the large British insurance organisations derive most of their income from overseas, as the following examples show:

(i) Source of 1988 premium income (in %)

	UK	USA and Canada	Other countries
Commercial Union	39	30	31
General Accident	37	43	20
Guardian Royal Exchange	50	13	37
Prudential	44	31	25
Royal	36	47	17

Source: Companies' Annual Reports 1988

(ii) Sedgwick: Brokerage by currency in 1988 (%)

US dollars	64.2
Sterling	14.4
European currencies other than sterling	8.5
Canadian dollars	5.5
Australian and NZ dollars	4.9
others	2.5
	100.0

Source: Sedgwick Group, Annual Report 1988

This highly international orientation of the British insurance industry produces a two-way relationship between the insurance industry on the one hand and the British balance of payments on the other. Insurance operations affect the balance of payments, and the balance of payments affects the insurance industry; the latter process mainly works through exchange rates.

12 HOW INSURANCE TRANSACTIONS AFFECT THE BALANCE OF PAYMENTS

If a non-resident of the UK buys insurance or reinsurance from a British insurer, the premium paid flows from the country of the insurance buyer to the UK. Claims under such policies lead to a flow of money in the opposite direction. If non-residents of the UK buy insurance from foreign subsidiaries of British insurance companies, the premiums and claims will normally not lead to any flow of money into or out of the UK, since the insurance fund will be kept outside Britain. However, the British balance of payments will then be affected by profit remittances from the foreign subsidiary to the UK parent company. Furthermore, the acquisition or sale of foreign investments leads to money flowing into or out of the UK, and so do brokers' commissions paid by insurance companies to brokers in other countries. The effects of insurance operations on the balance of payments can be summarised as follows:

Insurance transactions leading to an	
Inflow of money	**Outflow of money**
Premiums received from overseas	Claims paid to policyholders overseas
Claims payments received from abroad	Premiums paid to insurers abroad
Brokers' commissions received from abroad	Commissions paid to brokers abroad
Returns on overseas investments held by UK insurers, as well as profit remittances from overseas subsidiaries of UK insurers	Returns on UK investments held by foreign insurers, as well as profit remittances by UK subsidiaries of foreign insurers to their home countries
Sale of overseas investments held by UK insurers	Purchase of overseas investments by UK insurers
Purchases of UK investments by insurers overseas	Sales of UK investments held by foreign insurers

As the table shows, insurance transactions can lead to both inflows and outflows of money, but the net effect is nearly always an inflow of money into the UK. The insurance industry is an important source of 'invisible earnings' for the British balance of payments.

I3 HOW BALANCE OF PAYMENTS POLICY MEASURES AFFECT THE INSURANCE INDUSTRY

We have seen earlier that governments sometimes use monetary and fiscal policy measures to affect the balance of payments. These measures can affect the insurance industry even if it is not the intended target. For example, if the government reduces demand in the economy in order to slow down imports, the demand for insurance may well fall. If people buy fewer television sets, cars or, in the case of manufacturing industry, machinery, they do not need so much insurance cover.

Of particular importance in this area are the effects which exchange rates (and, especially, changes in exchange rates) have on the insurance industry. Suppose a British insurer sells fire policies in the USA and the year's results are as follows:

Premiums	$100
Claims	$90
Profit	$10

For simplicity, let us ignore all the other costs and revenues; we will talk about insurance company accounts more realistically in Chapter 13.

What is the result in sterling? If the insurance fund is kept in the USA, the result in sterling terms is the sterling equivalent of the $10. If the pound is worth $2.50, the profit in sterling terms is £4; if the exchange rate is $2 = £1, it is £5; and if a pound is

$1.50, the $10 translate into £6.67. So, the result of the overseas operations of this British insurer in sterling terms is affected by the exchange rate between the pound and the dollar; the lower the value of the pound, the more pounds will the overseas profit fetch.

If the insurance fund is kept in Britain, the result in sterling terms is not only affected by the **level** of exchange rates, but also by any **changes** in exchange rates between the time when premiums are received and the time when claims are paid. If the pound is always worth $2, the $100 of premiums becomes £50, the $90 claims cost the company £45, and there is a profit of £5 at the end of the year. If, however, the pound is worth $2 when the premiums are received and $2.50 when the claims are paid, the $100 premiums fetch £50, and the $90 claims cost £36, so the profit is now £14. If exchange rates move in the opposite way (i.e. £1 = $2.50 when premiums are received and £1 = $2 when claims are paid), the $100 premiums translate into £40, and the $90 claims cost the company £45, so there is a £5 loss. This simplified example shows that the same underlying foreign transactions can lead to very different results in sterling terms, depending on what happens to exchange rates.

The sterling value of investment income from overseas is also affected by exchange rates, and so is the sterling equivalent of commissions which British brokers receive from overseas. For example, Sedgwick say in their Annual Report for 1988 that the weakness of the US dollar had an adverse effect on their results.

Reference
1 Source : CSO Economic Trends, June 1989

8
SELF-ASSESSMENT QUESTIONS

1. A Londoner goes on holiday to Scotland. Does this affect the British balance of payments? Why (not)?

   NO — Money does not enter/leave Britain.

2. A Londoner goes on holiday to Spain. Does this affect the British balance of payments? Why (not)?

   yes — Money leaves Britain + goes to Spain —

3. What is the effect of a current account surplus?

   PSDR

   Balance of payments

4. What is the effect of a current account deficit?

   PSBR

   Balance of payments

5. What is the cause of current account surpluses and deficits?

   Spending more/less than income

6. Why do monetary and fiscal policies affect the balance of payments?

7. Why do changes in the exchange rate affect the balance of payments?

   Interest rates + people from other countries willing more to invest

8. How do exchange rates come about in a system of floating exchange rates?

   _____

   _____

   _____

9. Does Britain have fixed or floating exchange rates at the moment?

   _____

   _____

   _____

10. Suppose interest rates in Britain go up while interest rates elsewhere remain unchanged. What will be the consequence for the exchange rate of the pound in a system of floating exchange rates?

    _____

    _____

    _____

11. In what way does the insurance industry contribute to the British balance of payments?

    _____

    _____

    _____

12. In what ways do exchange rate fluctuations affect the insurance industry?

    _____

    _____

    _____

ANSWERS TO SELF-ASSESSMENT QUESTIONS APPEAR OVERLEAF

8

ANSWERS TO SELF-ASSESSMENT QUESTIONS

1. The British balance of payments is not affected, because no money enters or leaves Britain.

2. The British balance of payments is affected. The Londoner will have to spend money in Spain while he is there, and this is an outflow of money from Britain.

3. A current account surplus increases a country's overseas assets, or reduces its overseas liabilities.

4. A current account deficit reduces a country's overseas assets, or increases its overseas liabilities.

5. If a country spends more than it earns, it has a current account deficit. If it spends less than it earns, it has a current account surplus.

6. Monetary and fiscal policies affect the amount of spending in the economy. If people spend less, imports will fall.

7. A devaluation of the pound increases the cost of foreign goods in Britain and decreases the cost of British goods abroad. It therefore discourages imports and encourages exports. A revaluation of the pound has the opposite effect.

8. In a system of floating exchange rates, exchange rates are determined by supply and demand in the foreign exchange markets.

9. At the moment Britain has fixed exchange rates vis-a-vis the other EMS member currencies, and floating exchange rates with all other currencies.

10. Such a development will make sterling more atttractive as an investment currency. Some people will therefore buy pounds to benefit from the higher British interest rates. This increased demand for sterling will increase the price (the exchange rate) of the pound.

11. Insurance transactions with overseas policyholders lead to both inflows and outflows of money. For example, premiums received from overseas are an inflow, and claims paid to policyholders overseas are an outflow. In addition, the investment activities of insurance companies lead to flows of money into and out of the country, and so do brokers' commissions received from or paid to other countries. Even though insurance transactions lead to both inflows and outflows of money, the net effect for the British balance of payments is nearly always an inflow ('invisible earnings').

12. Exchange rate fluctuations affect the sterling equivalent of items such as premiums, claims, investment income and brokers' commissions which are denominated in foreign currencies, and therefore affect the profits of British insurance organisations.

8

ASSIGNMENT 4

You should work this assignment after studying Chapter 8. Answer any three questions, and allow yourself one and a half hours to complete it.

1.   Describe the main elements of the British balance of payments, distinguishing between visible trade, the invisibles and the current account.

2.   What is meant by current account deficits and surpluses? How do such deficits and surpluses affect the country concerned?

3.   Outline two ways in which a country can combat an unwanted current account deficit.

4.   What is meant by the term 'exchange rate'? How are exchange rates determined in a system of (a) fixed; (b) floating exchange rates?

PART II
THE OPERATIONAL ENVIRONMENT

9

TYPES OF BUSINESS: INTERACTION BETWEEN A BUSINESS AND ITS ENVIRONMENT

A   Business and non-business organisations

B   Categories of business

C   Factors affecting a business

LEARNING OBJECTIVES

After studying this chapter, you should be able to:

▷ explain the differences and similarities between business and non-business organisations;

▷ give examples of business and non-business organisations;

▷ outline several ways in which organisations can be categorised;

▷ give examples of businesses in those categories;

▷ explain in what ways the owner(s), workforce, customers and suppliers affect a business;

▷ explain in what ways legal regulations and moral considerations affect a business;

▷ give examples of how legal and moral rules differ between regions/countries;

▷ outline geographical factors which affect a business;

▷ comment on how changes in technology have affected the insurance industry.

A
BUSINESS AND NON-BUSINESS ORGANISATIONS

Most goods and services are produced in businesses or other organisations. The difference between a business and a non-business organisation is difficult to define. Most people would consider a farm, a factory, a shop or an insurance company to be a business, but many people would argue that a church, a trade union, a hospital or a museum is not a business. Still, all these organisations (whether one considers them to be businesses or not) have quite a lot in common. To begin with, they all have some goal or purpose.

Q   How would you sum up, in one sentence, the common goal or purpose of all these different types of organisation?

A   In general terms, the goal or purpose is often to provide goods or services to the public.

To provide those goods and services they have to employ people, and by doing that they offer jobs and careers to those who work for them. Depending on the size of the organisation, the people who work in it may be specialists to a greater or lesser extent, allowing them to concentrate on work they are good at and enjoy doing. Most organisations employ some people who work directly on the good or service offered to the public; and others whose contribution consists of coordinating the work of the people within the organisation, thereby making sure that 'the job gets done' and the organisation reaches its goal; a charity needs managers just as a factory does.

Sometimes one hears the argument that business is about making money whereas non-business organisations have other aims. Well, things are rarely as clear-cut as that. It is certainly true that some organisations try to make as much money as possible, whereas others are non-profit organisations. However, even non-profit organisations usu-

A finished product is the result of a number of different influences and processes

ally have to cover their costs or live within some kind of budget; if they constantly fail to do so they will sooner or later cease to exist. The aim of a church or a trade union may not be to make a profit, but if they fail to balance inflows and outflows of money they will sooner or later be unable to pay staff salaries as well as all the other costs of running the organisation.

So, we can say that most goods and services, as well as most jobs, are provided by business or other organisations. Since businesses play such an important part in our lives, let us try to find out a bit more about them, and in particular about how they interact with their environment. First of all, let us try to find an answer to the question: what kinds of businesses are there?

B
CATEGORIES OF BUSINESS

The question as to what kinds of business there are is not as easy to answer as it may seem at first sight. Businesses can be categorised in various ways. One way, for example, is to categorise them according to the goods or services they provide. Other possibilities would be to categorise them according to size (large, medium, small), ownership (e.g. one-man businesses, public limited companies, state-owned corporations), aim (e.g. profit- or non-profit-making), legal structure, and so on.

B1 CATEGORISING BUSINESSES BY PRODUCT

Suppose you buy a bar of chocolate in a shop. That bar of chocolate is the end-product of a production process which has involved a large number of people and organisations in many different parts of the world. The first stage in the production of that bar of chocolate is the production of the agricultural raw materials from which the chocolate is made, such as cocoa, milk and sugar. Farmers in different countries produce these raw

materials. A chocolate manufacturer then buys them and converts them into the finished product. In that process he needs the services of a large number of people in addition to those who work in the chocolate factory. For example, the raw materials must be transported to the premises of the chocolate manufacturer. This involves shipping companies, road haulage companies, railways and so on. While being transported the goods are probably insured, thus bringing in insurance companies and brokers. Then, payments must be made to the farmers, the transport companies, the insurers and others, and this is normally done through banks. In the production process the manufacturer needs electricity, and the activities of various people and organisations have to be co-ordinated; this requires communication between people, often by telephone or the postal service. And once the chocolate has been produced it is still not at its final destination: with the consumer. So, the next step will be for the manufacturer to sell the chocolate to a wholesaler or retailer where it ultimately reaches the consumer; and of course, to get the chocolate from the manufacturer to the retailer one again needs the services of a large number of people and organisations, like transport companies, telephone services, banks and insurance organisations.

Generalising from this story, we can say that many products go through **three stages** in the course of their production, using the services of a large number of companies along the way. The first of these stages is the **extraction** of raw materials from nature (examples are growing cocoa and mining iron ore). The second stage is to **convert** the raw materials into a finished product. This is done in some manufacturing process (such as converting cocoa, milk and sugar into chocolate; making shoes from leather). And thirdly, the finished product is **distributed** to the various consumers, usually through wholesale and retail companies. All along the way the services of businesses like transport companies, providers of post and telephone services, bankers, insurance people and many others have been used.

We can now categorise businesses according to the place they occupy within this production process. The following diagram gives an example.

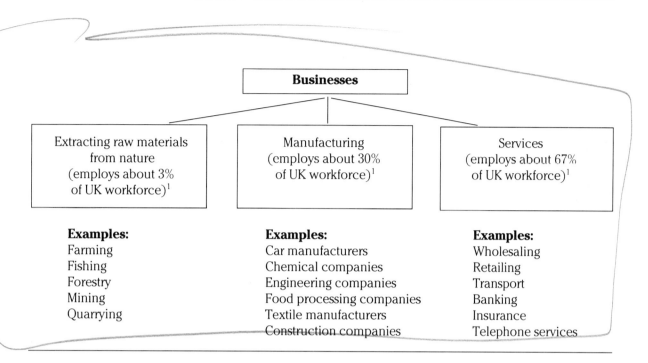

B2   CATEGORISING BUSINESSES BY SIZE

Businesses differ vastly in size. Some, for example small shops or small insurance broking businesses, are literally one-person businesses whereas others employ thousands of people, sometimes in many different countries.

Most of the businesses that are in existence are small and provide work for only a small number of people, or indeed for only one person (the owner). The following table provides some more information on this.

Number of people employed	Number of companies
1-9	105,936
10 - 19	17,152
20 - 49	16,533
50 - 99	7,350
100 - 199	4,768
200 - 499	3,240
500 - 999	913
1,000 or more	452
	156,344

Source : CSO, Annual Abstract of Statistics 1989

This table shows that about two thirds of all companies in Britain employ fewer than ten people, and only about three per cent of all companies employ more than a thousand. Nevertheless, a large part of the country's output and employment is provided by large businesses.

B3   CATEGORISING BUSINESSES BY OWNERSHIP

There are various ways in which a business may be owned. The major categories are discussed below.

B3A   Sole proprietor businesses

Many small businesses are owned by one individual who is owner and manager at the same time. That individual provides the capital, is entitled to all the profits (after tax), and can make all the decisions. The fact that the owner can make all the decisions means there is no need for the clumsy bureaucracy which is sometimes a feature of larger organisations.

? On the other hand, there can be considerable drawbacks to being sole owner of a business. Spend a minute making a list of those you can think of, before reading on.

Not only the profits but also the losses are for the account of the owner, and if the assets of the business are not sufficient to meet their claims, creditors can take the owner's personal assets as well (**'unlimited liability'**). A further disadvantage of the one-person business is that its ability to raise capital is very limited; limited, in fact, to the personal wealth of the owner plus any money he is able to borrow. And then, since the owner is the only manager, he has to do all aspects of the business's management whether he is good at them or not. Some managers are, say, good at finance but bad at purchasing. In a larger organisation, managers can specialise in what they are particularly good at, but such a specialisation is of course not possible if there is only one manager in the business.

From an employee's point of view, working in a sole proprietor business has both advantages and disadvantages; whether one likes it or not depends mainly on what one expects from one's job. On the one hand there is a more personal relationship with the owner than is the case in larger organisations, and there is no cumbersome bureaucracy. On the other hand, a business owned by one individual usually offers only very limited career prospects.

B3B   Partnerships

If a sole proprietor business grows, the owner may at some stage no longer be able to provide the necessary capital and/or management expertise. In this case the formation of a partnership may be the logical next step. In a partnership, each partner contributes a certain amount of capital and has a say in how the business is run. The partners can specialise in different aspects of management if they so wish. Profits and losses are shared among the partners. Partnerships are common among accountancy and law firms, insurance brokers, stockbrokers and the like.

B3C   Limited companies

Really large companies often need to raise capital from a large number of people who have no desire to take part in the management of the firm. The people who want to invest money in such companies do so by buying shares, and the shareholders are the owners of the company. They elect the board of directors whose task it is to run the company and who are answerable to the shareholders. The company is a legal entity in its own right, and shareholders cannot be sued for debts of the corporation. If things go wrong, the company can go bankrupt and the shares may become worthless, but this is the maximum loss shareholders can suffer ('limited liability'). The legal aspects will be discussed in more detail in Part IV, The Legal Environment. Most of the major companies in the private sector of the economy are limited companies, though in life assurance mutual offices are also common.

B3D   Mutual organisations

Some organisations, from small co-operative societies to giant life assurance corporations, are mutual organisations. The basic idea of a mutual organisation is that the people who use its services are its members and owners. For example, a mutual life office is owned by its policyholders. The members elect the board of directors, who are in charge of running the organisation.

B3E   State-owned businesses

Finally, a business can be owned by the state. In this case the government appoints the members of the board which runs the organisation. In Britain, many formerly state-owned businesses were sold to the private sector during the 1980s; examples of such privatisations include British Telecom, British Airways, British Gas, British Steel, and many water supply companies.

B3F Summary

The following diagram summarises the main forms of ownership

Businesses

Sole proprietor business
(owned by one individual)

Examples:
- small shops
- small insurance broking firms
- some businesses providing personal services: plumbers, hairdressers, etc.

Partnerships
(owned by several individuals)

Examples:
- many accountancy and law firms
- some stockbrokers and insurance brokers

Limited companies
(owned by shareholders)

Examples:
- BP
- ICI
- British Telecom
- proprietary insurance companies

Mutual organisations
(owned by members)

Examples:
- co-operative societies
- most building societies
- mutual life offices

State-owned corporations

Examples:
- BBC
- British Rail
- British Coal

C
FACTORS AFFECTING A BUSINESS

A business does not operate in a vacuum, isolated from the rest of the world. Businesses sell goods and services to customers, buy goods and services from suppliers, and use the labour of their work-force and the capital of their owners and creditors (more about the latter in Part III, The Financial Environment). They work within a legal frame-work laid down by the legislators of the countries they operate in, and are expected to adhere to certain ethical standards which, just like the legal framework, may differ from country to country. All these interest groups affect the business in one way or another, and often they expect different things from the business. Let us look at some of these interest groups in a bit more detail.

C1 THE OWNERS OR THEIR REPRESENTATIVES

Suppose you decide to set up a business of your own. What decisions will you have to make before you can even start doing business? To begin with, you will have to decide what exactly you want to do. Do you want to set up a shoe shop, or an insurance broking office, or do you want to manu-facture bicycles? What you finally decide to do will depend partly on your personal characteris-tics (personal interests, abilities, qualification and so on) and partly on factors outside your control. Among the latter will be points like the state of the market (is there a demand for your product?); competition (does it make sense to open yet another shoe shop in a small town where there are two such shops already?); and capital require-ments (normally a manufacturing business requires a larger capital investment than service industries).

Once you have decided what you want to do and your chosen business has started operations there are further decisions to be made. Assuming your business is profitable, what do you do with the profits? Do you withdraw all of them from the business as your personal income, or do you with-draw only as much as you need to survive and reinvest the remainder in your business so that it may grow and expand? There is no such thing as 'the right answer' to questions like this, and different businessmen have adopted different courses of action.

Some family businesses are set up to produce a certain income for their owners, with no plans for further expansion; other people would ideally want to see their business grow into a corporation doing business worldwide. So, every business has to make such basic decisions as 'what goods or services should the business produce?' and 'what size should the business aspire to?' In small businesses these decisions are made by the owner himself, and in a partnership where there are several owners the partners have to reach an agreement on these matters. In a public limited company, and also in large mutual organisations such as mutual life offices, these decisions will normally be made by the board of directors (elected by the shareholders or members) rather than by the owners themselves.

In many such large organisations the interest of the owners is largely financial, and most shareholders are quite happy to give a free hand to their directors as long as they are satisfied with the financial return on their investment. If they are dissatisfied, however, shareholders can do at least two things which have a profound effect on the business. Firstly, they can vote directors out of office at the next annual general meeting. Secondly, they can sell their shares. Of course, a shareholder can only sell his shares if somebody else is prepared to buy them, and if people are generally dissatisfied with the performance of a company or with the way in which it is run there will be many sellers and few buyers.

Q What will be the consequence of such a situation?

A Well, if supply exceeds demand, prices fall, as explained in Chapter 2. If many people want to sell their shares and few people want to buy them, the share price will fall. This is bad news not only for the shareholders, but also for the company.

One reason why a falling share price is bad for the company is that it makes it more difficult for the firm to raise more money by issuing more shares; and, perhaps more importantly, the lower the share price, the easier it is for outsiders to launch a takeover bid. Not only is it cheaper in such a situation to buy enough shares to gain control of the company, but shareholders who are disenchanted with their management are more likely to accept a bid from an outsider than are satisfied shareholders; let us not forget that ultimately it is the existing shareholders and not the bidder who decide whether or not the takeover bid will be successful, since the shareholders are the ones who decide whether to accept the bid or not.

So, the owners of a business or their elected representatives expect certain things from their business, and make decisions which affect the business. However, they are not the only ones who affect the business. Let us now turn to some of the other interest groups and see what influence they have.

C2 EMPLOYEES AND THEIR REPRESENTATIVES

No goods and services can be produced without human labour. So, if we ignore the case of the one-person business where the owner is the only supplier of labour, an organisation (business or otherwise) has to employ people in order to reach its goals. Since it is the employees who actually produce the goods or services, the quality of those goods and services and hence the standing of the organisation depends a great deal on its employees. If one organisation has more competent or more motivated employees than a rival, the company with the more competent workforce can either produce goods and services of a better quality than its competitor, or, if it produces exactly the same goods, it may be able to produce them more efficiently and hence at a lower cost. Being able to produce at a lower cost means that the company can either sell its goods at a lower price than its competitors do (thereby getting a competitive advantage in the market place), or sell its products at the same price as its competitors do and earn a bigger profit margin than they do. This is just one example to show that the quality of the workforce is of crucial importance to any business.

C2A The management

One sometimes hears the argument that if you

want to hire, say, five people you can select individuals who have exactly the characteristics you consider important for the job (technical ability, ability to get on with other people, intelligence, etc.), but if you want to hire a thousand people then the group you end up with will not differ much from any other group of a thousand you could have selected, and that with regard to any criterion you care to name. This may well be the case, and there is certainly a lot of statistical evidence for such a claim. However, even if the rank and file of the workforce consists of thousands of people, the top management will consist of only a few individuals. If one company has a better top management than its rivals it is obviously at an advantage.

In America, for example, the traditional idea of a respectable car used to be that of a huge fuel-guzzler doing 15 miles per gallon, and small cars were considered to be big jokes. During the first oil crisis in the early 1970s, which led to a trebling of the price of oil, a journalist asked the chairman of one of the leading American car manufacturers whether he did not think his company should now produce smaller and more fuel-efficient cars. The chairman replied: "I don't see any more smaller people about, so why do you want us to produce smaller cars?" However, the American public wanted smaller cars, because of the higher price of petrol. Since the American motor industry was extremely slow at adjusting to the new pattern of demand, Japanese and to a lesser extent European car manufacturers benefited by supplying the cars which Americans now wanted. So, the wrong decision by a small group of top executives (failing to adjust to a new pattern of demand) severely affected the American motor industry; one of the leading car manufacturers was almost bankrupt in the late 1970s, although it recovered later. The rank and file of the workforce of the American companies may have been every bit as good as their Japanese competitors, but if they were using their undoubted technical expertise to make cars nobody wanted to buy, they were really wasting their time. This highlights the importance of quality in the top layers of an organisation's management.

C2B The workforce

A satisfied workforce is obviously more likely to

produce good results than a dissatisfied one. Not only will a dissatisfied workforce lack the motivation to do good quality work, but dissatisfaction also leads to a high rate of staff turnover (i.e. many people leaving) and possibly to industrial relations problems like strikes. Since frequent strikes make a company an unreliable supplier, some customers may turn elsewhere. Depending on the type and size of the organisation and the nature of the problems, negotiations to improve working conditions can take place either directly between dissatisfied individuals and the company's management, or through representatives of the workforce like trade unions.

However, what makes a workforce satisfied? This is a difficult question to answer, since different individuals expect different things from the organisation they work for. Some people regard their job mainly as a source of income, will do their best as long as they are satisfied with their pay, and select jobs and employers accordingly. Others, however, consider the satisfaction they derive from doing their work to be as important or even more important than the pay cheque at the end of the month. Many nurses, for instance, could increase their income quite easily by quitting their job and doing work other than nursing. The fact that many of them do not do so indicates that nursing gives them a satisfaction which outweighs the higher monetary reward they could get elsewhere. Then, different individuals have different ideas about what constitutes the ideal work situation. Some people thrive in a dog-eat-dog atmosphere, whereas others prefer a more relaxed, co-operative style.

Each organisation has its own style and values, and to some extent will end up with employees who feel comfortable in that sort of environment. The reason for this is that the organisation will try to recruit people who 'fit in', and people who are not willing or able to accept the style of the organisation will often leave it sooner or later, either voluntarily or otherwise.

?   Take a few minutes to think about the style and values of your own organisation in this context. Is there a distinctive atmosphere; a 'corporate approach' to issues and problems? How is this reflected in the workforce?

So far in this section we have discussed some of

the ways in which the people who are already in an organisation affect it. There is, however, another part to this argument: since an organisation cannot produce its goods or services without suitable employees, the organisation will be in trouble if it cannot get the employees it wants to recruit. In spite of the unemployment still plaguing the country, there is a shortage of certain categories of workers, especially in the more prosperous regions like the south east of England. Referring to the Employment Report of the Organisation for Economic Co-operation and Development (OECD), the Financial Times wrote on 28 July 1989: 'The study notes reports of skill shortages in many member countries. In the UK and Canada labour scarcity has increased sharply since the end of the recession, while in Sweden the problem of labour shortage is pressing and immediate.' Some insurance companies have had difficulties in attracting suitable staff since the late 1980s, especially in urban areas in the more prosperous parts of Britain. This development has been caused at least in part by a fall in the number of school-leavers, which in turn is the consequence of a fall in the number of births in the 1970s.

C3 CUSTOMERS AND SUPPLIERS

A business produces goods and services in order to sell them to other people. The reason why your customers buy from your business is not, however, that they want to do you a favour: they want the goods and services in question, and they will buy from you as long as they think you are the best supplier. 'Best' in this context can mean the one who supplies goods of the best quality, or at the lowest price, or at the most convenient location, or who offers the most favourable conditions of payment (maybe one supplier allows two months' credit whereas others insist on immediate payment). If, in the opinion of your customers, you cease to be the best supplier, it is only rational from their point of view to buy elsewhere in the future. So, making sure his customers are satisfied with the goods or services he supplies is an important part of the work of every businessman: without customers he will not be in business for very long.

In addition to your customers' satisfaction with your product, their economic situation may affect the demand for your goods or services. Many shopkeepers in Britain's mining areas had a hard time during the miners' strike a few years ago, because their customers did not have as much money to spend as they used to have. The buoyancy of the demand for motor cars and air travel in the late 1980s benefited manufacturers of car and aeroplane components like GKN and Rolls Royce, whereas Westland suffered from the lacklustre demand for helicopters.

As far as insurance is concerned, people's attitude to risk, desire to save, awareness of insurance and desire to take out insurance changes over time; and both life and non-life insurance companies try to influence these determinants of the demand for insurance, by advertising and by other means. (This overlaps with the determinants of demand, which were discussed in Chapters 2 and 3.)

Customers certainly affect your business, and so do suppliers. Suppliers may not be as crucial in service industries like insurance as they are in retailing or manufacturing, but they are certainly not irrelevant. If your computer system breaks down, the speed with which the supplier of that system puts things right makes a lot of difference to your company, or at least to the section affected by the computer failure. Retailing or manufacturing companies simply cannot operate if they do not get the necessary supplies, and if company A has more reliable suppliers than company B, company A is at an obvious advantage.

C4 LEGAL REGULATIONS AND ETHICAL STANDARDS

A Robinson Crusoe can do on his island whatever he likes, but societies need rules so that people can live together peacefully. Businesses are affected by such rules, just as private individuals are. There are large numbers of legal and other regulations which businesses must adhere to, and the sanctions for failing to do so can be severe. For example, several directors of the National Westminster Bank, including the chairman, resigned in July 1989 after the publication of a report by the Department of Trade and Industry alleging misdemeanours in the context of an issue of shares on behalf of a customer. In Britain, businesses are subject to regulations laid down by law, by the relevant regulatory authorities (for example the Securities and Investments Board and various self-regulating organisations in the financial field), professional bodies and others. In some cases different rules may apply in different parts of the country; for example, government grants and other financial incentives may be available for investment in high-unemployment areas but not elsewhere.

Businesses operating in more than one country can be affected by legal and other regulations of all the countries they operate in. Countries with balance of payments difficulties sometimes impose restrictions on outward payments. In the late 1980s, for example, Zimbabwean exchange control regulations limited profit remittances to other countries to 25-50% (depending on the nature of the business) of the after-tax profit made in Zimbabwe.[2] Air France says in its 1987 annual report that it had the equivalent of about $40 million in 'blocked funds' in Algeria; these blocked funds came about because Air France had sold tickets to Algerians who paid in Algerian money, and then the Algerian government did not allow the airline to remit that money out of the country. British Caledonian (now part of British Airways) had similar problems in Nigeria a few years earlier.

The law, however, is not the only body of regulations a company has to obey. Most societies have moral and ethical conventions which individuals and companies are expected to obey. The chairman of the Bank of Montreal said in this context:

Ethics in a business context means more than just remaining within the law; everything which is legal is not necessarily ethical. The business which hopes to earn the trust of the public must aim for higher standards than this.

In recent years, the business world has experienced a number of ethical failures. Some have involved businesses engaged in the investment and safekeeping of other people's money; others, the misuse of privileged information. As a result of these ethical lapses and of an over-emphasis upon short-term gains ... the basic trust between business and society is under increasing pressure. We must ensure, therefore, that ethical principles and concern for the well-being of

our customers, employees and shareholders, as well as of the public, are integral components of every business relationship.

There should be no fundamental difference between the values of the market place and those we apply in other aspects of our daily lives. These include honesty, fairness, a decent respect for the standards of society, and acceptance of the obligation to give value and useful service in return for the rights and privileges which we enjoy and for the trust placed in us by our fellow citizens.[3]

Another example of how the expectations of society affect a company was given by Sir Peter Walters, then chairman of BP. He said:

BP has pledged itself for many years to being a careful company in all its operations - not solely for reasons of altruism, but because safety and environmental care are ultimately good business practice. Concern for the environment is becoming more focused. The Exxon Valdez accident in Alaska highlighted the potential costs - both financial and in terms of reputation - that industry can incur. In today's highly-charged atmosphere of concern for the natural world, no company can afford to ignore the effect that its activities may have on the environment.[4]

Insurance organisations are subject to a large number of legal and other regulations, for example the Companies Acts, the Insurance Companies Acts, the Insurance Brokers (Registration) Act, the Policyholders' Protection Act, and rules laid down by the Securities and Investment Board (SIB), the relevant self-regulating organisations (SROs), and professional bodies. Just as is any other sector of the economy, the insurance industry is affected by the expectations of society in general and those of its customers in particular. If, for example, people become more conscious of the surrender values of life policies, companies will find it in their own interest to become more generous on this issue, otherwise they will lose potential customers to more generous competitors. If society becomes more conscious of the environment, this may increase the demand from companies for liability insurance relating to environmental issues. And if the government introduces new tax-efficient forms of saving like the TESSAs (tax exempt special savings accounts) available from January 1991, some people may decide to save by making regular deposits to such an account rather than by paying premiums on an endowment policy.

C5 TECHNOLOGY

Technology has a profound effect on the way in which business is handled, both in insurance and elsewhere. Modern technology allows instant communication both within a company and between a company and its customers and brokers, and data processing is now much quicker and a lot less labour-intensive than it was before the days of computers. In the insurance industry, the computer and related technology is important not only as a means of quicker communications and data processing, but also as a labour-saving device, given that a large percentage of expenses (costs other than claims and commissions) consists of salaries.

The effect of modern technology will be discussed in more detail in Chapter 11.

References

1 Source : Employment Gazette, July 1989

2 Source : Reserve Bank of Zimbabwe, Quarterly Bulletin

3 Chairman's letter to shareholders in Bank of Montreal, Annual Report 1988

4 Letter from the Chairman in BP Annual Report 1989

𝟗
SELF-ASSESSMENT QUESTIONS

1. What decisions have to be made by the owners of a business, or their elected representatives?

   _____

   _____

   _____

2. What can shareholders do if they are dissatisfied with the management of their company?

   _____

   _____

   _____

3. In what ways does the quality of the workforce affect a business?

   _____

   _____

   _____

4. In what ways does the quality of top management affect a business?

   _____

   _____

   _____

5. In what ways do shortages of skilled personnel affect a business?

   _____

   _____

   _____

6. Why should a business keep itself informed about the needs of its customers?

   _____

   _____

   _____

7. How do legal regulations affect a business?

   _____

   _____

   _____

8. Give examples of rule-making bodies other than the government.

   _____

   _____

   _____

9. Give examples of regional differences in legal rules and ethical standards.

   _____

   _____

   _____

10. In what ways have changes in technology affected data processing in insurance organisations?

    _____

    _____

    _____

11. In what ways has modern technology changed the methods of communication between insurance companies and brokers?

    _____

    _____

    _____

12. What are the implications of modern technology for staffing in insurance organisations?

    _____

    _____

    _____

13.   What effects may increased awareness of the environment have on the demand for insurance?

_____

_____

_____

14.   How may the introduction of tax-exempt forms of savings, such as TESSAs, affect the demand for savings-based life assurance?

_____

_____

_____

9

ANSWERS TO SELF-ASSESSMENT QUESTIONS

1. Basic business policy; what goods or services to provide; what markets to operate in; and so on.

2. Shareholders can vote directors out of office; speak at the annual meeting to inform directors of their grievances; sell their shares; accept a takeover bid if and when such a bid is made.

3. A workforce which is capable and motivated will produce better goods and services than one with the opposite characteristics, thus leading to more satisfied customers. No business can survive in the long run unless customers are reasonably satisfied with its goods or services.

4. A business led by a good top management will produce goods or services which customers want to buy, will operate in profitable markets, and will have a sound financial structure. All these points give it an advantage over businesses which lack these characteristics.

5. A business cannot produce its goods or services without a suitable workforce. If a business cannot attract the people it needs, it will find it difficult or impossible to produce its chosen products.

6. In the long term, a business will survive only if it produces goods or services which its customers want to buy. Knowing what customers want is therefore necessary in order to be able to decide what to produce, what marketing methods to use, and so on.

7. Legal regulations say what a business can or cannot do; they may prescribe or forbid certain organisational structures; laws in other countries may make it profitable or unprofitable to operate in those countries.

8. Examples include professional organisations; the Securities and Investments Board; self-regulating organisations.

9. What is legal in one geographical area may be illegal in another. Some countries allow a free flow of money into and out of the country, others do not. Some countries allow foreign insurers to operate, others do not. Investment incentives are often available in high unemployment areas, but not elsewhere. Taking or giving bribes, or stock market dealing on insider information, is common business practice in some countries but not in others. You should keep your eyes open for specific instances of such differences.

10.   They have led to a shift from paper-based to electronic methods.

11.   Again, there has been a shift from paper-based to electronic methods.

12.   Fewer clerical staff are required. Staff should be able to work with modern technology.

13.   There is likely to be more demand for certain types of liability insurance.

14.   If people feel that TESSAs are a better or cheaper way of saving than life assurance, the demand for life assurance will fall.

10

THE STRUCTURE OF BUSINESS ORGANISATIONS

A 'One best way' versus the 'contingency' approach

B Size as a determinant of structure

C Limited companies

D Recent trends in the structuring of insurance companies

We have already seen that most goods and services are produced in business or other organisations. These organisations differ considerably with regard to size, aims, methods of doing business, structure, and the like. Let us now look at the structure of business organisations in some more detail.

A

'ONE BEST WAY' VERSUS THE 'CONTINGENCY' APPROACH

How should a business be structured?

There is no simple answer to this question, and approaches to solving this problem have varied over time. As the American professor Stoner has pointed out:

> **Early management writers attempted to find the 'one best way' or the 'universal' approach to designing organisations. They tried to establish a set of principles that would yield an organisational structure efficient and effective in most situations. Such an approach implied that organisational structure was affected by neither the organisation's environment nor its strategy - that a sound structure would succeed independent of external conditions and internal objectives. Today, management writers have moved from a 'one best way' approach to a contingency approach. They argue that an organisation is highly interdependent with its environment and that different situations require different structures. Managers, then, must identify the variables that affect their organisation so that they can design it appropriately.**[1]

In other words, the decision about the structure of a business cannot be made in isolation from the business's aims and environment. A business

---

LEARNING OBJECTIVES

After studying this chapter, you should be able to:

▷ distinguish between 'universal' and 'contingency' approaches to business structure;

▷ list factors which affect the structure of a business;

▷ explain why changes in the size of a business may make it necessary to change its structure;

▷ comment on the advantages and disadvantages of delegation of authority;

▷ explain the role of the board of directors;

▷ outline possible structures of a branch network;

▷ outline possible head office structures for general, life, and composite companies;

▷ explain the interaction between head office and branches;

▷ comment on recent trends in the structuring of insurance companies.

exists for a purpose; it has a goal or goals, and it should be structured in a way that makes it as easy as possible to reach the aims of the business in the environment it finds itself in. A structure which is optimal for one organisation may be inappropriate for another. It is unlikely that the Mafia will be structured in the same way as a charity, and a business in a rapidly changing environment will require a different structure from one in more stable surroundings.

B

SIZE AS A DETERMINANT OF STRUCTURE

One of the factors affecting the structure of an organisation is its size. A one-person business like a small shop or insurance broking office does not need any formal organisation or structure since all the work relating to the business is done by the one person. A sole proprietor business consisting of an owner and a few employees must have some kind of structure even if that structure is very informal. At least, each employee must know what he is supposed to do and what decisions (if any) he is allowed to make. In a partnership there must be some understanding on which partner does what. Take a firm of loss adjusters consisting of a number of partners. Should each partner deal with every aspect of the firm's work, and incoming work be directed to the partner who is least busy at the time, or should each of the partners specialise in a particular area (e.g. one may specialise in fire, another in liability,) and clients be referred to the partner who is a specialist on their particular problem? In a manufacturing business set up as a partnership, partners may specialise in different areas of the work to be done: one may deal with production, another with sales, a third with finance, and so on.

The larger a business becomes, the more specialisation and division of labour there will have to be; once the business reaches a certain size, no one individual will have the ability to oversee all that is going on in the business. This has often led to problems in growing businesses. As long as the business is small, the owner-manager can oversee every aspect of it, but this will no longer be the case once the business reaches a certain size. A different organisational structure is needed for the larger business, and problems will arise if that different structure is not implemented in good time. This has frequently led to problems because often people only realise that a different structure is required after the traditional structure has become inappropriate, and in many cases people may be reluctant to change the structure of their business. Especially, many owners of small businesses who have become used to the idea that they are in charge of every aspect of their business find it difficult to implement a structure under which they will no longer control every detail. Delegating authority is unavoidable if the business is to progress beyond a certain size, but equally unavoidably it leads to some loss of control for the one who delegates. Some owners of small businesses find it hard to come to terms with the idea that they can no longer control every aspect of their business.

The idea that no one individual can deal with all the aspects of a major undertaking is certainly not a new one. Probably the first 'management consultant' we know of was Jethro, Moses' father-in-law, who discovered that Moses was judging each and every dispute among the people of Israel. He said to Moses:

> **You and these people...will only wear yourselves out...Select capable men from all the people...Have them serve as judges for the people at all times, but have them bring every difficult case to you; the simple ones they can decide themselves. That will make your load lighter, because they will share it with you. If you do this and God so commands, you will be able to stand the strain, and all these people will go home satisfied.[2]**

A modern management consultant might express this by saying to a businessman: "You will have a nervous breakdown if you go on trying to do everything yourself. Select and train a few able subordinates, delegate the donkey-work to them, and concentrate your efforts on the really important matters."

Many businessmen could learn quite a lot from this Moses story, even though it is 3,500 years old!

C

LIMITED COMPANIES

In large limited companies, ownership and management are two different things.

Q Who owns a limited company, and who has responsibility for managing it? (You studied this in section 9B3C.)

A Such companies are owned by shareholders, most of whom hold their shares in the hope of making financial gains (by either dividends or rising share prices) and not because they want a say in how the organisation is run. Management is in the hands of a board of directors (elected by the shareholders) and the top executives appointed by the board of directors.

C1 THE BOARD OF DIRECTORS

The legal position of the board of directors, its chairman and the company secretary will be discussed in Part IV (The Legal Environment). What we need to know at this stage is that the job of the board of directors is to formulate the company's policy and to make the major decisions relating to the business: this includes problems like 'what lines of business should we pursue?'; 'what goods or services should we produce?'; 'what geographical area(s) should we operate in?'

An insurance company, for example, has to decide whether it wants to write only general insurance, or only life assurance, or both; and if it wants to do both it has to decide what percentage of premiums should come from each type of business. Furthermore, it has to decide whether it wants to enter areas outside the insurance field, such as the estate agency business or unit trusts. Then, it has to decide where it wants to do business: only in one particular part of Britain; or throughout Britain; or in other countries as well (and, if so, which ones). Different insurance companies have made different decisions in these regards.

Of course, these topics are not only relevant to insurance companies. A telephone company like British Telecom has to decide whether it wants to confine itself to providing telephone services or whether it wants to do other things as well (like manufacturing telecommunications equipment, or doing research in the telecommunications area). Some companies confine themselves to a fairly narrow range of activities; others prefer a wider range, but still within a given sector of the economy (like chemicals or banking or insurance); and some companies have diversified to such an extent that they end up with a large number of unrelated activities, like newspaper publishing in Britain, running hotels in Mexico and breeding bulls in Zimbabwe.

This is not to say that one strategy is any better or worse than any other. There are advantages and disadvantages both in confining oneself to a narrow range of activities and in becoming a conglomerate, and there are success stories and failures in either category.

Many people, including employees, just take it for granted that 'this company does X, but not Y'. This, however, does not change the fact that it is not a law of nature that this is so; rather, somebody has **decided** that this should be so, and this 'somebody' is ultimately the board of directors.

A board of directors usually consists of individuals with a variety of backgrounds and talents. For example, in 1989 British Telecom's board consisted of 14 members. Among these were the chairman and his deputy, the group managing director, the managing directors of British Telecom's three operating divisions (namely, British Telecom UK, British Telecom International, and Communication Systems), the group technology and development director, the group finance director, and six non-executive directors.[3] An **executive director** is a person who, in addition to holding his directorship, is employed by the company in question in an executive capacity. In many companies the chief executives of the main sub-sections of the company are members of the board (as with British Telecom). A **non-executive director** is not an employee of the company: his only contribution to the company is his work as a director (although he may of course have an executive position in another organisation). The role of non-executive directors is to contribute knowledge and experience from a wider area. In the case of British Telecom the six non-executive directors include a university professor, a politician, a solicitor, and three individuals holding directorships in other companies. The former chairman of ICI, Sir John Harvey-Jones, has said in this context:

> **We believe that it is helpful to the company and to the individual if he can be a non-executive member of one, or at most two, other boards. We have pursued this policy deliberately because it is one way of learning the many differences of approach in different boards, so that we can adapt in our continuous reviews of our own performance, and profit by others' experience.**[4]

So, the highest decision-making authority in a large company is the board of directors, which is elected by the shareholders or members of the organisation. The task of the board is to formulate the company's policy, decide what kinds of business it should do, and appoint the highest-ranking executives. To quote Sir John Harvey-Jones again:

> **The job (of the board) is to discern trends and to match the opportunities and skills which exist within your own company with the growing opportunities which you see in the changing world outside. The job of the board is all to do with creating momentum, movement, improvement and direction. If the board is not taking the company purposefully into the future, who is?**[5]

Well, what happens next? The board may well decide that the company should do X, Y and Z, but the formulation of aims and policies is one thing and implementing these policies is another.

So, the next step is to implement the policies decided by the board. However, no one person can oversee all aspects of the business of a large organisation. Consequently, we need a **structure** through which the decisions of the board can be implemented.

C2 HEAD OFFICE AND BRANCHES

To implement the strategies decided upon (one of which will invariably be to sell the goods or services the company has decided to produce), most insurance organisations have found it necessary to have a head office and a network of branches. There are, of course, some exceptions. Many reinsurance companies do not have a branch system, and neither does Lloyd's. Among insurance brokers the situation differs from company to company, which is not surprising when one considers that insurance broking businesses vary in size from one-man outfits to multinational organisations.

However, apart from these exceptions, most insurance companies, both life and general, find it desirable to have a network of branches throughout the country, or at least in that part of the country in which they want to do business. What work is done at branch level and what has to be referred to head office differs from company to company; some are more centralised than others. Furthermore, there is often more than one layer of branches. Many companies have a number of regional offices (some call them regional head offices) which supervise the work of the branches, sub-branches and so on in their area. This might lead to the following (hypothetical) structure of branches:

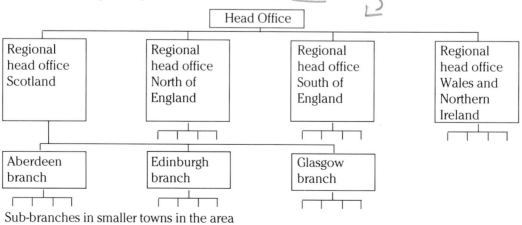

Sub-branches in smaller towns in the area

? How far is this structure reflected in the company for which you work? If your company has a similar structure, try to produce a similar diagram for it: this should help you to understand this section better. If you do not work for such a company, it would be worth your while trying to find out details of a company with which you have close contact.

As stated earlier, what kind of work is done at which level of the structure is a matter of company procedure and will differ from company to company. Some branches will be mainly sales outlets, whereas others may have authority to do their own underwriting up to a certain level, and do the accounting in relation to their work. Everybody in the company should know what he is supposed to (and allowed to) do, and to whom to report at the next higher level (be it within the same branch or further up the scale).

In some cases the 'branches' are actually subsidiary companies: companies incorporated in their own right in which the company in question owns all or most of the shares. There may be various reasons for such a structure. One is historical, stemming from the way in which the company has developed over time. All the leading British insurance companies have evolved at least partly by mergers, take-overs, acquisitions and so forth, and more often than not the acquired companies have been left intact and integrated into the structure of the group. In international operations it is sometimes advisable to incorporate offices in the country where they do business, for legal, political, tax and other reasons. Another reason for adopting a structure of subsidiary companies may be legal requirements. The **Insurance Companies Act 1982** specifies, for example, that no new composite insurance companies may be set up, largely for reasons of consumer protection. If a new insurance company now wants to do both life and general business, it can do so only through a 'holding company' structure, with a general and a life subsidiary :

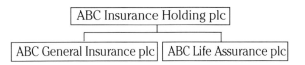

Each of the two subsidiaries can then have the usual structure of head office and branches, as explained earlier in this chapter.

C3   HEAD OFFICE STRUCTURE

Having looked at the regional structure regarding branches and/or subsidiary companies, the next step is to look at the structure of the company's head office. Again, details vary from company to company, and it would be useful for you to find out how exactly your company's head office operations are structured. You will find some information on this in your company's annual report. In fact, it would not do any harm if you looked at the structure of some other companies as well; loyalty to one's employer does not mean that one should be blind to what goes on elsewhere.

To begin with, there is one person who is formally in charge of the operations of the company as a whole. That person usually has a title like 'Chief General Manager' or 'Chief Executive Officer'. In North American companies he or she is often called the 'President' of the company. He or she reports to the board of directors and is, in fact, usually a member of the board.

Obviously, the chief general manager cannot run the entire company himself (think of the advice which Jethro gave to Moses back in 1450 BC). Under the chief general manager there will be several general managers, representing the various areas of operation of the company. The following organisation charts show possible structures of a composite insurance company and of a life office, down to general manager level:

Head office structure of a hypothetical composite insurance company

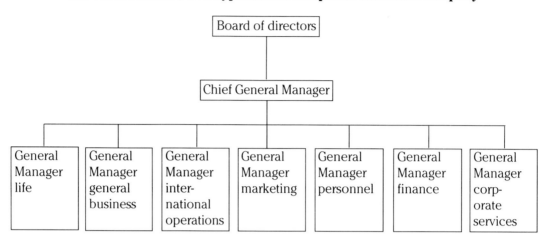

Head office structure of a hypothetical life office

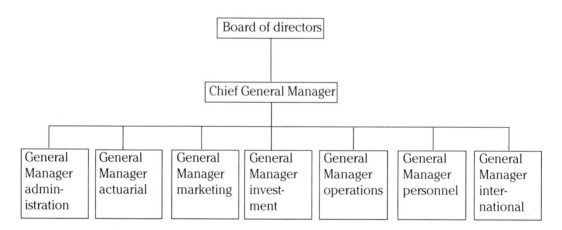

Obviously, the organisational structure does not stop at general manager level. Any one field of which a general manager is in charge is so large that no one person can run it by himself. Therefore, the work must be split up further, and different individuals given authority over the various sub-sections of the work. The following charts are examples of such further sub-divisions.

Composite company

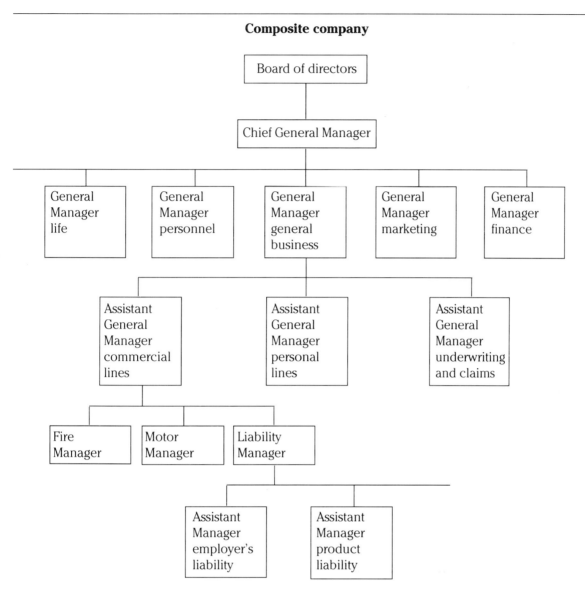

In the foregoing chart, a possible structure down to the level of assistant manager has been shown for one aspect of the company's work (general business, commercial lines). The other general managers will each have a similar structure under their authority.

Life office

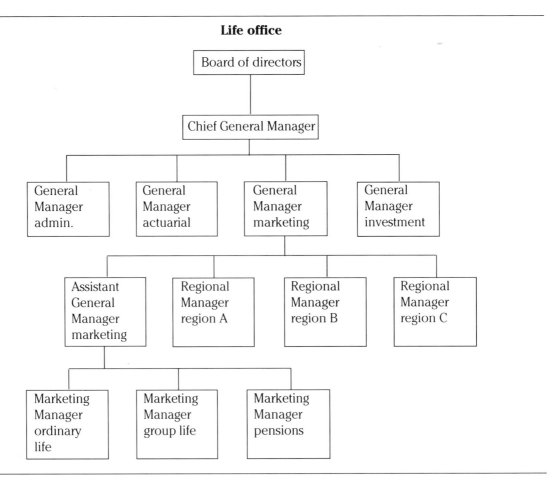

The foregoing chart shows one possibility of how the structure may develop down from the 'General Manager, marketing' level. Again, there will be similar structures following on from the other general managers. In the case of the example shown here, the further development may be based on product lines (the marketing of company pension schemes or pension schemes for the self-employed, for example), or on geographical lines, or a combination of the two.

C4 INTERACTION BETWEEN HEAD OFFICE AND BRANCHES

So far we have looked at head office and branches in isolation from each other. Most insurance companies have traditionally been based on the 'head office and branches' principle, and both the head office and the branch network must have a structure in the sense that responsibilities must be defined, overlaps and duplication of work avoided, and everybody in the organisation must know what he is supposed to do and whom to report to

at the next higher level. This leads to questions such as: how are the head office and the branches integrated into the work of the company as a whole? How do they 'fit together'? To whom at head office does a branch manager or regional manager report? In reality, branches and head office obviously do not exist side by side in isolation from each other (if they do, something has gone seriously wrong!). If a company decides that a head office and branches structure is the most appropriate one to achieve its goals, then head office and branches must complement each other so that the company's goals can be attained.

So, how can head office and branches be integrated in a coherent way? Again, it is impossible to prescribe any one method as the best solution. Such a 'best way', irrespective of the environment the company operates in, simply does not exist. Just like any other aspect of the company's structure, the co-ordination of the work of head office and branches cannot be done without due regard to the company's environment, the type of work involved, the general philosophy of the company

[handwritten: A chain of command must be established so employees know who they report to the whole way up the chain]

(some companies are more centralised than others), and so on.

Many people who work in a branch office will hardly ever have any direct contact with their company's head office. Instead, they report to someone higher up in the branch, and the branch manager may himself report to some regional office rather than to the head office directly. This leads us back to the organisation chart in section C2. The managers of the sub-branches report to the main branches, the managers of the main branches report to the regional head offices, and the managers of the regional head offices report to head office. The person at head office to whom regional head offices report varies from company to company. If the work of the branches is mainly sales-orientated, the whole branch network may be under the responsibility of the general manager, marketing. This is actually the case in some life offices, as shown in the life office organisation chart in C3 above. In other companies, the link between branches and head office may be the latter's administration, operations, or some other section.

D

RECENT TRENDS IN THE STRUCTURING OF INSURANCE COMPANIES

In sections C2, C3 and C4 we looked at what might be called the 'traditional' structure of many British insurance companies: head office and branches.

Q We mentioned in section C2 some exceptions to this pattern. Can you remember what they are?

A Lloyd's has never had a head office and branches structure, nor have the various reinsurance companies, whether on the general or the life side of the business.

D1 THE FUTURE OF THE HEAD OFFICE AND BRANCHES SYSTEM

Even in that part of the market where head office and branches used to be the usual form of organisation, one can now see changes. For example, the CU says in its 1988 annual report, 'Changes occurring within the financial services sector following the Financial Services Act are radically affecting the way business is being marketed', and the Royal states in its 1989 annual report, 'The Financial Services Act continues to affect distribution systems in the UK market. We broadened further the range of our channels, increasing the number of tied agents to 1350, giving us in total over 4000 outlets. This is now our single largest source of business, producing over 50% of sales.'

Full branch networks are no longer as important as they used to be. This is due to changes in the market place (such as the buying patterns of policyholders), staffing constraints, and advances in technology.

D2 CHANGES IN THE MARKETPLACE

Commercial insurances still tend to be sold through specialist brokers and other independent intermediaries. The most significant changes have occurred in the marketing and selling of personal insurances.

A distinctive feature has been the growth in **direct marketing** of personal insurance products to the general public. Several new direct insurance companies have been established, and large insurers have entered into or expanded their activities in this field. Methods used include newspaper and magazine advertisements containing coupons for obtaining quotations, television commercials, and direct mailing activities. You should keep an eye on the insurance press for the development of this trend, and the arguments surrounding it. Certain organisations like banks and building societies have extended their insurance activities by taking advantage of cross-selling opportunities to their substantial customer bases. In some cases, special 'branded' insurance products have been developed to facilitate this.

Brokers are also looking for ways to attract volume business, particularly motor, and recently there has been considerable expansion of chains of outlets by acquisitions or franchising.

The effect of this increasing competition from a variety of suppliers has been to produce increasingly sophisticated market segmentation, with close targeting of products and prices.

D3 STAFFING CONSTRAINTS

Insurance companies in cities and large towns are facing increasing competition when seeking suitable staff. The reduction in the number of school leavers in the late 1980s and the 1990s will add to the problems arising from the shakeout of experienced staff following mergers over the last 20 years. The net effect is a contraction in the experience and expertise available, which has increased pressure to concentrate that which is available in fewer, carefully chosen locations and to utilise it more effectively.

D4 TECHNOLOGY

The rapid growth in information technology which facilitates electronic data transfer, the expansion of computer systems and the proliferation of personal computers producing household and motor quotations have had profound effects on the way in which business is handled. Quotation systems allow rapid comparisons of the premiums charged by different insurance companies, and the sophisticated systems used by those companies facilitate processing at centralised locations. Some companies feel that it is no longer necessary to have their head office in a high-cost location like London, and computer bureaux can be located wherever they are most cost-effective; the Norwich Union, for instance, has moved its bureau to the Republic of Ireland.

D5 CONCLUSION

The three categories of factors described above have obvious implications for the ways in which business is sold and serviced. The conventional branch network (substantial sales, underwriting and processing units in numerous locations throughout the UK) is frequently neither cost-effective nor relevant to present needs. Therefore, many companies are concentrating most operations in one or a few carefully selected locations while maintaining small sales and servicing outlets to cater for local markets.

References

1 James A.F. Stoner : Management, 2nd edition p. 353 (Prentice Hall 1982)

2 The Bible, 2nd book of Moses (Exodus), chapter 18

3 Source of information : British Telecom's annual report 1989

4 Sir John Harvey-Jones: Making it happen: Reflections on leadership, p.158 (Collins 1988)

5 Sir John Harvey-Jones : op.cit. p.162

1.   List factors which affect the way in which a business should be structured.

     _____

     _____

     _____

2.   Explain what is meant by the 'contingency approach' to business structure.

     _____

     _____

     _____

3.   Why do rapidly growing businesses often face problems?

     _____

     _____

     _____

4.   In what circumstances does delegation of authority become necessary? What are its advantages and disadvantages?

     _____

     _____

     _____

5.   What is meant by 'separation of ownership and control' in large organisations?

     _____

     _____

     _____

6.   Who is the highest decision-making authority in a limited company?

     _____

     _____

     _____

7. What are the functions of the board of directors in a limited company?

   _____

   _____

   _____

8. Why do most insurance organisations have a 'head office and branches' structure?

   _____

   _____

   _____

9. Outline possible organisational structures for (a) a general insurance company; (b) a life assurance company.

   _____

   _____

   _____

10. In what way do head office and branches interact?

    _____

    _____

    _____

11. What changes have occurred in the structure of insurance companies since the late 1980s? What are the reasons for these changes?

    _____

    _____

    _____

ANSWERS TO SELF-ASSESSMENT QUESTIONS APPEAR OVERLEAF

10
ANSWERS TO SELF-ASSESSMENT QUESTIONS

1. Factors include the size of the business; its aims; the products it makes; the country or countries in which it operates; whether it operates in a stable or a rapidly changing environment.

2. There is no such thing as the one best way to structure a business. The optimal structure for a given business depends on its aims, products and so on.

3. Problems can arise because growth in a business often calls for a revision of the organisational structure. This should be done in plenty of time: rapid growth can leave a business with an inappropriate structure. Problems also arise if people who have had control of the smaller business are unwilling to delegate authority as it grows.

4. Delegation of authority becomes necessary when an organisation becomes too large for one person to oversee every aspect of its work. It also becomes necessary when a task requires the expertise of more than one person.

   Advantages Work can be spread over several people. Work can be done by a person who is particularly good at that type of work.

   Disadvantages Delegation leads to some loss of control for the one who delegates. It may lead to coordination problems.

5. In small businesses, the owner is usually also the manager. In large organisations, owners and managers are usually different people. A public limited company, for example, is owned by shareholders and managed by salaried employees.

6. The board of directors is the highest authority.

7. The directors' functions are to decide business policy; decide what markets to operate in; plan ahead; appoint the highest-ranking employees; and so on.

8. Most insurance companies have found that a head office and branches structure makes it easier than other structures to achieve their objectives. It is easier to generate sales if you are represented in many different locations. Head office co-ordinates the activities of the branches.

9. See the text, or the annual reports of such companies.

10. Details differ from company to company. Generally, decisions affecting the company as a whole are made at head office and are communicated to branches. Branches report to head office on a regular basis. Head office supervises branches.

11. The head office and branches structure is no longer taken as much for granted as it once was. This is because of changing methods of marketing, staffing constraints, developments in technology, and the like.

11

THE USE OF INFORMATION TECHNOLOGY

A   Information and information systems

B   Categorising information systems

C   Computer networks

D   Data Protection Act 1984

LEARNING OBJECTIVES

After studying this chapter, you should be able to:

▷ explain the role of information systems in business organisations;

▷ categorise information systems;

▷ explain the difference between organisational and public information systems;

▷ list ways in which (a) organisational; (b) public information systems are used in insurance organisations;

▷ explain the meaning of the term 'computer network';

▷ give examples of the use of computer networks in insurance;

▷ give examples of the use of computer networks in other sectors of the economy;

▷ list some of the risks associated with various information systems;

▷ list some of the risks particularly relevant to computer networks.

A

INFORMATION AND INFORMATION SYSTEMS

Information is an important 'commodity' in any organisation. A shopkeeper must control his stocks in order to know when to order fresh supplies, and a shopkeeper who knows of better or cheaper suppliers has a competitive advantage over those of his competitors who do not have that information. A manufacturer who is aware of the latest technological developments in his area is likely to be able to produce better or cheaper goods than competitors using the technology of yesteryear. An insurance broker who is well informed about market conditions can give better advice to his clients than a broker who is not so well informed. A well-informed investment manager can make better decisions than one who lacks the necessary information, and a military leader has a better chance of success if he has access to reliable intelligence information about what is happening on the other side. 'Awareness that possession of information is tantamount to a competitive edge is stimulating intensified efforts at gathering technical and economic intelligence at the corporate and national levels.'[1]

If we want to have access to a large amount of information, we must first of all gather that information, then store it in such a way that it can easily be retrieved; after all, information which 'exists somewhere' but which nobody knows where to find when it is needed, is pretty useless. In order to gather, store, and be able to retrieve information, we need **information systems** of some kind. Information systems have always existed, although the nature of those systems has changed over time, following the developments in technology. A personal diary, address book or list of family birthdays are (simple) information systems, and so are filing cabinets, boxes of record cards, and libraries. All these information systems continue to be used, but these systems alone would not allow us to handle the vast amount of information we are dealing with nowadays. The largest amount of information is now held in electronic information systems, like computers.

Computers and other electronic information systems are used widely in insurance and other organisations; insurance applications include storing data on policyholders, accounting, staff files, transmitting information by electronic mail or fax, and others.

USES

B

CATEGORISING INFORMATION SYSTEMS

To discuss the use of information systems in insurance and other organisations, it is useful first to categorise the various information systems. This can be done in a number of ways, for example as follows:

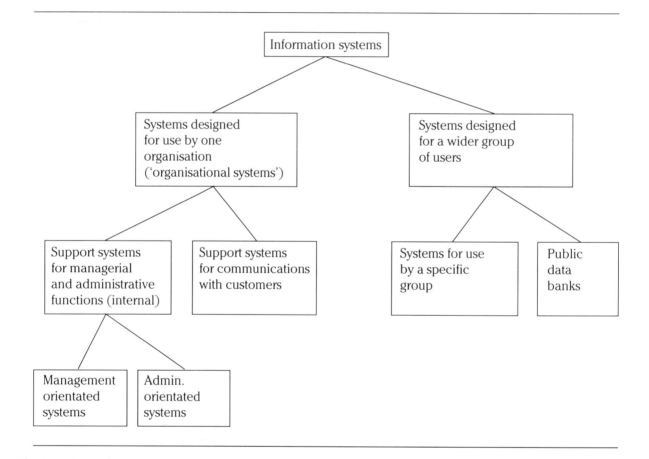

B1   SYSTEMS DESIGNED FOR USE BY ONE ORGANISATION

As stated at the beginning of this chapter, every organisation has to handle information in order to be able to conduct its business. As a first step it is useful to distinguish between systems designed for use by only one organisation (for example a company, government department, research institute) on the one hand, and systems designed for a wider group of users on the other. As we will see, insurance organisations make use of both types of system. In the past, information was mainly held on paper-based systems, whereas nowadays magnetic tapes, floppy disks and other electronic devices are increasingly taking over the role once held by (vast amounts of) paper. Obviously, information relating to a company's own operations is not available to the public in the form of a public data bank; much of this information may in fact be considered to be confidential. So, we are now talking about information systems designed to handle information relevant to one particular organisation, and accessible only to that organisation.

Such systems are used on a large scale by organisations of all kinds. Traders use such systems for stock control, manufacturers for technical data, insurance companies for recording details on policies and policyholders, and all organisations can use such systems for accounting, staff files and other record-keeping purposes.

As shown in the chart in section B, some of the systems designed for use by one organisation are used for internal purposes whereas others are designed to facilitate communication with customers (policyholders). The former include, on the one hand, data banks which contain information needed for decision-making by the company's management. Suppose an insurance company which has so far operated only in the UK wants to venture into foreign markets for the first time. Such a decision would have to be made by the board of directors. However, the directors will hardly toss a coin to decide whether or not to venture into foreign markets (and if they do, the shareholders will be well advised to make use of their right to send those directors packing!). The directors will need quite a lot of information before they can make a rational decision on such an issue.

Q What kinds of information would you advise the directors to obtain before making their decision?

A First of all, they must find out whether the company has sufficient capital to expand its operations. If it has, the next question is whether that expansion can best be done in the UK or abroad. If an expansion of the company's British business is not possible or not desirable, the directors will have to decide **which** foreign countries they want to start operating in, and what kinds of policies to offer there.

You may have thought also of other, equally relevant, items of information needed.

All these decisions require information. After all, there is no point in establishing a presence in California just because of its pleasant climate, if there is an over-capacity in that market already or if there are government regulations which make that US state unattractive for insurers (such as restrictions on premiums that may be charged). Some of the information required is general information about the economy of the country concerned. Such information can often be obtained from public data banks, as can information about the legal situation affecting insurance companies. To find out whether there is an insurance over-capacity in that country already, the company either will have to rely on its own market research or can try to get that information from a variety of other sources. The underwriting experience of other companies which already operate in that country can be a useful indicator of market conditions. So, to facilitate decision-making, companies will collect information about the various markets they operate in already, as well as on markets where they may consider doing business in the future. Such information can come either from publicly available sources such as government statistics or reports of other companies, or from the company's own research.

In addition to systems designed to facilitate decision-making, there are systems designed to aid internal administrative tasks. Examples include accounting, records on employees, inventory control, cash control (this may be part of the accounting system), and various office automation systems like electronic mail and word processors. As Québec Téléphone points out in its annual report 1988, an electronic mail system can significantly reduce administrative work and lead to a better spread of information within an organisation, which should allow that organisation to offer a more efficient service and thereby gain a competitive edge over its competitors.

Finally, there are those information systems which facilitate communications with customers (policyholders). An insurance company or broker must keep a record of certain details regarding its policyholders, such as personal details and information about what policies each person holds; renewal notices must be sent out a few weeks before a policy expires; there must be an established method of handling claims; claims must be paid and premiums collected; late payers have to be reminded, and so on.

Of course, an insurance company 100 years ago also had to keep such records, but due to changes in technology this information is usually handled in a different way now from how it was in the past. In the past, information systems were mainly based on paper. Nowadays electronic media dominate the scene, but future generations of information systems may well be based on optical rather than electronic impulses.

B2 SYSTEMS DESIGNED FOR A WIDER GROUP OF USERS

Systems designed for a wider group of users can be further sub-divided into information systems accessible to everybody who has the necessary equipment and is prepared to pay the fee charged by the provider of the information, and systems accessible to a specific group of users only. The former are **public information systems** or **data banks;** which provide information on a wide variety of topics: the latest political news, stockmarket prices, exchange rates, government and other statistics, weather reports and forecasts, information on sporting, cultural and other events in a given geographical area, catalogues of products and services, and many others. Some of these systems provide one-way communication only: they confine themselves to giving information to the user. Other such systems are **inter-active:** they

allow a two-way communication. With such a system a user could, for example, obtain information on goods and services offered by a certain producer, and then place an order for the goods or services of his choice. The Encyclopaedia Britannica says in this context, 'In the USA, on-line data-base vendors constitute a kind of evolving electronic supermarket.'[1]

Home banking is another example. The user of such a system can communicate with the bank's computer via a telephone line, and obtain statements of his account, instruct the bank to transfer money from his account to somebody else's (hopefully not the other way round!), and obtain a number of other financial services. Telephone companies are major beneficiaries of this development, since the communication between the user and the data base usually takes place via the telephone system. British Telecom commented in its 1989 annual report : 'There was particularly high growth in the newer services such as facsimile and information services.' Similar comments can be found in the reports of telephone companies in many other countries.

In addition to information systems available to everybody who has the necessary equipment and is willing and able to pay the required subscription charge, there are systems with access restricted to a certain group of users. Examples include the information systems used by stock exchange members or airlines. If you go to an airline office and say that you want to fly from London to Rome in ten days' time, go on from Rome to Athens three days later and return from Athens to London another five days later, the airline employee can call up all the relevant details on the VDU (visual display unit) in front of him or her, and tell you what flights are available, what the cost is, and so on. This is not a system confined to any one company; British Airways can tell you what flights there are from Rome to Athens even if they do not fly on that route at all. However, the system is confined to airlines and travel agents. The stock exchange has a similar system known as SEAQ (Stock Exchange Automated Quotations). Each market maker (that is, wholesaler of stocks and shares) feeds into the system the prices at which he is prepared to buy and sell stocks. A broker-dealer (stockbroker) who has a buy or a sell order from a client can then see on his VDU what prices the various market makers offer, and deal with that market maker who offers the most favourable price: the highest price if the client wants to sell, and the lowest if the client wants to buy. A further development of this system, known as SAEF (SEAQ Automated Execution Facility) even selects the best market maker automatically, and does all the required accounting and documentation. For the time being, however, SAEF is restricted to fairly small orders.

C
COMPUTER NETWORKS

The early computers were rather solitary animals. Hardware and software were kept in one particular location, the input and output of data had to take place at that same location, and one computer was not able to communicate with other computers. Consequently, if an organisation such as an insurance company wanted to use computer facilities, its computer was located at one particular point and information which was to be computerised had to be delivered to the computer by messengers, the postal service or some other means. As Hal Becker points out:

Reports may have been mailed from their source to the computer location on a daily, weekly or monthly basis and converted to a machine- or computer-readable form at the central location. Other information may have been telephoned in periodically and collected in files, which were then keypunched at the appropriate time. Many methods, including truck, messenger service, pneumatic tubes, and others, were used to get the information from its source to the location where it was to be processed. The results or output of the computer runs were delivered to the appropriate destination or destinations by similar means.[2]

Obviously, it is much easier, quicker and perhaps safer if information can be transmitted to the computer directly from the point where it originates. To do this, it takes two things: the person who wants to enter information into the computer, or get information from it, must have a suitable machine to do so; and there must be a link

between the two machines which can carry the data. Neither of these is a problem nowadays. Any office can have several minicomputers which can act as terminals, and the telephone system can be used to link the minicomputers to the company's central computer. Before long, it was not just a question of linking minicomputers in various branch offices to the company's central computer, but computers of all sorts could be 'taught' to communicate with other computers. Now we are talking about **computer networks.** Such a network is a system consisting of two or more computers connected by suitable communication lines. Once such networks have been set up:

Data in central storage units can be shared by large numbers of dispersed users, many having a small computer which can process data or provide an end-user dialogue which simplifies the access to information. Data of interest to one terminal user may reside in multiple distant computers, accessible via networks. When a computer program says GET, it may be accessing a file unit attached to a computer a thousand miles away.[3]

Such computer networks are used on a wide scale nowadays. All the public data banks and organisational information systems discussed in the previous sections are based on this principle. When you instruct a bank to send money to someone in another country, more likely than not the bank will use a computer network called SWIFT (Society for Worldwide Interbank Financial Telecommunication) to get the money to its destination. This is a system through which one member bank can send messages (like instructions to pay a certain amount of money to a named beneficiary) to another member bank. In insurance, such networks are used for communication within the company as well as for communication between companies and brokers. A broker can use such a system to get information on the products offered and the prices charged by various companies, and in some cases he can then decide which company he wants to deal with, enter the relevant details into his terminal, and a few seconds later have his terminal print out the policy document. The motor business is almost entirely computerised in this way. Large scale computerisation can make such transactions quicker and more efficient.

? Despite the advantages of computer networking, there are substantial potential drawbacks as well. Take a minute or two to list those you can think of before reading on.

A negative aspect from the point of view of small companies is that the modern methods are more capital-intensive than traditional ways of doing business. If a company cannot afford the technology, it will find it increasingly difficult to do business at all.

Another problem that needs to be mentioned in the context of computer networks is that of security and privacy. What do you do if important information stored in a computer is lost through some hardware or software failure, or if unauthorised users of a network get hold of confidential information? Some of the problems which may arise are:

► damage to or destruction of hardware;

► accidental or malicious modification or destruction of software;

► accidental or intentional disclosure of data to unauthorised persons;

► accidental or malicious modification of data;

► accidental or malicious destruction of data.

Some of these risks, like damage to hardware or software or the accidental loss of data, are a problem with any computer system, or even the old-fashioned solitary machine. Computer networks magnify those risks and create other risks in addition, because of the much larger number of authorised users and the possibility of unauthorised persons getting access to the system. The details of how network architects try to minimise those risks is mainly a technical matter which is not part of this course, but you should be aware of the problems that exist, and of the fact that computer security is a highly complex issue. No system can claim to be perfect; all one can do is try to make the probability of loss, abuse and so on as small as possible.

Security is a highly complex subject because there are so many different

aspects to it. A systems designer responsible for security needs to be familiar with all features of the system because the system can be attacked or security breached in highly diverse ways. Sometimes a great amount of effort is put into one aspect of security and other aspects are neglected. If a moat is seen as the way to make a castle secure, a great amount of security engineering could be applied to the moat. It could be very wide, and full of hungry piranha fish, and could have a fiercely guarded drawbridge. However, this alone would not make the castle secure. A determined intruder could tunnel under the moat. A security designer sometimes becomes so involved with one aspect of security that he fails to see other ways of breaking into the system. It takes considerable knowledge and ingenuity to see all the possible ways.[3]

D

DATA PROTECTION ACT 1984

This Act aims to prevent the misuse of information about individuals which is held or processed in non-manual systems.

Generally, it is an offence to hold such data unless the holder has registered as a 'data user' with the Data Protection Registrar. Full details have to be provided of the types of information which will be held, and the purposes for which it will be used. Knowingly or recklessly operating outside the registered categories is also an offence.

Individuals about whom data is held ('data subjects') have the right to examine the information held, and to be compensated if they suffer damage or distress through its misuse or loss.

Typical areas where insurance companies, brokers and so on will be affected by the Data Protection Act include:

► personnel records (although payroll and pension details may be excepted);

► management accounts, for example if the information can be interpreted as accounts for individual clients;

► client and agent files;

► mailing lists.

References

1 Encyclopaedia Britannica : 'Information Processing and Information Systems'

2 Hal B. Becker: Functional Analysis of Information Networks, (John Wiley & Sons, 1973)

3 James Martin: Computer Networks and Distributed Processing (Prentice Hall, 1981)

11
SELF-ASSESSMENT QUESTIONS

1. Explain the importance of information in running a business.

   _____

   _____

   _____

2. What information systems do you use (a) in your work ; (b) privately?

   _____

   _____

   _____

   What other information systems are used in your company?

   _____

   _____

   _____

3. In what ways does technology affect the nature of information systems?

   _____

   _____

   _____

4. Distinguish between public information systems and organisational information systems. Give an example in each case.

   _____

   _____

   _____

5. What information does an insurance company need about its policyholders?

   _____

   _____

   _____

6. In what way is such information usually stored now? How was it usually stored 50 years ago?

    _____

    _____

    _____

7. What information does head office need to assess the profitability of certain branches or certain lines of business?

    _____

    _____

    _____

8. What information does top management need (a) about its own company; (b) about the outside world, to be able to make rational decisions?

    _____

    _____

    _____

9. What public and organisational information systems may top management use to facilitate decision-making?

    _____

    _____

    _____

10. What is meant by the term 'computer network'?

    _____

    _____

    _____

11. For what purposes does your company use computer networks?

    _____

    _____

    _____

12. In what ways are computer networks used for communication between insurance companies and brokers? How did brokers and companies communicate before the development of computer networks?

_____

_____

_____

13. What are the risks of computerisation in general, and of the use of computer networks in particular?

_____

_____

_____

14. In what ways does increasing computerisation affect small insurance broking businesses?

_____

_____

_____

11

ANSWERS TO SELF-ASSESSMENT QUESTIONS

1. Without information you know neither your own strengths and weaknesses, nor the requirements of the market place. Without information it is unlikely that a business can operate successfully.

2. It would be worth your while to check your answer to this question with other people in your organisation.

3. Technology affects the way in which information is gathered, stored and retrieved. It also affects the speed with which information can be made available.

4. **Public information systems** may be used by anyone who has the necessary equipment and is willing to pay the fee charged by the operator of the system. **Examples:** News agencies (like Reuters); systems providing information on economic, political, cultural or sporting events.

   Organisational information systems are accessible only to the organisations that run them. **Examples:** a company's staff files.

5. Names, addresses, policies held, claims records, and similar details.

6. Nowadays such information is usually stored electronically (in computers); fifty years ago it was recorded on paper.

7. It needs to know the income and costs generated by those branches and lines of business.

8. (a) Its strengths and weaknesses; staff and capital availability; profitability and liquidity etc.

   (b) Market demand; profitability of various lines of business; government regulation; competition etc.

9. It may use systems providing information on costs and revenues of its various activities, and systems providing information on the outside world, such as economic variables which are likely to affect the company.

10. Two or more computers that communicate with each other.

11. Again, it may be worth checking your answer with a knowledgeable colleague.

12. Brokers can obtain information about premiums charged and policies offered by different insurance companies; in some cases business can be placed by a broker via a computer network. Before the development of computer networks, information had to be obtained from catalogues or company handbooks or brochures; business was placed by mailing a proposal form to the insurance company.

13. The risks comprise accidental or malicious damage to hardware or software, and accidental or malicious disclosure of information to unauthorised persons. Computer networks increase these risks because of the larger number of people who can get access to the system.

14. Computerisation requires large capital outlays. A small business which does not have the necessary capital will find it difficult to do business.

You should work this assignment after studying Chapters 9 to 11. Answer any three questions, and allow yourself one and a half hours to complete it.

1. Many goods go through several stages of production before reaching the consumer. Describe these stages, and give examples of businesses involved at each stage of production.

2. Businesses are affected by a large number of influences from the environment they operate in. Select any two such influences and describe how they affect businesses.

3. During the last one hundred years, organisation theory has moved from the 'one best way' to the 'contingency' approach to business structure. Explain the meaning of these two approaches.

4. Describe the use of information systems in insurance organisations. Distinguish between public and organisational information systems.

PART III
THE FINANCIAL ENVIRONMENT

12

FINANCIAL OBJECTIVES AND FINANCIAL INFORMATION

A   Financial objectives of organisations

B   Groups interested in information about an organisation

C   Annual reports and accounts

LEARNING OBJECTIVES

After studying this chapter, you should be able to:

▷ outline possible financial objectives of various organisations;

▷ explain the reasons for formulating financial objectives;

▷ explain the role of information in assessing whether financial objectives have been attained;

▷ list groups of people interested in financial information about an organisation;

▷ name the main sources of information about an organisation;

▷ list the main items to be found in the annual report and accounts of British companies;

▷ explain why insurance companies need information on other companies.

A
FINANCIAL OBJECTIVES OF ORGANISATIONS

We saw in Chapter 9 that organisations come in all shapes and sizes. There are business organisations like factories, farms, shops and insurance companies; professional organisations, like the Chartered Insurance Institute, the Law Society or the Royal Institution of Chartered Surveyors; governmental organisations, some of which are run more or less on business lines (like British Rail) whereas others are not (like the Department of Social Security or the Police); churches and other religious organisations; charities; political parties; criminal organisations and many others.

Given the diversity among organisations, it is of course impossible to say that the financial objective of an organisation is always such and such. Different organisations have different aims and different ways of doing business, and this is true of the financial aspect of their work just as it is of any other aspect of their activities. However, even if there is no such thing as **the one** financial objective shared by all organisations, one can nevertheless list a few sets of financial objectives which apply to certain types of organisation.

A1   NON-PROFIT-MAKING ORGANISATIONS

First of all: do all organisations have financial objectives? It may seem at first sight that the activities of a church or a golf club have little to do with money.

Q   Such institutions do need financial objectives. What might the financial concerns be of, say, a church or a charity?

A   Well, making money may not be the main aim of such organisations, but that does not mean that they can just forget about money altogether. A church has to pay its employees and maintain its buildings, and most charities need money and equipment to carry out their work. The Royal National Lifeboat Institution, for example, could not save lives at sea without suitable boats, and it costs money to buy and maintain such boats. So, even if making money is not the ultimate aim of an organisation, most organisations need money to pursue the purpose for which they exist. The financial objective of many non-profit-making organisations can therefore be described as procuring enough money to enable them to pursue the aims they have set themselves.

A2 GOVERNMENTAL ORGANISATIONS

Governmental organisations are a rather mixed bag as far as their financial objectives are concerned. Some of these organisations are run more or less on business lines: the Post Office and British Rail can serve as examples. These organisations offer a service for which users have to pay, and exactly the same can be said of any service industry in the private sector of the economy. Still, governmental organisations rarely aim at making the highest possible profit. It is more common for them to provide the services the government has decided they should provide, and fix their prices in such a way that they will cover their operating costs as well as provide a return on the invested capital which the government considers to be reasonable. Their financial objective, therefore, is to create sufficient revenues to cover their costs and to achieve the required rate of return on their capital.

Other government organisations, however, are not run on business lines. The Foreign Office and the Police do not have revenues derived from selling goods or services, so they are financed from taxpayers' money. This, however, does not mean that they can just spend any amount they like. They have a budget, and are expected not to spend more than their budget allows them. The financial objective of this kind of government organisation is to provide the services government has decided they should provide, by using no more money than has been allowed to them in their budget.

Some **public sector organisations** are on the borderline between those that are run on business lines and those which are not. This is true, for example, of universities and colleges. These institutions provide a range of services (like teaching, research and consultancy) for which the users have to pay. However, the fees paid by the users are often not designed to cover the whole cost of providing the service. In the UK, foreign students (other than those from EC countries*) pay fees which cover the entire cost of their tuition. British and other EC students, on the other hand, pay fees which are less than the full cost of providing their tuition. Therefore, colleges and universities receive grants from the government which are paid for ultimately by the taxpayers. The financial objective of public sector organisations in this category can be described as generating sufficient income from fees and grants to allow them to offer the services they have decided to provide.

A3 PRIVATE SECTOR BUSINESS ORGANISATIONS

In private sector business organisations, the financial objectives will usually be more profit-orientated than in the organisations discussed so far. Indeed, conventional economic theory often assumes profit maximisation to be the aim of just about any business, but most economists are agreed that this is a simplification of reality. The financial objective of many owners of small businesses (like small shops, one-person insurance broking businesses, self-employed plumbers and electricians), is to generate a 'reasonable' income for themselves and their families. What is 'reasonable' is partly a matter of personal opinion, but it is largely influenced by the amount which similar businesses earn and by what the owner of the business could earn by working as an employee in some other organisation. For instance, a baker could work as an employee in a large bakery or food processing company instead of running his own business, and the wage or salary he could earn in such a job will no doubt influence his expectations as to what he should earn as a self-employed person.

Some owners of small businesses are, of course,

---

* In 1990, the member countries of the EC (European Community) were Belgium, Denmark, France, Greece, Ireland, Italy, Luxembourg, the Netherlands, Portugal, Spain, the UK and Germany.

more ambitious and want to earn more than just an average income, either in order to enjoy a higher standard of living or in order to plough these earnings back into their business so that it may expand. (By the way, being more ambitious than the average person is in itself neither good nor bad; it is just a different attitude.) In this case, the financial objective may be either to earn a given amount of income, or indeed the profit maximisation postulated by traditional economic theory.

In larger businesses, the financial objectives are often more difficult to define than in smaller organisations. The reason for this is that in most large businesses ownership and control are in the hands of different groups of people. In a family business, the owner has a direct personal interest in the financial performance of his firm, because the firm's profit is his personal income. In large organisations the link between the performance of the business and people's personal incomes is a less direct one. As we have seen earlier (see Chapter 9) many large corporations take the form of public limited companies. Such companies are owned by shareholders, while control is in the hands of a board of directors elected by the shareholders. If the directors manage the company particularly well and profits go up, those profits accrue to the shareholders and not the directors. The directors may of course benefit indirectly from an increase in profits, perhaps by way of higher salaries, but the link is nevertheless a less direct one than in the case of a business managed by its owners. This does not mean, however, that the directors have no interest at all in earning money for the shareholders. After all, the directors are elected by the shareholders, and if the shareholders are dissatisfied with a director they can vote him out of office or make their dissatisfaction felt in other ways (see Chapter 10). Experience has shown, however, that shareholders are unlikely to rebel as long as their company's earnings do not fall too far behind the stockmarket average. As Stanlake puts it:

> **The status, prestige, and remuneration of managers is closely linked to the size of the firm and it is likely, therefore, that such people will be more interested in maximising sales rather than maximising profits. They cannot be indifferent to the profit and loss account of the firm, but, having achieved a level of**

profit which they believe will satisfy shareholders, managers are more inclined to make sales-maximisation their major objective.[1]

Sales in this context can be expressed either in terms of units of the company's products (for example so many tons of steel), in money terms, or in terms of market share. Alcan, a Canadian aluminium producer, says that its financial objective is 'to operate at a level of profitability which will ensure the long-term economic viability of the company by providing a return on the shareholders' investment which compares favourably with other industries of similar capital intensity and risk and will enable the company to attract capital adequate to support its growth.'[2]

? Try to summarise, from the material above, what the financial objective of a large private sector company will generally be.

Obviously, the exact financial objectives differ from company to company, but one can generalise these by saying that for many large private sector organisations the financial objective is to earn a return on investment which will satisfy shareholders, and which will allow the company to attract additional capital when needed to finance the company's planned expansion in the future.

Once a company has decided its financial objectives, it will implement the corporate structure which it thinks is most likely to allow it to fulfil its objectives. Several insurance companies, among them the Prudential, the Royal and the Sun Alliance, have adopted a holding company structure which in some way turns them from being insurance companies in the traditional sense of the word to being broader-based financial services organisations.

A4 WHY FORMULATE FINANCIAL OBJECTIVES?

In the preceding paragraph we talked about the financial objectives of various types of organisation. Formulating financial objectives is, of course, not an end in itself. There is no point in working out such objectives and circulating them to the relevant people in an organisation by way of memos if all these memos do is to disappear in various drawers and gather dust. So, what should come next?

Well, the logical next step is to make sure the organisation is on the right path towards attaining its stated financial objectives. Does a charity attract enough donations to enable it to finance its intended activities? Does a small business make enough money to provide its owner with what he considers to be a reasonable income? Is a large company profitable enough to satisfy shareholders, or does it at least generate enough cash to pay its bills on time? Losing control of one's financial affairs can have nasty consequences, not only for private sector enterprises but also for public sector entities like city administrations. People in the Belgian town of Liège learned this the hard way in September/October 1989 when the town's treasury suddenly ran out of money, apparently because it had overspent its budget. The town could not pay its employees, and when the dustmen did not get their wages they decided that it was more comfortable to sit at home in an armchair than to collect other people's rubbish. Rubbish piled up in the streets, other public services also ground to a halt, and a Dutch radio commentator described Liège at that time as "ungovernable and almost uninhabitable". All this inconvenience was the consequence of a city administration losing control over its financial affairs. So, it is essential to monitor whether an organisation is on the right course to attaining its financial objectives, and to take remedial action if it is not.

To be able to monitor an organisation in this way, one needs information about its financial objectives and its actual financial situation: you cannot say whether a ship is on the right course if you do not know where it is supposed to be going or where it is now. Much of this information will be in the format of accounting statements, like balance sheets, profit and loss accounts and so on, so we will have to look at such statements in more detail later on (see Chapter 13, Basic Accounting). Before doing that, however, let us look in some more detail at who exactly will need such information, and for what purposes.

B

GROUPS INTERESTED IN INFORMATION ABOUT AN ORGANISATION

There are five main groups who would have an interest in information about an organisation. We will look at each of these in turn.

B1 THE ORGANISATION'S MANAGEMENT

To begin with, the management of an organisation needs to know whether the organisation is 'on track' financially. Only if it has enough information about where the organisation is and where it should be (that is, about the organisation's actual financial situation and its financial objectives) can it decide what action, if any, has to be taken. For example, Royal Insurance says with regard to its operations in the USA, 'We plan to develop our business only in those geographical areas that promise a reasonable rate of return, consistent with our policy of maintaining adequate pricing for all products.'[3] Obviously, the management of Royal USA needs information about which geographical areas are profitable for the company before it can decide whether to further develop its business there or not. The Allstate Insurance Company (an American insurer) must have been thinking along similar lines when deciding not to renew its licence to sell insurance in Massachusetts, which expired in June 1989, because of persistent losses on its operations in that state.[4]

Of course, these considerations are not confined to the insurance industry. For example, British Home Stores decided in 1985 to stop selling groceries, and Air France decided in 1987 to reduce the number of flights between France and Algeria; in both cases the reasons for the decision were insufficient profits or actual losses resulting from those operations. On the other hand, many telephone companies have identified fax and data-bank-related services as an area where faster growth can be expected than in traditional telephone services. To add an example from the farming sector: under the headline 'Wild about boars - and doing very well', Michael Gailsford wrote in 'Farmers Weekly' of 13 October 1989 that a Somerset farmer had decided to switch from pig to wild boar production, saying "We have always had pigs on the farm here, but returns from conventional pigkeeping are nowhere near those that we are now achieving from wild boar farming" (and the article is accompanied by a lovely photo showing a litter of five Danish wild boars). Obviously, the farmer must have worked out the costs and benefits of pig as against wild boar production before he could make his decision to switch from the former to the latter.

In those sectors of the economy where prices or other conditions are decided by the government, the management or representatives of organisations sometimes use accounting information to underpin requests for more favourable conditions. Sheep farmers in the Highlands and Islands of Scotland, for instance, get higher support payments than do farmers in other parts of the UK. However, in 1989 they were of the opinion that the existing differential was not sufficient to compensate them for the less favourable weather conditions, higher transport costs, restricted choice of markets and other disadvantages of remoteness which they face. In the autumn of 1989 the Scottish Crofters' Union therefore sent a request to the Scottish Office, Highland and Island MPs, local authorities, the Highlands and Islands Development Board and other agencies, asking for 'a large increase in the existing supports payment differential between producers in the Highlands and Islands Development Board area and those in the rest of the UK.' [5] To back up its demand, the Scottish Crofters' Union referred to a survey conducted by the North of Scotland Agricultural College in Aberdeen 'which shows that the net average profit on 50 croft businesses (in 1988) was just £729.' [5] In this case, accounting information was used by an organisation to back up its demand for more favourable treatment by the government.

B2   SHAREHOLDERS

Turning now to groups other than an organisation's management, the shareholders are one of the groups who will be interested in information about their company. If you have invested some

of your money in a company, you will of course want to know how well (or otherwise) that company's management is handling your money. Is your company profitable? How do this year's results compare with those of previous years? How does the performance of your company compare with that of other companies in the same sector of the economy? These are some of the questions shareholders will ask themselves in order to decide whether they are satisfied with the performance of their company, whether they should re-elect or replace some of the directors, whether to keep their shares or to sell them and invest the proceeds in some other company, and, occasionally, whether to accept or reject a takeover bid.

In fact, not only will the existing shareholders be interested in information about the company, but so will potential future shareholders. Suppose you have decided to invest some of your money in British company shares, and for some reason you consider retailing and banking shares to be particularly attractive. Which shares do you buy? On the retailing side you could buy, for example, Storehouse (owners of British Home Stores, Habitat, Mothercare and other stores) or Marks and Spencer shares. Both companies are among the leading British retailers, but that does not mean that they are just the same. Indeed, their performance differed substantially in the late 1980s. On the banking side, there are considerable differences between the leading banks as far as their exposure to risky Third World debtor countries is concerned. Before you can make a rational decision as to which shares you should buy, you will need information about all the companies concerned.

Q   Where do you get this information from?

A   The main sources of such information are the company's annual report and accounts. These are dealt with in some detail in section C.

B3   THE GOVERNMENT

In addition to an organisation's management and its members or owners, a number of government departments will be interested in various aspects of its activities. The Inland Revenue will need information about the profit or loss a business has made in order to work out the amount of income or corporation tax it has to pay. Incorporated businesses such as limited companies pay corporation tax on their taxable profits. In the case of unincorporated businesses such as partnerships or sole traders, the profit is attributed to the owner(s) who then have to pay income tax on their share of the profits.

Income tax and corporation tax are examples of **direct taxes:** those levied on the income of an individual or an organisation. **Indirect taxes** are added to the price of goods or services. The Department of Customs and Excise handles indirect taxes, including import duties, special taxes on petrol, alcohol and tobacco, and value added tax (VAT). To assess the correct amount of VAT payable, the Department needs information on certain aspects of an organisation's activities; mainly on its sales.

Insurance is exempt from VAT, which means insurance companies need not add it to the premiums they charge. However, they still have to pay VAT on goods they buy, like office equipment or stationery, and they can reclaim that part of the VAT they have paid which relates to their overseas business. To simplify matters, the government has agreed to a proportional method of assessment: if an insurance company gets 30% of its premium income from overseas, it can reclaim 30% of the VAT it has paid. Apart from taxation matters, many organisations have to provide information about their activities to some government department on a regular basis. The most relevant of such items from an insurance point of view are the returns which insurance companies have to submit to the Department of Trade and Industry (DTI). These will be discussed in more detail in Part IV, The Legal Environment.

B4 INSURANCE COMPANIES

Insurance companies need information about other companies for the following reasons (among others):

▶ To work out whether sums insured are adequate. If a small company states in its balance sheet that its buildings are worth $300,000 but these buildings are insured for only $200,000, the insurance company will want to know whether these buildings are underinsured.

▶ To check the amount of claims. In property insurance, claims can be compared with relevant balance sheet data, and in consequential loss insurance claims can be compared with the profit and loss account, to establish whether they are reasonable.

▶ To assess whether a company's shares are suitable as an investment. Claims can only occur after premiums have been paid, and during the period between receiving a premium and paying a claim the insurance company can invest the money. Some of this money is usually invested in company shares, so the investment manager of the insurance company has to decide which shares he should buy. To be able to make rational decisions, the investment manager needs information on a large number of companies so that he can select those which he thinks are most suitable as an investment.

B5 OTHER INTERESTED PARTIES

This is a rather open-ended category, because it is simply not possible even to find out all the people who might be interested in an organisation.

? Try to list some of these interested people for yourself, with reasons for their interest, before reading on.

Among the more obvious parties are employees and their representatives, like trade unions. For example, there is no point in making huge wage claims if the company is in financial difficulties. If such wage claims 'succeed' they may well push the company into insolvency, and that can hardly be in the interest of its workforce. If, on the other hand, the company is very profitable, it is only legitimate for the workforce to get some benefit from those profits, be it in the form of profit-sharing schemes or higher wages and salaries: after all, it is the workforce who, together with the capital provided by the owners, have created those profits. So, to decide what wage claim is reasonable and realistic, a trade union or individual employee must be informed about the financial situation of the company, its future prospects and so on.

In addition to existing employees, potential future employees may want some information about an organisation. It is a good idea to read a company's annual report before going to a job interview. Many job applicants know very little about the company to which they have applied for a job. A selection panel cannot fail to be impressed if an applicant shows that he or she knows a bit about the company already, for example by asking specific questions about some aspect of the company's activities.

Furthermore, banks, stockbrokers, chambers of commerce, research institutes, data bank operators and others collect information about companies for a variety of reasons. Lastly, the commercial sections of embassies often compile information about the main companies in their area, for use by companies in their own country or their government.

C

ANNUAL REPORTS AND ACCOUNTS

The main sources of information about a company for existing and potential future shareholders are the company's annual report and accounts. You will find it easier to understand the following pages if you actually get the annual reports of a few companies, preferably from various sectors of the economy. If you are a shareholder in a company, you will get that company's annual report sent to you automatically, and some companies prepare special reports for their employees. To get the annual reports of other companies, just write to the secretary of the companies concerned. Companies are, of course, under no obligation to send copies of their annual report to people other than their shareholders (and the Registrar of Companies), but most companies will send a copy to anyone who asks for it.

So, what information will you find in the annual report?

According to the **Companies Act 1985,** every company must hold an annual general meeting once every year, and each such meeting must take place no more than 15 months after the previous one. It is at these meetings that shareholders elect the directors and the auditors, and at each such meeting the directors and auditors elected at the previous meeting report to the shareholders. The Act specifies further that:

> **in respect of each financial year of a company the directors shall lay before the company in general meeting copies of the accounts for that year.*** ... For the **purposes of this Act, a company's accounts for a financial year are to be taken as comprising the following documents:**
> **(a) the company's profit and loss account and balance sheet;**
> **(b) the directors' report;**
> **(c) the auditors' report;**
> **(d) where a company has subsidiaries..., the company's group accounts. ****

In addition to these legal requirements, the relevant Statement of Standard Accounting Practice*** (laid down by the professional bodies of the accountants) also requires the publication of a source and application of funds statement in the case of all but the very smallest of companies. Companies listed on the Stock Exchange must also produce a source and application of funds statement to comply with the Stock Exchange's listing requirements. Nearly all companies also include a chairman's statement (American companies call this 'letter to shareholders') in their annual report, but they are not required to do so by law. To comply with the Companies Act, the annual report and the notice of meeting (which is the official invitation of the shareholders to the annual general meeting and is normally incorporated into the annual report) must reach the shareholders at least 21 days before the date of the annual general meeting.

To comply with all these requirements and conventions, the annual reports of British companies usually contain the following items (not necessarily in this order):

(i) the notice of meeting;
(ii) the chairman's statement;
(iii) the directors' report;

---

* Companies Act 1985, section 227
** Companies Act 1985, section 239
*** SSAP number 10

(iv) the auditors' report;

(v) the profit and loss account for the latest financial year, and the year before that;

(vi) the balance sheet for the latest financial year, and the year before that;

(vii) the source and application of funds statement for the latest financial year, and the year before that;

(viii) if the company has subsidiaries, the group accounts.

It would be useful for your understanding of these matters if you compared the list above with the table of contents in the annual reports of a number of British companies. You should find there all the items listed above, and probably more. Most companies include far more information in their annual report than they have to.

Let us now discuss each of the items in the list above in some more detail.

C1 THE NOTICE OF MEETING

As stated earlier, the Companies Act requires companies to hold an annual general meeting once every year, and shareholders must be given at least 21 days' notice of that meeting. The notice of meeting tells shareholders where and when the meeting will take place, and what business will be on the agenda of the meeting. The ordinary business of an annual general meeting consists of four points, namely:

▶ the consideration of the annual report and accounts;

▶ the consideration of the dividends proposed by the directors;

▶ the election of directors;

▶ the election of auditors;

Any other business conducted at the annual general meeting is called **special business.** Such special business may include decisions to increase or reduce the company's share capital, and changes in the company's articles of association (more about this in Part IV, The Legal Environment). Shareholders who cannot attend the meeting in person can vote 'by proxy': they can authorise another shareholder or one of the directors to vote on their behalf.

C2 THE CHAIRMAN'S STATEMENT

This is usually a fairly general description of the business of the company, its financial situation and prospects, and developments in the outside world which affect the company.

C3 THE DIRECTORS' REPORT

This report is usually more detailed than the chairman's statement, and there are some legal regulations as to its contents. Section 235 of the Companies Act says:

(1) In the case of every company there shall for each financial year be prepared a report by the directors

    (a) containing a fair review of the development of the business of the company and its subsidiaries during the financial year and of their position at the end of it, and

    (b) stating the amount (if any) which they recommend should be paid as dividend and the amount (if any) which they propose to carry to reserves.

(2) The directors' report shall state the names of persons who, at any time during the financial year, were directors of the company, and the principal activities of the company and its subsidiaries in the course of the year and any significant changes in those activities in the year.

C4 THE AUDITORS' REPORT

In this report the auditors indicate whether, in their opinion, the company has kept proper accounts during the financial year under review, and whether those accounts give a true and fair view of the state of affairs of the company. A report by satisfied auditors might look as follows (taken from British Steel's annual report 1988-89):

To the members of British Steel plc.
We have audited the accounts on pages ... in accordance with approved auditing standards.

In our opinion the accounts give a true and fair view of the state of affairs of the Company and the Group as at 1st April 1989 and of the profit and source and application of funds of the Group for the financial year then ended and comply with the Companies Act 1985.
(name of auditing firm)
(date)

The Companies Act 1985 lays down the duty of auditors in more detail. Section 236 says:

(1) A company's auditors shall make a report to its members on the accounts: examined by them, and on every balance sheet and profit and loss account and on all group accounts, copies of which are to be laid before the company in general meeting during the auditors' term of office.

(2) The auditors' report shall state
   (a) whether in the auditors' opinion the balance sheet and profit and loss account and (if it is a holding company submitting group accounts) group accounts have been properly prepared in accordance with this Act;
   (b) without prejudice to the foregoing, whether in their opinion a true and fair view is given
      (i) in the balance sheet, of the state of the company's affairs at the end of the financial year,
      (ii) in the profit and loss account (if not framed as a consolidated account) of the company's profit and loss for the year, and
      (iii) in the case of group accounts, of the state of affairs and profit or loss of the company and its subsidiaries dealt with by those accounts, so far as concerns members of the company.

Section 237:

(1) It is the duty of the company's auditors, in preparing their report, to carry out such investigations as will enable them to form an opinion as to the following matters

(a) whether proper accounts have been kept by the company ...
(b) whether the company's balance sheet and ... its profit and loss account are in agreement with the accounting records and returns.

(2) If the auditors are of the opinion that proper accounts have not been kept... (they) shall state that fact in their report.

C5   THE PROFIT AND LOSS ACCOUNT

Basically, the profit and loss account adds up all the organisation's revenues, deducts all the costs, and so arrives at the profit or loss that has been made during the period to which the account refers. The technical aspects of profit and loss accounts and the main items one normally finds in them will be discussed in Chapter 13.

C6   THE BALANCE SHEET

Basically, the balance sheet lists the values of all the organisation's assets (machinery, buildings, vehicles, and so on), deducts all the liabilities (for example bank loans), and so arrives at the organisation's net worth, which belongs to its owners (the shareholders).

The technical details of balance sheets, as well as the main items one usually finds in them, will be discussed in the next chapter.

C7   THE SOURCE AND APPLICATION OF FUNDS STATEMENT

Basically, a source and application of funds statement lists all the inflows and outflows of money, works out what the net inflow or outflow is, and explains how any net inflow has been used (applied) or how any net outflow has been financed.

At first sight this may seem similar to a profit and loss account, but there are some differences. For example, buying a machine certainly constitutes an outflow of money, but it is not a loss to the company that buys the machine. This will be discussed in more detail in the next chapter.

C8 GROUP ACCOUNTS

Group accounts, also known as 'consolidated accounts', are really another set of balance sheets, profit and loss accounts and source and application of funds statements. An ordinary balance sheet deals with the assets, liabilities and owners' funds of one company. If a company has three subsidiaries, one can work out the balance sheets of each of the subsidiaries as well as that of the holding company (for an explanation of the term 'holding company' see section 10C2.) The group accounts then comprise the assets, liabilities and owners' funds of the entire group of companies; those of the three subsidiaries as well as those of the holding company.

An example will be given in Chapter 13.

References

1 G.F. Stanlake : Introductory Economics (4th ed.), Longman Publishers 1983

2 Alcan Aluminium Ltd: Alcan, its purpose, objectives and policies; Montreal 1987.

3 Royal Insurance, Annual Report 1988 , page 8

4 Source of information : The Wall Street Journal, 15.11.1988

5 Douglas MacSkimming : Poor sheep returns putting us on the line, say crofters; Farmers Weekly, 13.10.1989, page 28

12

SELF-ASSESSMENT QUESTIONS

1. Do all organisations have financial objectives? Why (not)?

2. What are typical financial objectives of:

   (a) charities; (b) small businesses; (c) public limited companies; (d) government departments?

3. For what purposes do: (a) management; (b) shareholders; (c) insurance companies need information about an organisation?

4. What are the main sections of the annual report and accounts of British companies?

5. What is the difference between the chairman's statement and the directors' report in the annual report of British companies?

6. What information is provided in the auditors' report?

7.   What is the difference between a balance sheet and a profit and loss account?

   _____

   _____

   _____

8.   What does the term 'group accounts' mean? Which companies have to prepare group accounts?

   _____

   _____

   _____

ANSWERS TO SELF-ASSESSMENT QUESTIONS APPEAR OVERLEAF

12
ANSWERS TO SELF-ASSESSMENT QUESTIONS

1. All organisations whose activities involve the use of money will have financial objectives.

2. (a) To generate a sufficient inflow of money to finance the charity's intended activities.

    (b) To generate what the owner considers to be a reasonable income for himself.

    (c) To generate profits that will satisfy shareholders.

    (d) To generate a sufficient cash inflow to pay for their costs, and to achieve the return on capital prescribed by the government or to provide the services demanded by government by spending no more than allowed in the budget.

3. (a) To see whether the organisation meets its objectives.

    (b) To see whether their organisation is performing in what they consider to be a satisfactory way.

    (c) To check the adequacy of sums insured; to verify claims; to assess the suitability of a company as an investment.

4. Notice of meeting; chairman's statement; directors' report; auditors' report; profit and loss account; balance sheet; source and application of funds statement; group accounts, if applicable.

5. The chairman's statement is usually a fairly general comment on the affairs of the company and the state of the environment it operates in. The directors' report is more concerned with details, and its contents are prescribed by the Companies Act.

6. In the auditors' report, the auditors say whether the company has kept proper accounting records, and whether the accounts give a true and fair view of the situation of the company.

7. A balance sheet shows a company's assets and liabilities at a certain point in time. A profit and loss account shows what profit or loss the business has made during a given period of time.

8. Many companies have subsidiaries. Such companies have to prepare group accounts. The group accounts (also known as consolidated accounts) show the state of affairs of the company and all its subsidiaries.

13

BASIC ACCOUNTING

LEARNING OBJECTIVES

After studying this chapter, you should be able to:

▷ name the three main accounting documents;

▷ explain what kind of information is provided in balance sheets, profit and loss accounts

▷ and source and application of funds statements;

▷ list typical assets and liabilities of individuals;

▷ list typical assets and liabilities of companies;

▷ prepare a balance sheet in horizontal or vertical format, given the assets and liabilities of the organisation concerned;

▷ explain the layouts of balance sheets, profit and loss accounts, and source and application of funds statements;

▷ understand the published accounts of insurance companies and brokers.

We saw in the previous chapter that the main accounting documents are balance sheets, profit and loss accounts, and source and application of funds statements. We know already what kind of information is provided in each of these (see section 12C), but we still have to look at the practicalities: what does a balance sheet look like, and how have the figures we see in a balance sheet come about? The same questions can be asked about profit and loss accounts and source and application of funds statements.

To answer these questions, we will first look at balance sheets of individuals. It may be rare for individuals to work out balance sheets for themselves, but since balance sheets of individuals are a bit easier than are balance sheets of businesses (if only because most people are more familiar with the financial affairs of individuals than they are with those of companies), working out a balance sheet for an individual is a useful way to understand the basic principles of balance sheets.

Next, we will go one step further and apply this knowledge to businesses. We will look at the balance sheet, profit and loss account, and source and application of funds statement of a small business. This will enable us to understand published accounts; balance sheets and other accounting statements as we can find them in the annual reports of British companies. These will be discussed in section C.

A

BALANCE SHEETS OF INDIVIDUALS

A balance sheet gives a picture of the assets and liabilities of an individual or organisation, and the manner in which that information is provided is extremely important. We will look below at how the information is put together, and at the various ways in which it can be presented.

A1 ASSETS AND LIABILITIES

We know already that a balance sheet tells us something about the assets and liabilities of the organisation or the individual to whom it refers.

Q Well, what kind of assets and liabilities does an individual normally have? It would be useful for you to pause for a while at this point and think of the various assets and liabilities you yourself have.

A Typically, an individual will own some cash, and some money in a bank, building society, the Post Office or some other financial institution. Then, nearly all individuals have some household equipment, like furniture, pots and pans, a fridge, washing machine, radio, television set, and so on. If you live with your parents, it may be difficult to ascertain which of these things are actually owned by you and which are owned by your parents.

In addition, many people have a car, some own the house or flat they live in, some have investments like company shares or government securities, some own personal 'chattels' like jewellery; the list could be continued. All these are examples of **assets** which are typically owned by individuals.

By way of example, let us assume that Mr Jones has the following assets on 1 January 1991:

► A house, worth £75,000 (if you find this figure outrageously high or ridiculously low, remember that house prices vary considerably from one part of the country to another);
► household equipment (furniture etc.) worth £10,000;
► a car, worth £8,000;
► investments (company shares etc.) worth £5,000;
► money in the bank: £1,800;
► cash: £200.

We can see from these figures that the total value of all the assets owned by Mr Jones is £100,000. Does this mean, however, that his personal wealth amounts to £100,000?

Maybe it does, but this is by no means certain. We just cannot tell from the information we have got so far. Why is that? Why could it be that Mr Jones's personal wealth amounts to less than £100,000 if he owns assets worth that amount?

The answer becomes clear once we find out how he financed the purchase of his house. Does every housebuyer just open his wallet and pay out the purchase price in cash? Of course not. Many, probably most, people who buy a house borrow money to finance at least part of the purchase price; a loan to buy property is usually called a mortgage. Suppose Mr Jones owes his building society* £60,000. In that case it is obvious that Mr Jones's personal wealth does not amount to £100,000. True, he owns assets worth £100,000, but at the same time he has a debt of £60,000. That means that his personal wealth is £40,000 and not £100,000. If he has other debts in addition to his mortgage, we have to deduct those debts as well if we want to work out his personal wealth. Let us assume that he has borrowed money from a bank in order to help him with the purchase of his car, and that at the moment £2,000 of that loan are still outstanding. In that case Mr Jones's total debt is £62,000. Deducting this from the value of the assets he owns (£100,000) produces a net personal wealth of £38,000.

This is the kind of information contained in a balance sheet. A balance sheet shows all the assets and the **liabilities** of a given individual or organisation at a certain date. So, what does Mr Jones's balance sheet look like on 1 January 1991?

A2 PRESENTATION

Now we are talking about the methods of presenting balance sheets. There are two widely used formats for balance sheets; the vertical (or columnar), and the horizontal (or side by side) format. Both formats contain exactly the same information; they are just two different ways of showing an individual's (or a company's) assets and liabilities. At the moment, the vertical format is more common in published accounts of British compa-

---

* Note for overseas readers: Building societies are financial institutions which accept deposits from savers and use most of the money obtained in this way to give mortgages to people who want to buy property.

nies, but if you look at the annual report of a North American or continental European company you will almost certainly find the horizontal method of presentation. Some British companies (particularly banks) also continue to use the horizontal method, and it is listed as a permissible method of presentation in Schedule 4, one of the annexes to the **Companies Act 1985**. So, we have to be familiar with both balance sheet formats. The vertical format of the balance sheet starts by listing all the assets, and then works out their total value. It then lists all the liabilities and establishes their total. And the last step is to deduct the liabilities from the assets in order to find the individual's personal wealth. (This description is accurate as far as balance sheets for individuals are concerned; in the case of balance sheets of businesses the presentation is slightly more complicated, as we will see in the next section.)

A2A Vertical format

Using the vertical format first, Mr Jones's balance sheet looks as follows:

Balance sheet of Mr Jones on 1 January 1991

	£	£
Assets:		
house	75,000	
household equipment	10,000	
car	8,000	
investments	5,000	
banks	1,800	
cash	200	100,000
Liabilities:		
mortgage	60,000	
car loan	2,000	62,000
Personal wealth:		38,000

The basic idea behind the vertical format of balance sheets is:
Total assets less total liabilities = personal wealth.

A2B Horizontal format

Now that we know the vertical presentation of bal-

ance sheets, let us turn to the horizontal method of presentation. Balance sheets based on this principle have two sides. We can just call them left and right if we want to, or we can talk of the asset side and the liability side. In Britain assets are listed on the right hand side and liabilities on the left hand side. In most other countries it is the other way round. Recording the information we have on Mr Jones in a horizontal balance sheet, we would, as a first step, get the following:

Balance sheet of Mr Jones on 1.1.1991 (£)

Liabilities		Assets	
mortgage	60,000	house	75,000
car loan	2,000	household equipment	10,000
		car	8,000
		investments	5,000
		bank	1,800
		cash	200
			100,000

This, however, is not yet a complete balance sheet. The basic idea of the horizontal presentation of balance sheets is that a balance sheet must balance. That means that both sides must add up to the same total. We can see above that Mr Jones's assets total £100,000. The liabilities we have recorded on the liability side so far total £62,000. So, what does the difference of £38,000 represent? Well, if Mr Jones owns assets worth £100,000 and he has debts of £62,000, his personal wealth is £38,000; and that is the missing factor in our balance sheet. These £38,000 are now inserted on the left hand side of Mr Jones's balance sheet. We then get the following:

Balance sheet of Mr Jones on 1.1.1991

Liabilities		Assets	
mortgage	60,000	house	75,000
car loan	2,000	household equipment	10,000
personal			
wealth	38,000	car	8,000
		investments	5,000
		bank	1,800
		cash	200
	100,000		100,000

Now the balance sheet balances, as by definition it must. The basic idea of the horizontal presentation of balance sheets is: **all the assets must have been financed somehow, either from the individual's own resources (personal wealth) or from borrowed money.** The asset side tells us what assets the individual has. The liability side tells us how these assets have been financed. In Mr Jones's case, he owns assets worth $100,000, as we know already. These $100,000 have come partly from borrowed money ($62,000), and partly from Mr Jones's personal wealth ($38,000).

B

BALANCE SHEET OF A SMALL BUSINESS

In the previous section we have become acquainted with the basic principles of balance sheets. Let us now apply our knowledge to a small business. On 1 January 1992, Mr Smith, a shopkeeper, has the following assets:

cash	$500
money in the bank	$2,500
stock of goods for resale	$2,000
shopfittings	$10,000
delivery van	$10,000

When he started trading a year ago, his uncle lent him $10,000 to enable him to buy the delivery van.

What does the balance sheet of Mr Smith's business look like?

Let us start with the horizontal format. The basic principle is the same as that for balance sheets for individuals which we discussed in the previous section: the right hand side tells us about the business's assets, and the left hand side about the amounts owed and the businessman's own money that has been invested in the business. On the asset side, however, accountants usually distinguish between two different types of assets: **fixed assets** on the one hand, and **current assets** on the other. Fixed assets are those which are in the business more or less permanently, or at least for a couple of years; in Mr Smith's case this would apply to the shopfittings and the delivery van. Current assets are assets of a more 'liquid'

and less permanent nature; in our example cash, money in the bank and the stock of goods for resale would be in this category. To highlight the difference: the shopfittings will remain in the shop for a long time, maybe for as long as the shop exists. Stock, on the other hand, is a different matter. A clothing retailer does not buy shirts or trousers in the hope that they will stay on the shelves forever. The sooner they can be sold, the better.

With this information we can now draw up the balance sheet of Mr Smith's shop. It looks as follows:

Balance sheet of Mr Smith's shop, 1.1.1992 ($)

Liabilities		Assets		
loan from				
uncle	10,000	**Fixed assets**:		
capital	15,000	shopfittings	10,000	
		delivery van	10,000	20,000
		Current assets:		
		stock	2,000	
		bank	2,500	
		cash	500	5,000
	25,000			25,000

The word 'capital' denotes the amount of Mr Smith's own money invested in the business. If the business has assets worth $25,000 and debts of $10,000, the owner's stake in the business is $15,000.

The vertical version of the balance sheet is as follows:

	$	$	$
Assets:			
Fixed assets:			
- shopfittings	10,000		
- delivery van	10,000	20,000	
Current assets:			
- stock	2,000		
- bank	2,500		
- cash	500	5,000	25,000
Debt: Loan from uncle			10,000
Capital (owner's funds):			15,000

What is likely to happen next? Well, a shopkeeper earns his living by buying and selling goods. Let us assume that our shopkeeper Mr Smith knows from experience that the $2,000 worth of stock he has on 1 January 1992 is not sufficient for the sales he expects to make in January. He therefore decides on 3 January to buy an additional $5,000 worth of goods for resale. $1,000 worth of these goods are bought from a supplier who insists on immediate payment, so Mr Smith gives him a cheque for $1,000. The supplier of the other $4,000 worth of goods, however, allows Mr Smith one month's credit; this means that Mr Smith gets the goods now, but he will only have to pay for them in one month's time. Such arrangements are very common in business. They allow a shopkeeper to sell the goods before he has to pay for them, which means he does not have to find the money straight away.

Q What effect will these purchases of stock have on Mr Smith's balance sheet?

A The impact on the balance sheet of the first transaction ($1,000 worth of goods paid for by cheque) is easy to see: stock goes up by $1,000, and the bank balance goes down by that amount.

The second transaction ($4,000 worth of goods bought on one month's credit) is a bit more complicated. Stock again increases, this time by $4,000. Bank and cash remain unchanged, since those goods have not yet been paid for. This does not mean, however, that we can just increase the stock figure by $4,000 and leave the rest of the balance sheet unchanged (in fact, the balance sheet would not balance if we did that). As a result of this transaction, Mr Smith owes his supplier $4,000; in other words, he has incurred a $4,000 liability which must be recorded on the liability side of his balance sheet.

Just as liquid or short-term assets are shown under the heading 'current assets', so short-term liabilities (like this $4,000 debt payable next month) are

shown under the heading **'current liabilities'.** Suppliers to whom we owe money are known as creditors (in fact, some people now use this word for just about any debt, not only debts to suppliers).

If we sell goods to other people on credit, those buyers are known as debtors, and the amount they owe us is shown as a current asset.

What will Mr Smith's balance sheet look like after these purchases of stock? We have to start with the earlier balance sheet (the one showing the assets and liabilities of his business on 1 January 1992). As we have seen, the purchase of $1,000 worth of goods paid for by cheque increases stock by $1,000 and reduces the bank balance by the same amount. The purchase of $4,000 worth of goods on credit increases stock by $4,000, and the $4,000 Mr Smith now owes this supplier are shown as a current liability on the liability side of the balance sheet.

Balance sheet of Mr Smith's shop on 3.1.1992 ($)

Liabilities			Assets		
Capital:	15,000		**Fixed assets:**		
Long-term debt: loan from			shopfittings	10,000	
uncle	10,000		delivery van	10,000	20,000
Current liabilities:			**Current assets:**		
creditors	4,000		stock	7,000	
			bank	1,500	
			cash	500	9,000
	29,000				29,000

When presenting this balance sheet in the vertical format, we have to keep in mind that in the vertical method of presentation current liabilities are usually deducted from current assets and the balance is shown as **'net current assets'**. This item is also known as **'working capital'**. This leads to the following vertical balance sheet:

Balance sheet of Mr Smith's shop on 3 January 1992

	£	£
Fixed assets:		
- shopfittings	10,000	
- delivery van	10,000	20,000
Net current assets:		
- stock	7,000	
- bank	1,500	
- cash	500	
- less current liabilities	4,000	5,000
Total assets less current liabilities		25,000
Debt: loan from uncle		10,000
Capital:		15,000

The following transactions take place between 3 January 1992 (the date of the balance sheet above) and the end of the month:

▶ Mr Smith sells all his stock for £10,000. His customers pay in cash.
▶ Mr Smith makes the following payments by cheque:

wages paid to an assistant	£500
rent and rates	£200
electricity, telephone, petrol	£100
interest paid to uncle (1% per month)	£100

▶ At the end of the month Mr Smith keeps £1,000 cash in the till and pays the rest into the bank.

 Q What will the balance sheet look like at the end of January? Try to fill in the blank sheet below before reading on.

Balance sheet of Mr Smith's shop on 31 January 1992

	£	£
Fixed assets:		
- Shop fitting	10,000	
- Van	10,000	20,000
Net current assets:		
- Stock	—	
- Bank	10,100	
- Cash	1,000	
- Liabs (Curr)	4,000	7,100
Total assets less current liabilities:		27,100
Debt:		10,000
Capital:		£17,100

Well, if Mr Smith sells all his stock and does not buy any new stock, there will obviously not be any stock at the end of the month. Cash has gone up by £10,000 as a result of the cash sales. The bank balance is reduced by £900 due to the payments for wages, rent and rates, electricity, telephone and petrol, and interest. Before paying that part of the cash balance which exceeds £1,000 into the bank account, the shopkeeper has £10,500 cash and £600 in the bank. After paying the cash exceeding £1,000 into the bank, he has £1,000 cash and £10,100 in the bank. None of the other balance sheet items (except capital) have changed during January. Therefore, the balance sheet at the end of January is as follows:

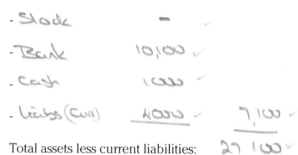

Balance sheet of Mr Smith's shop on 31 January 1992

	£	£
Fixed assets:		
- shopfittings	10,000	
- delivery van	10,000	20,000
Net current assets:		
- stock	0	
- bank	10,100	
- cash	1,000	
- less current liabilities	4,000	7,100
Total assets less current liabilities:		27,100
Debt: loan from uncle		10,000
Capital:		17,100

Q Mr Smith paid his uncle £100 in January. Why is the debt to his uncle still £10,000 at the end of the month? Why has his debt not gone down by £100 as a result of the money paid?

A The £100 paid to the uncle are interest, not a partial repayment of the loan. Paying interest on a loan does not reduce the amount owed.

C
PROFIT AND LOSS ACCOUNT OF A SMALL BUSINESS

Comparing the balance sheet as on 31 January 1992 with that of 3 January you see that the capital at the end of January is £2,100 higher than it was at the beginning of the month. Why is this so?

Well, the business has made a **profit** in January. The goods which Mr Smith sold for £10,000 had cost him only £7,000, as shown in the balance sheet on 3 January. In the balance sheet, stock is always valued at the cost price: the price the business has paid for those goods. (The only exception to this is when the stock can only be sold at less than the cost price; in this case it will be shown at the lower sales price. However, let us ignore this rare case to avoid confusion.)

Deducting the cost of goods sold (£7,000) from the sales (£10,000) gives us the gross profit, which in this case is £3,000. However, the cost of goods sold was not the only cost of running the business. The shopkeeper also had to pay wages to his assistant, rent and rates for his shop, electricity and telephone bills, he had to buy petrol for his delivery van, and he had to pay interest to his uncle on the £10,000 loan. The wages, rent and rates, and electricity, telephone and petrol costs are known as 'other operating expenses': other expenses resulting from actually running the business. Deducting the other operating expenses from the gross profit gives us the operating profit, and if we deduct the interest paid from the operating profit we get the actual profit made during the month.

Now we have all the information we need to compile the profit and loss account for January.

Profit and loss account for Mr Smith's shop for January 1992

	£	£
Sales		10,000
less: cost of goods sold		7,000
Gross profit		3,000
Other operating expenses:		
wages	500	
rent and rates	200	
electricity, telephone and petrol	100	800
Operating profit		2,200
Interest paid		100
Profit for January		2,100

This profit of £2,100 is the reason why the capital, as shown in the balance sheet, has gone up from £15,000 to £17,100 during the month. Profits increase the owner's stake in the business provided they are left in the business. If Mr Smith had taken £500 out of his shop's bank account to pay for his living expenses, the shop's bank balance would have been £500 lower at the end of the month and so would the capital (check this against the balance sheet as at 31 January 1992, and make sure you fully understand this before you proceed). We can say therefore that the capital at the end of the month is equal to the capital at the beginning of the month plus any profits (or less any losses) made during the month, less any money taken out of the business by the owner(s).

D
SOURCE AND APPLICATION OF FUNDS STATEMENT OF A SMALL BUSINESS

When Mr Smith sees that his profit for January is $2,100 he is pleasantly surprised, but he wonders why his **liquid assets (cash and bank)** have gone up by much more than that amount. For the sake of simplicity let us first look at the period 3 to 31 January 1992. On 3 January the business had $500 cash and $1,500 in the bank, so its liquid assets totalled $2,000. On 31 January, however, cash and bank add up to $11,100. How can a profit of $2,100 increase the shop's liquid assets by $9,100 (from $2,000 to $11,100)?

This is the sort of question answered by the source and application of funds statement. Why, in our example, have liquid assets gone up by $9,100 if the profit has only been $2,100? Where has the other $7,000 come from? We can find the answer to this question by comparing the balance sheets of 3 and 31 January. On 3 January the business had $7,000 worth of stock; by the end of the month that stock had been sold, and no new stock was bought between 3 and 31 January. If you sell stock, you generate cash. The fact that the business has reduced its stock by $7,000 has increased its holding of liquid assets by that amount. This explains why liquid assets went up by $9,100 even though the profit was only $2,100.

Source and application of funds statement for Mr Smith's shop 3.1.92 - 31.1.92

	$	$
Sources of funds:		
Profit	2,100	
Reduction of stock (see Note 1)	7,000	9,100
Applications of funds:		0
Increase in liquid assets		9,100

Note 1: Stock is valued at the purchase (or cost) price. Any profit made on selling it is already included in the profit figure, so it must not be taken into account a second time here.

Technically speaking, any increase in an asset (for example, buying stock or fixed assets) is an application of funds which reduces the business's liquid assets. Any decrease of assets (for example selling stock or fixed assets) must consequently be a source of funds which increases the amount of liquid assets. Any increase in a liability (for example borrowing money from a bank or from suppliers of goods; or paying in additional capital, as capital is shown on the liability side of the balance sheet) is a source of funds which increases liquid assets. Finally, any decrease in a liability (repaying a debt or repaying money to the owners of the business) is an application of funds which reduces liquid assets. In this context the horizontal presentation of the balance sheet is perhaps a bit clearer than the now more common vertical one, especially since the horizontal method shows the owners' funds (capital) on the liability side.

Armed with this knowledge, we can now work out the source and application of funds statement for Mr Smith's shop for the whole of January and not just for the period from the 3rd to the 31st which is what we have done so far. Profits for January, as we know already, are $2,100. Liquid assets were $3,000 on 1 January as against $11,100 on 31st. So, why have liquid assets gone up by £8,100 during the month?

Well, to begin with there is the £2,100 profit. Then, stock has gone down from £2,000 at the beginning of the month to nil at the end, and this constitutes another source of funds amounting to £2,000. Finally, creditors have gone up from nil at the beginning of the month to £4,000 at the end. This is like borrowing from suppliers, and any such increase in a liability (as explained above) constitutes a source of funds. Now we have all the information we need to compile the source and application of funds statement for January as a whole.

Source and application of funds statement for Mr Smith's shop in January 1992

	£	£
Sources of funds:		
Profit	2,100	
Reduction of stock	2,000	
Increase in creditors	4,000	8,100
Applications of funds:		0
Increase in liquid assets		8,100

Applications of funds are shown as zero. In case you wonder whether wages and similar costs are not an application of funds: they are, but they have already been included in the profit figure. Apart from profit and, as we will see in the next section, depreciation, the source and application of funds statement concentrates on items listed in the balance sheet. All the relevant items of the profit and loss account (with the exception of depreciation) are already taken care of by the profit figure.

E

ACCOUNTS OF A SMALL BUSINESS: SOME AMPLIFICATIONS

We now know how balance sheets, profit and loss accounts, and source and application of funds statements are compiled and what information

they contain. However, in the previous section we have left a few points out for the sake of simplicity; we now have to look at these topics to make things more realistic. In particular, we have to consider the following three points:

- ▶ stock at the end of the period;
- ▶ drawing by the owners(s);
- ▶ depreciation.

In the previous section we assumed that the shopkeeper has no stock at all at the end of the month. This assumption made the bookkeeping a bit easier, but it is hardly a realistic assumption unless the owner had intended to close his business down. So, we have to allow for stock at the end of the period.

The drawings (money drawn out of the business by the owner) have already been mentioned briefly. A shopkeeper runs a shop to earn a living, so he will have to withdraw money from his business from time to time in order to pay for his living expenses.

Turning now to depreciation, fixed assets (with the exception of land) do not last forever. Consequently, they must be replaced at the end of their useful lives if the business is to continue. If the owner spends all the profit his business generates without allowing for depreciation, he will have no money to replace fixed assets when some such asset reaches the end of its useful life. It makes sense, therefore, to allow for depreciation by writing down the value of fixed assets at regular intervals. If the delivery van in our example has an expected life of 50 months, it would make sense to depreciate it at the rate of two per cent per month: to reduce its value in the balance sheet that amount each month and charge this amount to the profit and loss account. The example below will show how this works.

Let us now rewrite the accounts of Mr Smith's shop in January, incorporating these three points. The balance sheet on 1 January is again the starting point.

Balance sheet of Mr Smith's shop on 1 January 1992

	£	£	£
Assets:			
Fixed assets:			
- shopfittings	10,000		
- delivery van	10,000	20,000	
Current assets:			
- stock	2,000		
- bank	2,500		
- cash	500	5,000	25,000
Debt: loan from uncle			10,000
Capital:			15,000

We can adopt the following transactions from the previous example:

► Mr Smith thinks his stock is too low for the sales he expects to make in January. He therefore buys an additional £5,000 worth of stock. £1,000 is to be paid immediately by cheque; the other £4,000 is payable in one month's time.

► During January, Mr Smith makes the following payments by cheque:
wages paid to an assistant	£500
rent and rates	£200
interest paid to his uncle	£100
electricity, telephone, petrol	£100

► At the end of the month, Mr. Smith leaves £1,000 cash in the till and pays the rest into the shop's bank account.

Differently from the previous example, however, let us assume that:

► Sales during the month total £6,000. All customers pay cash. The closing stock (stock at the end of the month) is £3,000.

(The closing stock can only be found by checking what is actually in stock at the end of the month and valuing it at the cost price. It cannot be found from opening stock and sales, because the former is valued at cost and the latter at the business's selling price.)

► During the month, Mr Smith takes £500 cash from the shop's till to pay for his living expenses ('drawings').

► Since the shopfittings have an expected life of 100 months and the delivery van has one of 50 months, they are written down by 1% and 2%, respectively, per month. This results in the following depreciation charges:

depreciation of shopfittings:	£100
depreciation of delivery van:	£200

These are all the transactions that take place in January 1992. What is the balance sheet at the end of January, the profit and loss account for January, and the source and application of funds statement for January?

? Try to work out the balance sheet for yourself, before looking at the answer below.

Balance sheet of Mr Smith's shop on 31 January 1992

	£	£
Fixed assets:		
shopfittings (see note 1)	9,900	
delivery van (see note 2)	9,800	19,700
Net current assets:		
stock (note 3)	3,000	
bank (note 4)	5,600	
cash (note 4)	1,000	
less creditors (note 5)	4,000	5,600
Total assets less current liabilities		25,300
Debt: loan from uncle		10,000
Capital:		15,300

Note 1:	value of shopfittings on 1.1.1992	£10,000
	less 1% depreciation	£100
	value of shopfittings on 31.1.92	£9,900

Note 2: value of delivery van on 1.1.92 £10,000
   less 2% depreciation £200
   value of delivery van on 31.1.92 9,800

Note 3: information provided in the question.

Note 4:

cash on 1.1.92	£ 500	bank balance	£2,500
plus sales	£6,000	on 1.1.92	
less drawings	£ 500	less purchase	£1,000
		of stock	
		less wages	£ 900
		rent etc.	
transfer to bank	£5,000	plus transfer	£5,000
		from cash	
closing balance	£5,600	closing balance	£5,600

Note 5: £4,000 of purchases still unpaid
   (see question).

Profit and loss account of Mr Smith's shop for January 1992

	£	£
sales		6,000
less: cost of goods sold (see note 1)		4,000
gross profit		2,000
other operating expenses: wages	500	
rent and rates	200	
electricity, telephone, petrol	100	
depreciation (note 2)	300	1,100
operating profit		900
interest paid		100
profit for January		800

Note 1: The opening stock (stock on 1 January 92) was £2,000. During January, another £5,000 worth of stock was bought. That means that £7,000 worth of goods (valued at cost price) were available for sale in January. However, £3,000 worth of goods were still unsold at the end of January (closing stock). So the business sold £4,000 worth of goods, valued at the cost price. This is the cost of goods sold. The cost of goods sold can be calculated by using the following formula:

Opening stock + purchases - closing stock = cost of goods sold

Note 2: £100 for shopfittings and £200 for the delivery van. See notes 1 and 2 to the balance sheet.

Q Now that we have worked out the balance sheet at the end of January as well as the profit and loss account for January, try to explain why capital as shown in the balance sheet has gone up by £300 during January.

A

capital on 1.1.92	15,000
plus profits	800
less drawings	500
capital on 31.1.92	15,300

Source and application of funds statement for Mr Smith's shop in January 1992

Sources of funds	£	£
profit	800	
depreciation (see note 1)	300	
increase in current liabilities	4,000	5,100

Applications of funds		
drawings	500	
increase in stock (note 2)	1,000	1,500
increase in liquid assets (note 3)		3,600

Note 1: Depreciation has been deducted in the profit and loss account even though it does not reduce liquid assets. The business does not actually spend any money on depreciation. For this reason, it is the profit **before** depreciation which is relevant for the source and application of funds statement. Therefore, depreciation must be added back on to the profit shown in the profit and loss account.

Note 2:	stock on 31.1.92	3,000
	stock on 1.1.92	2,000
	increase in stock	1,000

Note 3:	liquid assets (cash and bank)	
	on 31.1.92	6,600
	liquid assets (cash and bank)	
	on 1.1.92	3,000
	increase in liquid assets	3,600

F
PUBLISHED ACCOUNTS

With the knowledge we have gained in sections A to E we are able to understand the published accounts of British (and other) companies. In this section we will discuss the accounts of three well-known British companies from various sectors of the economy. Once you have studied this section you should not have any problems in understanding the reports of other companies either.

Basically, a balance sheet provides the same information about the organisation to which it relates no matter what kind of organisation we are talking about: it tells us about the value of the assets and liabilities of the organisation in question. However, different organisations need different assets to do their business. A retailer needs stocks of goods for resale, shopfittings, and a shop; incidentally, the shop itself will be listed in the shopkeeper's balance sheet if the shopkeeper owns it, but not if he rents it. In the latter case, the shop will show up in the balance sheet of the individual or the organisation that owns it.

A manufacturing company needs a factory hall, machines, tools, a stock of raw materials, and so on. The main assets of a transport company will be the buses, lorries, ships or aeroplanes which it uses to transport its passengers or freight. On the liability side of the balance sheet we will in all these cases find some mixture of borrowings and owners' funds (capital). A bank's main liabilities are deposits: money deposited by savers and other customers. Those deposits are a liability for the bank because it owes this money to the depositors (you could also say: it has borrowed this money from its depositors). And what does the bank do with this money? It lends it out, so its main assets are loans.

Since the example we used in the previous section related to a shopkeeper, let us start our discussion of published accounts with a retailing company. As you will see in the course of this section, the presentation of balance sheets, profit and loss accounts, and source and application of funds statements varies a bit from one company to the next, but those minor differences should not cause much of a problem if you have understood the basic principles outlined in sections A to E.

F1 PUBLISHED ACCOUNTS OF A RETAILING COMPANY

Group balance sheet at 31.3.1989 of Marks & Spencer

	£m	£m	£m
Fixed assets:			
land and buildings		1,947.7	
fixtures, fittings and			
equipment		320.4	
miscellaneous		87.4	2,355.5
Net current assets:			
stocks	364.4		
debtors	192.6		
liquid assets	102.1	659.1	
less: current liabilities		743.1	(84.0)
total assets less current			
liabilities			2,271.5
creditors: amounts falling due			
after more than one year			343.7
provisions for liabilities and			
charges			5.1
net assets			1,922.7
The net assets are made up as follows:			
shareholders' funds		1,918.6	
minority interest		4.1	
		1,922.7	

Source: Marks and Spencer's annual report 1989

Is this balance sheet not surprisingly similar to that of our hypothetical shopkeeper in the previous section, apart from the amounts involved? This similarity shows that once you have understood one balance sheet you can understand almost any. Insurance companies are probably the main 'odd one out': their accounts will be discussed in section G. Let us now look at the Marks and Spencer balance sheet in some detail.

It starts by saying 'Group balance sheet at....(date)'. What does this mean? As we have seen in section 12C, a company which has sub-

Under Companies Act 1985
a Company which has Subsidiary
Must Publish group accounts
Those Show Activities of the
whole Group

sidiaries must publish group accounts or consolidated accounts (those two terms mean the same thing) to comply with section 239 of the **Companies Act 1985**. These include the assets and liabilities of the whole group of companies: those of the parent company as well as those of all the subsidiaries. A subsidiary is a company in which the parent company owns more than 50% of the capital.

The first two items under the 'fixed asset' heading should be self-explanatory. The miscellaneous fixed assets, according to the company's annual report, consist of 'assets in the course of construction' and the net assets of the company's financial activities (store credit card business and so on).

Turning now to the current assets, stocks are the goods for resale which you can find on the shelves and in the store rooms. Debtors are people or organisations which owe the company money and which have to pay in the fairly near future, for example customers who have bought goods on credit. Also included here are prepayments. Sometimes the company has to pay in advance for goods it orders from manufacturers or others, and until those goods are delivered such prepayments are shown in the balance sheet under the 'debtors' heading. If the supplier cannot deliver the goods, he will have to return the money. Liquid assets consist of cash, money in the bank, and short-term securities.

The current liabilities are described in the annual report as 'creditors: amounts falling due within one year'. These are amounts the company owes individuals or other companies, which must be paid within one year. Examples include short-term debts to suppliers (for goods received but not yet paid for), prepayments received from others for goods or services to be delivered in the near future, money payable to the tax authorities or the Department of Social Security (think of National Insurance contributions for its employees), and dividend payments due to shareholders in the near future.

The 'creditors: amounts falling due after more than one year' are long-term borrowings, and the 'provision for liabilities and charges' are amounts which the company **may** have to pay in the future.

The term 'net assets' denotes the value of the company's assets less all the amounts which will or may have to be paid to others (debts, for example). Most of these net assets are in fact the shareholders' funds. The shareholders are the owners of the company, so they own the net assets. A small item ($4 million is a fairly small amount when compared to the net assets of nearly $2,000 million) is shown as 'minority interests'. This is an item one finds very frequently in group accounts. Current accounting practice is to include all the assets of subsidiaries in the asset figures shown in the balance sheet. If you do not own 100% of the subsidiary (you may, for example, own 80% and some other people own the remaining 20%), then whatever part of these assets you do not own is shown as 'minority interests' in the balance sheet. In fact, Marks and Spencer could also have deducted the minority interests from the net assets and shown the shareholders' funds as the bottom line.

As we have seen earlier, balance sheets can be presented in the vertical or the horizontal format. Marks and Spencer have chosen the vertical method of presentation.

? It would be a good exercise for you to rewrite the balance sheet in the horizontal format. You will find the solution at the bottom of the next page.

What conclusions can we draw from this balance sheet? (No matter whether we take the vertical or the horizontal one; they both contain the same information.) We will discuss the interpretation of balance sheets in more detail in the context of ratio analysis in Chapter 14, but there are a few conclusions we can mention already at this stage. The shareholders' funds amount to about two thirds of the total assets (this can be seen more easily in the horizontal balance sheet). This is a very prudent way of financing a business; generally speaking, the higher the level of debt, the greater the risk. Secondly, the amount of the fixed assets is roughly the same as the amount of the shareholders' funds plus the long-term debt, and the amount of current assets is roughly the same as the current liabilities. That means that the long-term assets (fixed assets) have been financed by long-term capital, and the more short-term (current) assets have been financed by current (short-term) liabilities. Again, this is a very cautious way of financing a business. It is not a good idea to finance long-term assets (say, buildings) by short-term bank overdrafts. Why not? Well, the bank may demand repayment of an overdraft at short notice, and if you have invested this money in a long-term asset like a building you will not be able to repay the bank. This cannot happen if you match the time-scale of your liabilities with that of your assets. There is nothing wrong with financing current assets out of short-term liabilities, but fixed assets should be financed by more long-term liabilities like long-term debt or shareholders' funds.

Now that we have discussed the balance sheet, let us turn to the profit and loss account.

Marks and Spencer: Consolidated profit and loss account for the year ended 31.1.1989

	£m
turnover	5,121.5
cost of sales	3,458.5
gross profit	1,663.0
other expenses (note 1)	1,099.3
operating profit	563.7
interest payable	21.6
profit before profit-sharing and taxation	542.1
profit-sharing	13.1
profit before tax	529.0
taxation	185.1
profit after tax	343.9
minority interests	1.0
profit attributable to shareholders (note 2)	342.9

Note 1:
The 'other expenses' are made up as follows:

staff costs	594.7
occupancy costs (rentals etc.)	193.4
depreciation	103.4
miscellaneous	207.8
	1,099.3

Note 2:
The profit was used as follows:

dividends paid to shareholders	149.7
retained in the business	193.2
	342.9

Source: Marks and Spencer's annual report 1989

Most of the items in the profit and loss account should be self-explanatory if you have understood section C. Turnover is the amount of sales (sales revenues). Cost of sales is the amount it cost the business to buy the goods it has sold to its customers. The gross profit is the difference between the turnover and the cost of sales. Deducting the other expenses which are explained in note 1 we arrive at the operating profit, and by deducting the interest paid on the company's borrowings we get the profit before profit-sharing and taxation. Many companies have profit-sharing schemes as an incentive for their employees, and if we deduct the amount of profit used in this way we get the profit before tax. Deducting tax, obviously, produces the profit after tax.

Answer to the question on the previous page:

Group balance sheet of Marks & Spencer at 31.3.1989 (£ millions)

Liabilities			Assets		
shareholders' funds	1,918.6		Fixed assets:		
minority interests	4.1		land and buildings	1,947.7	
provisions	5.1		fixtures, fittings,		
long-term debt	343.7		and equipment	320.4	
current liabilities	743.1		miscellaneous	87.4	2,355.5
			Current assets:		
			stocks	364.4	
			debtors	192.6	
			liquid assets	102.1	659.1
	3,014.6				3,014.6

The minority interests have been explained in the context of the balance sheet. The minority interests shown in the balance sheet indicate the net assets in subsidiaries owned by other shareholders, and the minority interests in the profit and loss account indicate what amount of profit belongs to those other shareholders. Deducting the amount of profit due to such minority interests, we arrive at the profit attributable to Marks and Spencer shareholders. Note 2 explains how much of this amount was paid out to shareholders as dividends and how much was retained in the business. The dividends paid by a public limited company can be compared with the drawings in a small business (see section E).

Now that we have discussed the profit and loss account, let us turn to the source and application of funds statement.

Marks and Spencer: Consolidated source and application of funds statement for the year ended 31.3.1989

Sources of funds

	£m	£m	£m
Funds generated from operations:			
profit before tax	529.0		
depreciation	103.4		
sales of fixed assets	8.0	640.4	
Other sources:			
borrowing	239.4		
shares issued	15.7		
miscellaneous	18.5	273.6	914.0

Applications of funds

	£m	£m
dividends	139.8	
taxation	186.1	
purchase of fixed assets	208.2	
acquisition of US subsidiary	472.2	
increase in working capital	52.9	
miscellaneous	85.0	1,144.2
change in liquid assets		-230.2

Source: Marks & Spencer's annual report 1989

Again, the source and application of funds statement shown here follows basically the same lines as that in section D. However, in published accounts it is customary to split the sources of funds into two categories; namely funds generated from operations, and other sources. The former include the funds provided by the normal day-to-day operations of the business, the latter any other sources. The main items among the funds generated from operations are nearly always profits and depreciation (for an explanation as to why depreciation is a source of funds, see section E). The main items under the 'other sources' are usually borrowings and money raised by issuing shares or other securities. Sales of fixed assets are a borderline case. Marks and Spencer listed them under funds generated from operations; other companies may have included them among the 'other sources'.

The application should be self-explanatory, with the possible exception of the 'increase in working capital'. 'Working capital' is just another expression for net current assets. These can go up if current assets (like stock or debtors) go up, or if current liabilities go down. If you buy more stock, lend more to customers so that they can buy from you, or repay creditors, then you **apply** funds; this is why the increase in working capital is listed among the applications of funds. A reduction in working capital would be a source of funds.

Turning now to the amounts, we can see that the sources of funds add up to £914m and the applications total £1,144.2m. Consequently, there is a shortfall of £230.2m, and this was financed by allowing the company's liquid assets to fall by that amount. Another way of interpreting the figures would be to say that the company generated £640.4m from operations and applied a total of £1,144.2m. The difference of £503.8m was financed partly (£230.2m) by allowing the company's liquid assets to decrease, and partly (£273.6m) from other sources like borrowing, issuing shares, and so on.

If you are a careful reader, you may have noticed that the amount of dividends shown in the source and application of funds statement is not the same as that shown in the profit and loss account. The company does not say in its annual report how this difference has come about. A possible reason is the timing of dividend payments. A final dividend may be payable some time after the end of the financial year, so it would not affect the source and application of funds statement for the year in question. The same is true of taxation.

Having discussed the published accounts of a retailing company in some detail, we can now explain those of some other companies more briefly.

F2 PUBLISHED ACCOUNTS OF A MANUFACTURING COMPANY

British Steel: Group balance sheet at 1.4.1989

Fixed assets	£m	£m	£m
land and buildings	227		
plant and machinery	1,465		
assets in course of construction	230		
loose plant, tools, and spares	219		
investments	489		2,630

Net current assets

stocks	1,074		
debtors	1,148		
liquid assets	671	2,893	
less current liabilities		(1,399)	1,494

Total assets less current liabilities		4,124
creditors: amounts falling due after more than one year		(210)
Net assets		3,914

The net assets are made up as follows:

shareholders' funds	3,910
minority interests	4
	3,914

Brackets indicate that the amounts concerned must be deducted.

British Steel: Consolidated profit and loss account for the financial year ended 1.4.1989

	£m
turnover	4,906
operating costs (note 1)	(4,250)
trading profit	656
share of profits of related companies	35
net interest and other income	42
	733
exception items (note 2)	(140)
profit before tax	593
tax	(31)
profit after tax	562
minority interests	(1)
profit attributable to shareholders (note 3)	561

Note 1:	Operating costs:	
	employment costs	920
	raw materials	1,987
	maintenance	398
	depreciation	198
	miscellaneous	747
		4,250

Note 2: The main item is 'redundancy and other rationalisation costs' of £131m.

Note 3: Dividends of £100m to be paid to the shareholders;

the other £461m to be retained in the business.

British Steel: Consolidated statement of source and application of funds for the financial year ended 1.4.1989

Sources of funds

	£m	£m	£m
Funds generated from operations:			
profit before tax	593		
depreciation	198		
miscellaneous	105	896	
Funds generated from other sources:			
sale of fixed assets	70		
miscellaneous	4	74	970
Applications of funds			
tax paid	2		
purchase of fixed assets	365		
increase in working capital	9		
reduction in borrowings	68		
miscellaneous	48	(492)	
Increase in liquid assets			478

Source: British Steel, annual report 1988-89

Any surprises? The main surprise is probably how easy it is to read the accounts of British Steel now that you have understood those of Marks and Spencer, even though the companies are entirely different. The main fixed assets of British Steel are plant and machinery; this is so in most manufacturing companies. The headings under net current assets are the same as in the Marks and Spencer example. However, whereas current liabilities were slightly greater than current assets in the case of Marks and Spencer, the current liabilities are only about half the current assets in the case of British Steel.

Longer-term borrowings (amounts falling due after more than one year) make up only 5.4% of net assets; for Marks and Spencer this ratio is 17.9%, so British Steel relies even less on such borrowings than does Marks and Spencer (more about this in the context of ratio analysis in Chapter 14).

In the profit and loss account, raw materials play an important part; again, this is typical of manufacturing companies. The source and application

of funds statement shows that the sources of funds exceeded the applications of funds, so that the company's liquid assets increased during the year. With Marks and Spencer, applications of funds exceeded the sources, leading to a reduction in liquid assets. The reason why the £100 million dividend mentioned in the profit and loss account does not show up in the source and application of funds statement is that it is payable after the end of the financial year, and the difference between the tax figures is due to the same reason.

Now that we have studied the accounts of a manufacturing company, let us conclude this section by seeing what the accounts of a transport company look like.

F3 PUBLISHED ACCOUNTS OF A TRANSPORT COMPANY

British Airways: Group balance sheet at 31.3.1989

Fixed assets	£m	£m	£m
fleet	2,012		
property	271		
equipment	184		
investments	111		2,578
Net current assets			
stocks	32		
debtors	796		
liquid assets	88	916	
less current liabilities		(1,748)	(832)
Total assets less current liabilities		1,746	
creditors falling due after more than one year			(896)
provision for liabilities and charges			(100)
net assets			750

The net assets are made up as follows:

shareholders' funds	749
minority interests	1
	750

British Airways: Group profit and loss account for the year ended 31.3.1989

	£m
turnover	4,257
cost of sales	(3,816)
gross profit	441
administration	(105)
operating surplus	336
other income and charges	18
profit before interest and taxation	354
interest payable and similar charges	(86)
profit before tax	268
tax	(93)
profit after tax	175

Of the profit after tax, £56m are to be paid as dividends to shareholders and £119m are to be retained in the business.

British Airways: Group source and application of funds statement for the year ended 31.3.1989

	£m	£m	£m
Sources:			
From operations:			
profit before tax	268		
depreciation	307		
disposal of assets	22		
miscellaneous	(7)	590	
Other sources:			
borrowing etc.		260	850
Funds applied:			
Tax paid	78		
dividends paid	52		
acquisition of fixed assets	699		
increase in working capital	100	(929)	
Change in liquid assets:			(79)

Source: British Airways, annual report 1988-89

Again, the layout of the account is very similar to that of the companies discussed earlier. Not surprisingly, the fleet of aeroplanes is British Airways' main asset. Current liabilities exceed current assets quite substantially. The current liabilities consist partly of normal trade creditors like purchases of fuel or other supplies not yet paid for, and partly of what the airline calls 'sales in advance of carriage'. Many passengers buy and pay for their tickets a few days or even weeks before they fly, and between the day of receiving the money and the day when the passenger travels the amounts involved are creditors as far as the airline is concerned.

Creditors falling due after more than one year amount to 119% of net assets, indicating that British Airways relies more on this type of finance than do British Steel or Marks and Spencer. The main items making up the provisions for liabilities and charges are pensions obligations, litigation provisions, and 'costs still to be incurred' following the acquisition of British Caledonian (contract termination payments and so on).

In the profit and loss account, the cost of sales includes expenditure on staff salaries, fuel, landing fees and other costs incurred in providing the airline's services. The other items in the accounts should be self-explanatory.

G

ACCOUNTS OF INSURANCE ORGANISATIONS

As the accounts produced by various insurance organisations have their differences, it is helpful to consider broker and company accounts separately.

G1 INSURANCE BROKERS

The accounts of insurance brokers do not differ substantially from the accounts of companies in other sectors of the economy. Their format is, in fact, very similar to that of the accounts of other service industries, notably travel agents. The main revenue for insurance brokers is the commissions they receive from the insurance companies with which they place business, and the main cost items are the various costs of keeping the office going and, if applicable, staff salaries. As for the balance sheet, the main fixed assets are office equipment and property, and the main current assets are liquid assets such as money in the bank, and money (commissions) due from insurance companies. The latter are referred to in the balance sheet as 'insurance broking debtors'. Among the liabilities, the biggest single item is usually premiums owed to insurance companies ('insurance broking creditors'); in addition one may find loans that have been raised to finance the business and provisions for liabilities and charges that may have to be met. The remainder are the owner's (or owners') funds.

Example: Sedgwick, Profit and loss account 1988

	£m	£m
Revenue:		
broking commissions and fees	544	
investment income	54	598
Expenses:		
salaries and associated expenses	311	
other expenses	205	516
operating profit		82
share of profits in other companies		8
interest payable		(12)
profit before tax		78
taxation		(26)
other items		1
profit attributable to shareholders		53

Sedgwick : Balance sheet 31.12.1988

	£m	£m		£m	£m
Shareholders' funds		246	Fixed assets:		
borrowings		103	properties	222	
provisions for liabilities			office equipment	66	
and charges		83	vehicles	11	
			subsidiary companies etc.	62	361
Current liabilities			Current assets:		
insurance broking			insurance broking debtors	899	
creditors	1,155		cash and deposits	490	
other items	293	1,448	other items	130	1,519
		1,880			1,880

Source: Sedgwick Group, Annual Report 1988

G2 INSURANCE COMPANIES

While the accounts of brokers are very similar to the accounts of non-insurance businesses, the accounts of insurance companies are a rather different species. The following examples demonstrate this.

	CU 1988		GRE 1988	
Revenue account	£m	£m	£m	£m
premiums written less reinsurance		2,187		1,578
premiums earned		2,138		1,503
less: claims	1,595		1,105	
commissions	398		233	
expenses	274	2,267	181	1,519
underwriting result		(129)		(16)

Profit and loss account				
underwriting result		(129)		(16)
investment income		247		217
shareholders' part of life assurance profits		84		30
profit before tax		202		231
taxation		(79)		(75)
other items		8		(4)
profits attributable to shareholders		131		152

The profit attributable to shareholders was used as follows:

dividends		80		77
retained		51		75
		131		152

Balance sheets on 31.12.1988

	CU 1988		GRE 1988	
Assets	£m	£m	£m	£m
investments	3,720		2,847	
assets relating to the life business	7,399		5,326	
other assets	1,313	12,432	1,295	9,468

Liabilities				
outstanding claims and provisions	2,342		2,168	
unearned premiums	657		648	
liabilities relating to life business	6,996		5,326	
other liabilities	1,168	11,163	65	8,207

Shareholders' funds		1,269		1,261

Source: Companies' annual reports 1988

While you probably did not find it difficult to read the insurance broker's accounts in section G1, you will probably find it much more difficult to make sense out of the insurance company accounts shown here. So, let us work our way through them step by step.

G2A Legal requirements

To comply with the Insurance Companies' Acts, insurance companies must provide the Department of Trade and Industry with an audited annual revenue account, profit and loss account, and balance sheet (more about reporting requirements in Part IV, The Legal Environment). If a company writes both life and general business, the assets and liabilities relating to the life business must be shown separately from the rest.

G2B The revenue account

As the examples in section G2 show, the revenue account, which relates to the general business only, starts with 'premiums written less reinsurance'. The total premiums collected by the CU in 1988 amounted to £2,655m. Out of this, reinsurance premiums amounting to £468m were paid, so that £2,187m actually accrued to the CU; the latter is the figure shown in the revenue account. Next, the revenue account says (for the CU): 'Premiums earned: £2,138m'. These premiums earned are then the basis for the calculations that follow. What is the difference between **premiums written** and **premiums earned?** To explain this, let us use a highly simplified example. Suppose a company sells an annual policy for £200 on 1 July 1990, another for £100 on 1 January 1991, and yet another for £300 on 1 July 1991. In this case, the premiums written in 1991 are £400. However, only half the premium received on 1 July 1991 relates to 1991: the other half is still **unearned** at the end of that year and relates to 1992. By the same token, only half the premium received on 1 July 1990 relates to 1990: the other half is earned in 1991. So, the premiums earned in 1991 are:

The premiums written in 1991	£400
less: unearned premiums at 31.12.1991	£150
plus: unearned premiums at 31.12.1990	£100
equals: premiums earned in 1991	£350

This simple example shows why premiums earned and premiums written are not the same thing. The rest of the revenue account is based on the premiums earned and not on the premiums written.

As the CU and GRE examples show, claims, commission and expenses are deducted from the premiums earned to arrive at the underwriting result. Just like premiums, claims are adjusted for any reinsurance recoveries. In 1988, the CU had to pay £1,908m of claims, but could recover £313m from reinsurers. That part of the claims which is paid by others (reinsurers) obviously does not affect the CU's profit, and that is why only the claims net of reinsurance recoveries (£1,908m - £313m = £1,595m in the case of the CU) are shown in the revenue account.

Commissions are moneys paid to brokers and other intermediaries who have placed business with the company, and 'expenses' is really a catch-all for all other outgoings (some companies also include commissions in their definition of expenses).

If the total of claims, commissions and expenses is less than the premiums earned, the company makes an underwriting profit; if these three items add up to more than the premiums earned, the company makes an underwriting loss. Nearly all British insurance companies make underwriting losses, and the two companies used as examples here are no exception.

The fact that they make underwriting losses, however, does not mean that those companies actually lose money. The reason for this is that underwriting is only one out of several sources of income for insurance companies. The chairman of the Eagle Star insurance company said in his 1984 annual report:

The earnings of a composite insurance company are generally recognised as arising under three headings: the general insurance underwriting result, that is earned premiums less incurred claims and expenses; investment income on the general or shareholders' funds ... ; and the shareholders' proportion of the distributable surplus of the life fund.

G2⑦ The profit and loss account

As we have seen, the revenue account deducts claims, commissions and expenses from the earned premiums and so arrives at the underwriting result. At this point the profit and loss account takes over. It starts with the underwriting result, adds investment income and the shareholders' part of the life profits, and so arrives at the profit before tax. As we have seen earlier, a claim can only arise after a premium has been paid, and in the meantime the money can be invested and earn interest; this is how investment income comes about. In mutual life offices the entire profit of the life fund accrues to the with-profit policyholders; in proprietary offices, a small part of the life profits (usually about ten per cent) accrues to shareholders and the rest goes to with-profit policyholders. If a company writes only general business, there are obviously no life assurance profits.

The company then has to pay tax on its profits, and there may be a few other items which may increase or reduce profits slightly. These may include realised capital gains or losses, gains or losses resulting from fluctuations in exchange rates (to the extent that these are not already reflected in the underwriting result or the investment income: see section 8l3). Taking all these factors into account, we arrive at the profit attributable to shareholders, which as usual can either be paid out to shareholders in the form of dividends, or retained in the business.

G2⑧ The balance sheet

In addition to the revenue account and the profit and loss account, insurance companies have to publish a balance sheet, and the assets and liabilities relating to the life business must be shown separately from the assets and liabilities of the general business. The asset side of an insurance company's balance sheet consists mainly of investments.

Q Before we go any further, are you sure you know how these investments come about? Try to answer this question before you read on.

A Claims can only arise after premiums have been paid, and in the meantime the money can be invested.

The investments shown in the balance sheets in section G2 are investments relating to the companies' general business. The assets relating to the life business are mainly the investments held by the life funds. The other assets consist mainly of money owed to the company by brokers and policyholders, but also includes some liquid assets as well as the companies' fixed assets like office equipment.

Turning now to the liabilities, let us start with the liabilities relating to the life assurance business. This is the actuarially determined liability of the companies under the life policies in force at the date of the balance sheet. Since all the liabilities resulting from the life business are comprised in this item, the other three liabilities shown in the balance sheet relate to the general business. The outstanding claims and provisions are, in the words of the CU, 'the estimated ultimate cost of all claims incurred but not settled at the date of the balance sheet, whether reported or not, together with the related administrative expenses.' The 'incurred but not reported' claims (sometimes referred to as IBNR claims) are a particularly tricky business (think of risks like AIDS or asbestosis) and can only be estimated in the light of the company's experience. Since it is almost impossible for outsiders (and that includes auditors) to judge what level of provision for **IBNR** claims is appropriate, some companies may use this device to build up hidden reserves.

The next item on the balance sheet, unearned premiums, has already been explained in the context of the revenue account when explaining the difference between written premiums and earned premiums. In the words of the CU, 'unearned premiums are those proportions of the premium that relate to the periods of risk subsequent to the balance sheet date. They are computed principally on either the daily or monthly pro-rata basis.' So, if somebody pays an annual premium on 1 December, eleven twelfths of that amount would be regarded as unearned at the end of the calendar year.

Some companies use the term 'general insurance funds' or simply 'insurance funds' to describe the total of outstanding claims and provisions and unearned premiums. (Purists may object to the use of the word 'funds' in this way, since these items are not 'funds' in the sense of cash: if they were, they would be on the asset side of the balance sheet.)

The 'other liabilities' consist mainly of money due to brokers and other companies, but also of some borrowings as well as taxes and dividends that have to be paid in the near future.

The difference between the assets and the liabilities is, as usual, the stake of the shareholders in the business.

G2e Summary

Summarising, we can say that insurance companies publish three items of accounting information:

(i) the revenue account, which works out the underwriting result;

(ii) the profit and loss account, which works out the total profit or loss made by the company;

(iii) the balance sheet, which shows the company's assets, liabilities, and, if applicable, shareholders' funds.

Now that we know how to read published accounts, we can turn to the interpretation of such accounts and to explaining the various uses to which accounting information is put in the control and planning processes of a business. We will do this in the next chapter.

13

SELF-ASSESSMENT QUESTIONS

1. Terry owns a car worth $6,000. Is this an asset or a liability?

   Asset, provided no o/s loan on car.

2. Lesley has borrowed $30,000 by way of a mortgage. Is this an asset or a liability?

   the R30 000 is a liab any value of the property above R30k is an asset

3. Why is the personal wealth of an individual not necessarily the same as the value of all the assets he owns?

   because all assets may not have been purchased for cash. Some may have been bought with the aid of a loan

4. You buy $50 worth of goods from a shopkeeper on credit. Is this $50 an asset or a liability (a) for you; (b) for the shopkeeper?

   *(a) liab to you as you owe money
   (b) Asset to shop as they are owed the money*

5. Explain the term 'cost of goods sold'.

   Goods Sold = Value of opening Stock plus any purchases less Closing stock

6. Explain the term 'depreciation'.

   Fixed assets do not last forever so value must be reduced each year as the move toward the end of their working life

7.   Explain what information is provided in:

     (a)   a balance sheet;

     Assets + liab of a comp
     on a given date.

     (b)   a profit and loss account;

     the incommings + out goings
     which make up a firms
     profit or loss at the end of a
     period

     (c)   a source and application of funds statement.

     how any funds were
     used and where they came
     from.

8.   What is the difference between fixed assets and current assets? Give an example in each case.

     Fixed asset, Property, is
     one of a perm nature
     Current, Money, liquid nature

9.   What is the difference between 'funds generated from operations' and 'other sources' in a statement of source and application of funds?

     from operation used to fund
     operating profit
     other help find gross profit

10. What do you think is the largest asset (in money terms) of:

    (a) a manufacturing company;

    Plant machinery

    (b) a retailer;

    Stock

    4/5

    (c) a shipping company;

    Ships

    (d) a gas or water distribution company;

    Tanks/ Resources pipes

    (e) an insurance broker?

    Knowledge / Staff   X   _Debtors_

11. Why can insurance companies survive even if they make underwriting losses year after year?

    May make enough from investments to cover loss.

12. What is the difference between an insurance company's revenue account and its profit and loss account?

    Revenue account is purely to do with profit or loss from insurance activities

    $\dfrac{10 \, 4/5}{12.} = 90\%$

13

ANSWERS TO SELF-ASSESSMENT QUESTIONS

1.   An asset.

2.   A liability.

3.   Personal wealth is the value of assets less liabilities (debts).

4.   You owe the shopkeeper £50 in this case. This is a liability from your point of view, and an asset from the shopkeeper's.

5.   The cost of goods sold is the amount of money it cost the business to buy or make the goods which it sold during a given period of time. It can be calculated as follows: **cost of goods sold = opening stock + purchases - closing stock.**

6.   Depreciation is an allowance made for the loss in value of assets which have a limited life (e.g. wear and tear of machinery). It is treated as a cost item in the profit and loss account.

7.   (a) A balance sheet shows the assets and liabilities of a company (or occasionally an individual) at a given point in time.
      (b) A profit and loss account shows what profit or loss a business has made during a given period of time.
      (c) A source and application of funds statement shows the sources and amounts of cash that has flowed into a business, and what the business has done with that cash.

8.   **Fixed assets** (e.g. buildings and machinery) are assets with a relatively long life. **Current assets** (e.g. stock of goods for resale, debtors, cash) are more liquid assets.

9.   **Funds generated from operations** are funds that have been earned by the company's ordinary activities. **Other sources** indicate funds which have been injected into the company from outside (such as a bank loan).

10.   (a) Buildings; machinery.
      (b) Stock of goods for resale; maybe property (if he owns the shop).
      (c) Ships.
      (d) Gas or water mains; storage tanks.
      (e) Debtors (money due from insurance companies).

11.   Underwriting is only part of the story. Since claims can occur only after a premium has been paid, the money can be invested in the meantime and the company can earn investment income. If the investment income is sufficiently large, a company can earn reasonable profits in spite of underwriting losses.

12.   The **revenue account** works out the underwriting profit or loss. The **profit and loss account** works out the total profit or loss.

ASSIGNMENT 6

You should work this assignment after studying Chapters 12 and 13. Answer any three questions, and allow yourself one and a half hours to complete it.

1. Explain typical financial objectives of (a) charities; (b) public sector organisations; (c) private sector businesses.

2. List three parties (individuals or organisations) interested in information about the financial aspects of a company's operations. Explain for what reasons those parties want such information.

3. List and explain the contents of any four of the sections one usually finds in the annual report and accounts of British companies.

4. From the following information about Jim Miller's newsagent's shop in 1992, compile that business's profit and loss account for 1992, and balance sheet at the end of 1992 (the horizontal and vertical methods of presentation are equally acceptable):

	£
cash held on 31.12.92	1,000
bank balance on 31.12.92	4,000
purchases during 1992	36,000
sales during 1992	50,000
depreciation charge	1,000
mortgage outstanding on 31.12.92	20,000
mortgage interest paid during 1992	2,000
value of the shop on 31.12.92	35,000
value of shopfittings on 31.12.92	10,000
expenses for heating, cleaning and repairs	1,000

You may assume there is no stock of goods for resale either at the beginning or at the end of the year.

FINANCIAL ANALYSIS, CONTROL AND PLANNING

LEARNING OBJECTIVES

After studying this chapter, you should be able to:

▷ outline the reasons for analysing a company's performance;

▷ explain the reasons for using accounting ratios;

▷ name the main categories of standard accounting ratios;

▷ list some ratios in each category;

▷ explain the reasons for using sub-ratios;

▷ understand the use of ratios for the purposes of financial analysis, control and planning;

▷ understand the main ratios commonly used to analyse the performance of insurance companies.

A
INTRODUCTION TO RATIO ANALYSIS

In Chapter 12, we discussed financial objectives of various types of organisation. Formulating objectives is of course not an end in itself. In fact, it is definitely a waste of time if one formulates objectives and then forgets about them. Formulating objectives only makes sense if one checks later whether or not one has met them, and takes appropriate action if not.

However, how do we know whether we have met our objectives?

Financial aims are usually expressed in terms of sales, profits, liquidity, and the like, and here the accounting information discussed in Chapter 13 comes in handy. We will often be able to see whether we are on track by analysing the balance sheet, profit and loss account, and source and application of funds statement. In fact, analysing these statements will not only allow us to see whether we have met our objectives: it will also allow us to make comparisons. For example, we can compare the performance of a company this year with the performance of the same company in previous years, to see whether things have got better, got worse, or stayed the same. Alternatively, we can compare the results of different sections of a given company during a certain period; a chemical company may find, for example, that its plastics division has performed satisfactorily whereas its agricultural chemicals business has not. And then we can compare different companies. It often happens that one company does badly whereas other companies in the same sector of the economy do well. Comparing different companies is useful both for the directors or managers of those companies (to see what can be achieved in their particular sector of the economy) and for investors (to help them decide which company to invest in).

For these and other reasons, it is often necessary to:

- analyse the performance of a company in the past; and
- draw conclusions from this past performance as to what action should be taken now or in the future.

How can this be done?

Often, a figure from the balance sheet or the profit and loss account does not convey much useful information if one looks at it in isolation. To see why this is so, suppose somebody told you that company XYZ made a profit of £30,000 last year. Is this a good result or a bad one? It is impossible to tell, unless we know a bit more about the business in question. If we are talking about a small greengrocer's or newsagent's shop, then a £30,000 profit per year is an excellent result, but if we are talking about a business the size of BP or ICI then a profit of only £30,000 is pretty atrocious. Likewise, it is impossible to say without further information whether any given level of debt is sustainable or not. A small business may not be able to pay the interest on a debt of £50,000, whereas a large company may have no difficulty in servicing a debt of £50 million.

These examples show that it is often not meaningful to look at some figure from the balance sheet or the profit and loss account in isolation: to make it meaningful, the figure must be put into some relevant context by comparing it with other figures for the business under scrutiny. For example, the profit made by a business can be compared to its sales, by expressing the profits not in money units such as pounds but as a percentage of sales.

Now we are talking about **accounting ratios,** and in fact much of the analysis of company accounts takes the form of working out and interpreting such ratios.

Having said that figures often become meaningful only when compared with other figures, the logical next step is to ask: what should be compared with what? To quite a large extent this is for the analyst to decide. There simply is no such thing as a right ratio or a wrong ratio. If somebody decides that his ratio is the annual turnover of a business divided by the shirt collar size of its owner, then this ratio is not wrong. The reason why not very many people will find it a good ideal to spend time and effort on working out such a ratio is not

that it is 'wrong', but that it does not provide any useful information about the business. So, the emphasis is very much on **usefulness rather than correctness.**

What is useful depends largely on the type of business. Insurance companies often compare claims to premium income, airlines find it useful to know the fuel cost per passenger mile, retailers often work out the annual sales per square foot of selling area, and British Steel uses the number of man hours required to produce one tonne of liquid steel as an indicator of their productivity, and publish that figure in their annual report. None of these ratios would have much relevance to businesses in other sectors of the economy. There are, however, a few ratios which people have found useful in a wide range of situations and which can be applied to a large number of businesses. These are the ratios which one usually finds in accountancy textbooks. Beginners may find it useful to start with these standard ratios, but knowing these should not stifle your imagination. With a bit of knowledge about a business, it is not difficult to come up with other ratios which are equally relevant to the business in question even though they are not mentioned in any textbook.

B
FREQUENTLY USED RATIOS

The standard ratios referred to above fall into five categories:

- profitability ratios;
- productivity ratios;
- liquidity ratios;
- activity (or turnover) ratios;
- gearing ratios.

Let us now discuss these five types of ratio in more detail.

B1 PROFITABILITY RATIOS

Profitability ratios, as the name implies, are a tool to analyse the profit of a business. The basic idea is to compare the profit, however defined, with other relevant data from the balance sheet or the profit and loss account.

Shareholders will be interested to know how well (or otherwise) the management of their company has used their money. They will want to know what profit has been made in relation to the money they have invested in the business. A suitable ratio to indicate this would be:

Return on shareholders' funds =

$$\frac{\text{profit attributable to shareholders}}{\text{shareholders funds}} \times 100$$

The reason for the multiplication by 100 is to express the figure as a percentage rather than as a fraction.

Just to say that company A has made £1 million profit does not convey much useful information to the shareholders.

Q   Why is it not much use to them?

A   If the shareholders' funds invested in the business amount to £5 million, then the £1 million profit amounts to a return on shareholders' funds of 20%, and that is a very good result. If, however, shareholders' funds amount to £50 million, then the same £1 million profit amounts to a return on shareholders' funds of just 2%, and that is a very poor rate of return: in fact, the shareholders would then have been better off putting their money into a deposit account with a bank or a building society. This example shows that a ratio provides more useful information than a figure taken from the balance sheet or the profit and loss account and looked at in isolation.

If you feel that it is fairer to assess the management of a company by reference to profits before tax, since tax rates are fixed by the government and not the company, you can express the above ratio on a pre-tax basis:

Return on shareholders' funds before tax =

$$\frac{\text{profit before tax}}{\text{shareholders funds}} \times 100$$

Sometimes you may want to know how well a business has used the entire capital at its disposal, rather than just the shareholders' funds. In that case you could say that the business works with two different types of money: shareholders' funds (these being the amounts originally paid in by the shareholders plus any retained profits), and borrowed money. What reward do the providers of these two types of money get for their investment? Well, shareholders are entitled to the profits, and lenders are entitled to interest on their loans. We can say, therefore, that the total amount of money invested in the business is the shareholders' funds plus the borrowed money, and the total reward to the providers of money is the profits plus the interest paid. This ratio is always expressed on a before-tax basis. The reason for this is that the taxation of the interest depends on the tax position of the lender. The 'interest paid' figure in the company's profit and loss account is therefore before tax; it is consistent to add the profit before tax to this figure, but it would not make sense to add the interest before tax to the profit after tax.

Taking these factors into account, we arrive at the following ratio:

Return on total capital before tax

$$= \frac{\text{profit before tax plus interest paid}}{\text{shareholders funds plus borrowed money}} \times 100$$

$$= \frac{\text{profit before tax plus interest paid}}{\text{total assests less current liabilities}} \times 100$$

In some countries of continental Europe it is quite common to express the profit before tax plus interest paid as a percentage of the balance sheet total as shown in the horizontal balance sheet. This, however, is not very common in Britain.

So far, we have compared profits to the money invested in the business. An alternative is to compare profits to sales. In this case we get the various profit margins, which again can be based on gross profit, net profit, and so on. One example of such a ratio would be:

$$\frac{\text{profit attributable to shareholders}}{\text{sales}} \times 100$$

Another ratio often worked out by analysts is the

dividend cover. It is defined as follows:

$$\text{Dividend cover} = \frac{\text{profit}}{\text{dividend}}$$

What useful information does this ratio provide?

Well, it indicates how **safe** the dividend is. Suppose company A makes a profit of £1,100 and pays dividends of £1,000; its dividend cover is $\frac{1,100}{1,000} = 1.1$

Company B also pays dividends of £1,000, but its profits amount to £2,000; its dividend cover is 2. Which company's dividends are safer?

A fairly small fall in profits may force company A to reduce its dividend, whereas company B's prof-its can fall quite substantially before it will find it necessary to cut its dividend. So, the higher the dividend cover, the safer is the dividend. Companies particularly exposed to the ups and downs of the business cycle, like mining companies, transport companies, and steel manufacturers, often aim at having high dividend covers in order to be able to continue paying their dividends during lean periods. Companies which operate in a more stable environment (such as food retailers, electricity suppliers or water works) feel they can afford to have a lower dividend cover because their profits are not likely to fall very much in a recession.

Let us now apply the ratios we have discussed so far to the three companies whose accounts we looked at in Chapter 13. The results are as follows:

		Ratios for		
Name of ratio	Definition	British Airways	British Steel	Marks and Spencer
Return on shareholders' funds after tax	$\dfrac{\text{Profit attributable to shareholders}}{\text{shareholders funds}}$ x 100	$\dfrac{175}{749}$ x 100 = 23.4%	$\dfrac{561}{3,910}$ x 100 = 14.3%	$\dfrac{342.9}{1,918.6}$ x 100 = 17.9%
Return on shareholders' funds before tax	$\dfrac{\text{Profit before tax}}{\text{shareholders funds}}$ x 100	$\dfrac{268}{749}$ x 100 = 35.8%	$\dfrac{593}{3,910}$ x 100 = 15.2%	$\dfrac{529.0}{1,918.6}$ x 100 = 27.6%
Return on total capital before tax	$\dfrac{\text{Profit before tax + interest paid}}{\text{net assets less current liabilities}}$ x 100	$\dfrac{354}{1,746}$ x 100 = 20.3%	$\dfrac{593*}{4,124}$ x 100 = 14.4%	$\dfrac{563.7}{2,271.5}$ x 100 = 24.8%
Net margin	$\dfrac{\text{Profit attributable to shareholders}}{\text{turnover}}$ x 100	$\dfrac{175}{4,257}$ x 100 = 4.1%	$\dfrac{561}{4,906}$ x 100 = 11.4%	$\dfrac{342.9}{5,121.5}$ x 100 = 6.7%
Dividend cover	$\dfrac{\text{Profit attributable to shareholders}}{\text{dividend}}$	$\dfrac{175}{56}$ = 3.125	$\dfrac{561}{100}$ = 5.61	$\dfrac{342.9}{149.7}$ = 2.29

* British Steel was a net receiver of interest, not a net payer. Consequently, profit before tax + interest paid is the same as profit before tax.

These figures show that British Airways achieved the highest return on shareholders' funds, both before and after tax. When it comes to the return on total capital, Marks and Spencer comes first. British Steel has the highest net margin and the highest dividend cover. Interestingly, British Airways has the lowest margin but the highest return on shareholders' funds. How is this possible? We will explain this apparent paradox in section B6.

B2 PRODUCTIVITY RATIOS

Here we have to start by explaining what 'productivity' actually means, and how it differs from profitability. Some people use those two terms almost interchangeably, but one should keep them apart because they are not the same.

Any business produces some goods or services, and gets a money income by selling those goods or services. However, it cannot produce those goods or services from nothing, but needs factors of production like human labour and machinery as well as raw materials in the production process. This can be summarised in the following diagram:

INPUTS   **OUTPUTS**

labour ⟶ goods

machinery ⟶ Business and

raw materials ⟶ services

Profitability and productivity both compare inputs and outputs, but they do so in different ways. Profitability compares the money value of the outputs with the money value (the cost) of the inputs; the difference between the two is the profit which can then be expressed either as an amount of money or as a ratio (see section B1). Productivity also compares inputs and outputs, but it does not use money as a measuring rod; it compares inputs and outputs directly. An airline, for example, can work out its fuel efficiency by working out how much fuel (input) it needs for a certain flight (output). A coal mine can measure its productivity of labour by dividing the output of coal by the number of man hours worked; this productivity ratio will then take the form of 'so many kilos of coal per man hour'.

Of what use are such figures? There are several applications. One is to work out how much it costs the business to produce its output. Another is to make comparisons, which are often a useful basis for management decisions. An airline, for example, can compare the fuel efficiency of different types of aeroplanes, and take this into account when deciding which one to buy. When considering the performance of a company as a whole, one can either compare the productivity of that company in a given year with the productivity of the same company in previous years, or one can compare its productivity with that of another business in the same sector of the economy. If the productivity of one company is lower than that of others, management may find it useful to think about whether there are good reasons for that difference or whether it is just due to inefficiency.

B2A Example 1: Comparison over time

The productivity of labour at British Steel

Years ended 1 April	Steel output: millions of tonnes (tonnes per year)	Number of employees	Productivity of labour: output per employee
1985	9.3	74,000	126
1986	9.6	67,000	143
1987	10.4	55,000	189
1988	12.2	54,000	226
1989	13.1	55,000	238

Source: British Steel, annual report 1988-89

The 'output per employee' column shows that British Steel's productivity of labour increased considerably between 1985 and 1989. In 1989 the output per employee was almost twice as much as it had been in 1985. From the point of view of technological and economic efficiency such a development is certainly desirable. There was of course a social cost in this process: a reduction in the number of people employed. This does not mean, however, that those jobs would have been saved if the company had stayed as inefficient as it was in 1985. Had it stayed at that level of productivity, it would now be far behind its overseas competitors; in fact, it might well have gone bankrupt, and in that case even more jobs would have been lost. So, operating inefficiently is not a very reliable way of creating employment, at least in the long run.

B2B   Example 2: Inter-company comparison

Productivity of labour in various electricity generating companies (all of which are predominantly coal-based) in 1988-1989:

Company	Electricity generated (million kwh)	Number of employees	Output per employee (million kwh per year)
Central Electricity Generating Board (CEGB, England)	239,125	47,442	5.04
China Light and Power Company, Hong Kong	18,709	6,260	2.99
Eskom (South Africa)	136,630	56,726	2.41
TransAlta Utilities (Alberta, Canada)	21,170	2,548	8.31

Source: Companies' annual reports

These figures show that as far as the electricity generated per employee is concerned, the CEGB is doing better than China Light or Eskom, but less well than TransAlta Utilities. If we include other companies in our comparison, we can see that power companies which generate the bulk of their electricity from nuclear power often have a lower output per employee than have coal-based companies. For example, the South of Scotland Electricity Board produces about 2 million kwh per employee per year and Electricite de France 2.5 million.[1] Both these figures are considerably below that for the CEGB. Hydroelectric power stations have a wide range of productivity ratios, for example 1.8 million kwh per employee per year in Namibia, about 4 million in Austria, and nearly 8 million in the US state of Idaho.[1]

B3   LIQUIDITY RATIOS

The future of a company which makes losses year after year is obviously bleak. Interestingly, however, most bankruptcies are not caused by a lack of profitability, but by companies' inability to pay creditors on time: by a lack of **liquidity.** The reason for this is that shareholders rarely find it in their interest to close down their company even after several years of losses, whereas the first creditor who is not paid on time can take the delinquent company to court and start bankruptcy proceedings. In this context, the word 'creditor' refers to anybody to whom the company owes money: this can be a supplier of raw materials; a gas, water or electricity supplier; or an individual or an organisation that has lent money to the company. It is therefore necessary for the survival of the business that it can pay its creditors on time, and it will only be able to do this if it has sufficient liquidity. Liquid assets are all those assets which either **are money** (like notes and coin) or can be **turned into money** at short notice (like short-term deposits with banks or other financial institutions, or short-term securities). Debtors are also fairly liquid since they will pay in the near future. To what extent stock is a liquid asset depends on what kinds of goods we are talking about. A jeweller may hold stocks of gold or other precious metals; such stocks are perfectly liquid since they can be sold at any time, although their value will fluctuate in line with the market prices of the metals concerned. The stock of a car manufacturer or dealer, on the other hand, consists of unsold cars. Such stocks are much less liquid since you cannot just sell them whenever you wish.

To assess a company's liquidity, it is again pretty useless just to look at the amount of liquid assets held. £10,000 in the bank are more than enough for a small butcher's shop but insufficient for a large company.

Q What additional information would you want in order to make use of your knowledge about the liquid assets held?

A What is particularly important in this context is not the absolute amount of liquid assets held, but the amount of liquid assets compared to the short-term (current) liabilities. If you have to pay somebody £5,000 later today, you are in trouble if you do not have at least £5,000 now. If, on the other hand, the next payment you have to make is due in one year's time, you can theoretically do without any liquid assets at the moment. Therefore, we have to compare a business's liquid assets with its current liabilities if we want to assess its liquidity position.

Three ratios frequently used to assess the liquidity position of a business are:

▶ the **current** ratio, defined as

$$\frac{\text{current assets}}{\text{current liabilities}}$$

▶ the **liquid** ratio, defined as

$$\frac{\text{current assets excluding stock}}{\text{current liabilities}}$$

$$= \frac{\text{liquid assets plus debtors}}{\text{current liabilities}}$$

▶ the **acid test** ratio, defined as

$$\frac{\text{liquid assets}}{\text{current liabilities}}$$

Since in this area both the terminology and the exact definitions vary, it is useful to define the ratios one uses, rather than just to say that the liquid ratio of company XYZ is such and such.

The **current** ratio, as defined above, compares the entire current assets with the current liabilities. The idea behind this approach is that the current assets denote the amount that is, or shortly will be, available to pay the current liabilities. Liquid assets like cash or bank deposits are available immediately, debtors will pay in the near future, and stock will be sold in the near future. If all this works out as intended, a company should not face any liquidity problems if its current assets are approximately equal to its current liabilities. Since some things may not work out as intended (for example, some debtors may go bankrupt, or some of the stock may not find buyers), many accountants recommend that the current ratio should be somewhat greater than 1 (perhaps about 1.5) to be on the safe side.

Another way of trying to be on the safe side is for

management to make sure that the more liquid parts of the current assets alone are sufficient to pay the current liabilities. Stock is clearly the least liquid part of the current assets, except in rare cases where the stock consists of goods (like gold or copper) for which there is a ready market. Most debtors pay when due, and the liquid assets like cash and bank balances can be drawn upon at any time. So, if the current assets excluding stock (which is the same thing as liquid assets plus debtors) are sufficient to meet the current liabilities, the business is in an even better liquidity position. This would indicate a **liquid** ratio (as defined above) of 1.

The **acid test** ratio indicates what fraction of the current liabilities could be paid off with the liquid assets the company has at the moment, without relying on receiving payment from debtors or selling stock.

Traditionally, many accountants and accountancy textbook writers have recommended that the current ratio should be somewhere near 1.5 and the liquid ratio somewhere near 1, although admitting that some companies may need more liquidity than others to steer clear of danger. At the moment many large businesses operate on (sometimes considerably) lower liquidity ratios. Only the future can tell whether the traditional advice has been excessively cautious or whether the current practice is a rather risky way of running a business.

Turning now to the three companies whose accounts we have studied earlier, we get a current ratio of just over 2 for British Steel, 0.89 for Marks and Spencer, and 0.52 for British Airways. The ratio for British Steel is very cautious. That for Marks and Spencer is a bit low by traditional standards, but not very far out of line with the practice of the late 1980s. British Airways' current ratio of 0.52 looks extremely low, but here we have to take into account a peculiarity of the structure of its current liabilities. For most companies, current liabilities are amounts which will have to be paid in the near future. As explained earlier, however, some of British Airways' current liabilities consist of 'sales in advance of carriage' (£557 million in 1989), and these are unlikely to produce outflows of money. Deducting this amount from the company's current liabilities produces a (slightly manipulated) current ratio of 0.77. This example shows that one has to take the nature of a business into account when interpreting its liquidity ratios.

A truly atrocious liquidity position is revealed by the following (slightly simplified) balance sheet of the Canadian oil company Dome Petroleum:

Balance sheet of Dome Petroleum, end 1982 (millions of Can.$)

Liabilities		**Assets**		
shareholders' funds	1,164	Fixed assets		8,707
long-term debt	5,019	Current assets:		
current liabilities	3,734	stock	376	
		debtors	831	
		liquid assets	3	1,210
	9,917			9,917

Source: Dome Petroleum, annual report 1982

The current ratio of Dome Petroleum at the end of 1982 was $\dfrac{1{,}210}{3{,}734} = 0.32$

and its acid test ratio was almost zero. Incidentally, Dome Petroleum no longer exists (no prizes for having guessed that!).

Two widely used ratios in this area are:

▶ the **gearing** ratio, defined as

$$\frac{\text{borrowings}}{\text{net assets}} \times 100 \text{ or}$$

$$\frac{\text{borrowings}}{\text{shareholders' funds}} \times 100$$

▶ the **interest cover,** defined as

$$\frac{\text{profit before interest paid and tax}}{\text{interest paid}}$$

B4   GEARING RATIOS

We have seen earlier that a business can be financed either by shareholders' funds or by debt. The gearing ratios indicate to what extent a business is debt-financed.

$$\frac{5019}{1164} \times 100 = 431\%$$

Q Incidentally, what is the difference between 'net assets' and 'shareholders' funds'? Consult the balance sheet of any of the companies discussed in section 13F if you do not remember.

A The difference lies in the minority interests. **Net assets = shareholders' funds + minority interests** (which is the same as saying: shareholders' funds = net assets – minority interests).

In countries where the balance sheet is normally presented in the horizontal form, gearing is often measured by a **ratio of indebtedness,** which expresses total debt (current liabilities plus long-term debt) as a percentage of the balance sheet total. This ratio is, however, rarely used in Britain. In this country, 'borrowings' in the gearing ratio are nearly always taken to mean the non-current liabilities only; the 'creditors: amounts falling due after more than one year', as this item is called in the accounts of the three companies we have used as examples earlier on.

The gearing ratio is easy to understand. It expresses borrowings as a percentage of net assets or shareholders' funds. The higher this ratio, the more the business in question relies on debt finance. For the three companies whose accounts we discussed in section 13F we get the following gearing ratios (defined as long-term debt, divided by net assets, multiplied by 100):

Marks and Spencer : $\dfrac{343.7}{1,922.7}$ x 100 = 17.9%

British Steel : $\dfrac{210}{3,914}$ x 100 = 5.4%

British Airways: $\dfrac{896}{750}$ x 100 = 119%

These figures clearly show that of these three companies, British Steel relies least on debt finance and British Airways most. And what was the gearing ratio of Dome Petroleum (see section B3) at the end of 1982? Work it out for yourself, and then compare your result with the answer at the bottom of the next page.

Why is it useful to know gearing ratios? Why does it matter whether a company is highly geared or

not? Well, the problem with debt is that interest must be paid on the debt, and the debt itself must be repaid on the due date no matter how well or badly the company is doing at that particular time. Any creditor who is not paid what is due to him can start bankruptcy proceedings against the company. If a company which has no debt has a bad year, it need not pay any dividends to its shareholders; a debt-financed company, however, still has to pay interest on its debt, and inability to pay such interest can be the end of the company. So, the higher the level of debt, the greater the risk. This leads to the question of why companies borrow at all. If borrowing increases the risk, why not sell more shares instead of borrowing? One of the reasons is that the borrowing option may be more profitable to the shareholders. The following simplified example explains why this is so.

Balance sheets at 31 December 1992

	Company A	Company B
assets	100	100
debt	20	80
shareholders' funds	80	20

Profit and loss account for 1992

sales	50	50
operating costs	40	40
interest	2	8
profit	8	2

Let us assume that the two companies, A and B, are identical in all respects except in the way they are financed. Both have assets of 100, but in company A that 100 consists of shareholders' funds of 80 and debts of 20 whereas company B has debts of 80 and shareholders' funds of 20. Sales and operating costs are the same in both cases. Assuming that both companies have to pay 10% interest on their borrowings, company A will have to pay interest of 2 and company B, 8. The resulting profit (8 for company A and 2 for company B) amounts to 10% of shareholders' funds in both cases. So, if we only look at the profitability and ignore the gearing, a shareholder may feel that it does not really matter whether he invests his money in company A or company B since in both cases the profit amounts to 10% of shareholders' funds.

So, why does the gearing matter? Suppose the following year (1993) is a particularly good year for the two companies, in that both of them can increase their sales by 10%. If sales go up by 10%, it makes sense to assume that operating costs will go up as well; let us assume they also rise by 10%. In this case, we get the following profit and loss accounts for 1993:

	Company A	Company B
sales	55	55
operating costs	44	44
interest	2	8
profit	9	3

Now, the return on shareholders' funds is 9/80 x 100 = 11.25% for company A and 3/20 x 100 = 15% for company B. So, the shareholders of company B benefit more from this improvement in the business climate than do the shareholders of company A, and the reason for this is the higher gearing of company B. The increase in profit by 1 amounts to a larger percentage of shareholders' funds if those funds are smaller.

If 1994 turns out to be a bad year for the two companies, with sales and operating costs 10% lower than in 1992, we get the following profit and loss accounts for 1994:

	Company A	Company B
sales	45	45
operating costs	36	36
interest	2	8
profit	7	1

Now, the return on shareholders' funds is 7/80 x 100 = 8.75% for company A and 1/20 x 100 = 5% for company B. The shareholders of company B suffer more from the business downturn than do the shareholders of company A. We can conclude that highly-geared companies (those with a high level of debt) benefit more in good times, but suffer more in bad times, than do companies with a lower level of debt. A high level of debt makes a company's performance more volatile than if the indebtedness is lower. The performance of low-geared companies is more stable over time.

The potential danger of a high level of debt is also highlighted by the second ratio mentioned at the beginning of this section, namely the **interest cover.** For the three companies investigated earlier, we get the following figures:

Marks and Spencer $\frac{563.7}{21.6} = 26.1$

British Steel — net receiver of interest

British Airways $\frac{354}{86} = 4.1$

Marks and Spencer's profit before tax would allow that company to pay its interest 26.1 times over. British Airways, which has a higher level of gearing, can pay its interest 4.1 times over. For British Steel this ratio is not meaningful, since that company is a net receiver and not a net payer of interest (a mathematical purist may want to express the ratio as infinite (∞) in this case since you divide the profit before tax and interest by zero, but ignore this if you find it confusing

Dome Petroleum in 1982 had a profit before tax of 280 million Canadian dollars and interest charges of 649 million Canadian dollars, giving it a loss of 369 million dollars and an interest cover of 280 ÷ 649 = 0.43.

The higher the interest cover, the safer is the company. This becomes particularly clear if we consider the case of a company with an interest cover of only slightly more than 1; say, 1.1. A slight fall in profit would then mean that the company does not earn enough to pay interest on its debt and, as we know already, any creditor who is not paid what is due to him can start bankruptcy proceedings against the company.

B5 ACTIVITY (OR TURNOVER) RATIOS

A company's assets or shareholders' funds do not generate any cash by themselves. They do enable

---

Answer to the question on the previous page:

Dome Petroleum's gearing ratio =

$$\frac{5,019}{1,164} \times 100 = 431\%$$

Note: Dome Petroleum's net assets are the same as the shareholders' funds the company to produce goods or services, and it is from the sale of those goods or services that the company generates its income. Therefore the profit the company makes will depend, among other things, on the activity (measured, for example, by the volume of sales) generated by the company's assets, shareholders' funds, or some other balance sheet item.

Activity ratios compare some aspect of the company's activities (usually sales or purchases) to some relevant balance sheet item. When comparing sales over a longer period of time, it may be advisable also to take inflation into account.

Some frequently used ratios are as follows.

B5A Shareholders' funds

▶ The **shareholders' funds turnover ratio** =

$$\frac{\text{sales}}{\text{shareholders' funds}}$$

This ratio indicates how may pounds ($) of sales are generated by each pound of shareholders' funds invested in the business.

Examples (relating to 1989):

Marks and Spencer: $\dfrac{5,121.5}{1,918.6} = 2.67$

British Steel $\dfrac{4,906}{3,910} = 1.25$

British Airways $\dfrac{4,257}{749} = 5.68$

It would not make sense to criticise British Steel for not achieving the same amount of sales per pound of shareholders' funds as the other two companies do. Steel-making is a much more capital-intensive business than retailing or air transport, which means one needs more assets to achieve a given amount of sales. However, the above ratios are meaningful if one wants to explain the level of profitability of the various companies (more about this in section B6), and of course one can compare the shareholders' funds turnover ratio of one business with that of another business in the same sector of the economy. For

example, Storehouse (owners of British Home Stores, Mothercare and other retailing companies) had sales of £1,221 million and shareholders' funds of £512 million in 1989: each pound of shareholders' funds generated 1,221 ÷ 512 = £2.38 of sales, which is about 11% less than the corresponding figure for Marks and Spencer.*

B5B Stock

▶ The **stock turnover ratio** = $\dfrac{\text{sales}}{\text{stock}}$

This ratio is used to investigate a company's stock-holding policy. If a company has annual sales of 120 and holds an average stock of 20, the stock is turned over six times per year, or once every two months. Changes in this ratio affect a business's liquidity. If the stock is turned over more slowly, less cash is generated and relatively more cash is tied up in stock.

Some people prefer to express stock as a percentage of sales. This in fact leads to the ratio

$$\frac{\text{stock}}{\text{sales}} \times 100,$$

which is the inverse of the stock turnover ratio, multiplied by 100. The information provided by this ratio is of course the same as that provided by the stock turnover ratio.

B5C Debtors and creditors

▶ The **debtor turnover ratio** =

$$\frac{\text{sales}}{\text{debtors}} \quad \text{or} \quad \frac{\text{debtors}}{\text{sales}} \times 12 \text{ months}$$

When expressed in the form $\dfrac{\text{annual sales}}{\text{debtors}}$

this ratio indicates how often the amount of debtors is turned over each year: sales of 120 per year and average debtors of 20 would product a

---

*These calculations are based on figures shown in the balance sheets. If differences in the valuation methods of property were taken into account, the difference between the shareholders' funds turnover ratios of the two companies would be even greater.

debtor turnover of six times per year. This is the same thing as saying that debtors are turned over once every two months, which is the information provided by the second version of this ratio (see above). To say that debtors are turned over once every two months is also the same thing as saying that they stay on the books for two months: they take, on average, two months to pay. This is the average credit period the business allows its customers.

Alternatively, this ratio can be expressed in the form

$$\frac{\text{debtors}}{\text{sales}} \times 100,$$

which expresses debtors as a percentage of annual sales.

▶ The **creditor turnover ratio** =

$$\frac{\text{purchases}}{\text{creditors}} \quad \text{or} \quad \frac{\text{creditors}}{\text{purchases}} \times 12 \text{ months}$$

This ratio is based on the same principle as the stock and debtor turnover ratios, but since creditors come about when the business buys something it should be based on purchases and not on sales.

If our purchases amount to 120 per year and our average amount of creditors is 10, our creditor turnover is 12 times per year or once a month. This means that we receive one month's credit from our suppliers.

Just like changes in the stock turnover ratio, changes in the debtor or creditor turnover ratios affect the liquidity of the business. If debtors take longer to pay, the business will have less cash at any one point in time than it would have had if the debtors had paid sooner. Working out the debtor turnover ratio (or the length of credit given) for a number of consecutive periods shows whether debtors now absorb more or less liquidity than they did in the past.

Since creditors are a current liability, an increase in the credit period increases the liquidity of the business. If we take longer to pay our suppliers, the effect is the same as if we borrowed more money to pay them; the business has more liquidity than it would have had otherwise.

B6 SUB-RATIOS

Often, additional information can be obtained from a ratio if we break it up into two or more sub-ratios. For example, the return on shareholders' funds

$$\frac{\text{profit}}{\text{shareholders' funds}} \times 100$$

can be broken down as follows:

$$\frac{\text{profit}}{\text{shareholders' funds}} \times 100 =$$

$$\left(\frac{\text{profit}}{\text{sales}} \times 100 \right) \times \left(\frac{\text{sales}}{\text{shareholders funds}} \right)$$

It is easy to see that mathematically the two sides of the equation are the same. On the right hand side the sales appear once as the numerator (above the line) and once as the denominator (below the line), so they cancel each other out and we are back at the ratio shown on the left hand side of the equation. However, both the sub-ratios on the right- hand side convey useful information about the business. The first one,

$$\frac{\text{profit}}{\text{sales}} \times 100,$$

is the profit margin, and the second one,

$$\frac{\text{sales}}{\text{shareholders' funds}}$$

is the shareholders' funds turnover.

Splitting the profitability ratio in this way can explain apparent contradictions like the one we found in section B1, where British Airways had the highest return on shareholders' funds but the lowest profit margin of the three companies we investigated. Let us now compare British Airways and British Steel by splitting the profitability ratio into the two sub-ratios shown above:

$$\frac{\text{profit}}{\text{shareholders' funds}} \times 100 =$$

$$\frac{\text{profit}}{\text{sales}} \times 100 \times \frac{\text{sales}}{\text{shareholders' funds}}$$

British Airways:

$$\frac{175}{749} \times 100 = \frac{175}{4,257} \times 100 \times \frac{4,257}{749}$$

23.4% = 4.1% x 5.68

British Steel:

$$\frac{561}{3,910} \times 100 = \frac{561}{4,906} \times 100 \times \frac{4,906}{3,910}$$

14.3% = 11.4% x 1.25

(Multiplying the two figures on the right may not produce exactly the result shown on the left hand side; this is due to rounding errors.)

What information does this calculation provide?

Well, in the case of British Airways the shareholders' funds turnover is 5.68: £1 of shareholders' funds generates sales of £5.68 per year. The profit margin is 4.1%. That means, the £5.68 of sales generated by each pound of shareholders' funds generate a profit amounting to 4.1% of £5.68, which is (approximately) 23.4 pence. Conclusion: £1 of shareholders' funds generates £5.68 of sales which in turn generate a profit of 23.4 pence; the profit amounts to 23.4% of shareholders' funds.

British Steel has a higher profit margin, but a lower turnover of shareholders' funds. In that company, £1 of shareholders' funds generates sales of £1.25 which, given the 11.4% profit margin, produces a profit of 14.3 pence; the profit amounts to 14.3% of shareholders' funds.

The higher profit margin of British Steel does not produce a higher profit per pound of shareholders' funds than is the case with British Airways: because in British Steel each pound of shareholders' funds generates a lower level of sales than is the case with British Airways; in relation to shareholders funds, British Steel has a higher profit margin on a lower volume of sales.

Theoretically, one can argue that in the long run the return on shareholders' funds should be roughly the same in all sectors of the economy; if this was not so, nobody would invest in the sectors offering lower returns. Since some sectors of the economy have a high asset (or shareholders' funds) turnover ratio due to the nature of their business (examples are food or petrol retailing), these sectors will normally have fairly low profit margins. On the other hand, sectors which are very capital intensive and therefore have a low rate of shareholders' funds turnover (such as the steel industry or electricity generation) will need above-average profit margins to give them the 'normal' rate of return on shareholders' funds.

In our comparison of British Airways and British Steel we used sub-ratios to explain why those companies have performed the way they have. The same method can be used to compare the performance of one company over a number of years. If, for example, the profitability of a business has fallen, the split-up of the profitability ratio in the way outlined above allows management to see whether the reason for this fall has been a decrease in shareholders' funds turnover or a decrease in the profit margin. Knowing what has caused an undesirable development should make it easier to decide what to do to improve the situation.

The profitability ratio can of course be split up in more detail to pinpoint even more precisely where problems have arisen. For example, a manufacturing business could use the sub-ratios we have just studied to find out whether an observed change in the profitability ratio has been caused by changes in the profit margin or by changes in the shareholders' funds turnover. If we find that it is the profit margin which has changed, it can be analysed in more detail, for example as follows:

$$\frac{profit}{shareholders'\ funds} \times 100 = \frac{profit}{sales} \times 100 \times \frac{sales}{shareholders'\ funds}$$

$$= \frac{sales - cost}{sales} \times 100 \times \frac{sales}{shareholders'\ funds}$$

$$= (1 - \frac{cost}{sales}) \times 100 \times \frac{sales}{shareholders'\ funds}$$

$$= (1 - \frac{raw\ material\ cost + labour\ cost + other\ costs}{sales}) \times 100 \times \frac{sales}{shareholders'\ funds}$$

$$= (1 - \frac{raw\ material\ cost}{sales} - \frac{labour\ cost}{sales} - \frac{other\ costs}{sales}) \times 100 \times \frac{sales}{shareholders'\ funds}$$

If necessary, we can proceed by splitting up the raw material ratio into ratios for different kinds of raw materials. The same can be done with the labour cost, and the 'other costs' can also be split up into their components.

By working out these figures for a couple of years, we can find out exactly which cost item has caused the change in profitability, and knowing this should place the company's management in a better position for making decisions. Just as a doctor can only treat a patient effectively if he knows the cause of the symptoms, so a manager can only make worthwhile decisions if he knows the cause of the situation his business is in.

C
THE USE OF RATIOS (SUMMARY)

? Before going on, run through in your mind the various uses to which we have seen that ratios can be put. Jot down those which you can think of, before reading through the suggestions below.

Ratios can be used:

▶ To analyse the performance of a business.

▶ To compare the performance of a company over time, by working out a set of relevant ratios for a number of years. Seeing how the various ratios have changed over time helps management to pinpoint problem areas.

▶ To compare the performances of a number of businesses (see our comparison of British Airways, British Steel and Marks and Spencer in section B5). Comparisons with similar businesses give managers and shareholders an idea of what performance can reasonably be expected. By comparing a number of businesses investors can decide which company is most suitable as an investment.

▶ To compare the performance of various sections of a business. Technically, this is the same as comparing different companies. Just as one can compare the performance of businesses A, B and C, so one can compare activities D, E and F of any one of these companies. Such an analysis tells a company which of its activities are most profitable, which are least profitable and, perhaps, which activities make losses. Such information can then be the basis for deciding which activities should be expanded and which should be discontinued, or it can simply identify problem areas which demand more attention from management.

▶ To set targets (**planning**). It is all very well to say, "We must improve our liquidity", but such an instruction is nevertheless rather vague. Suppose in the following year liquidity does improve slightly; should you praise the manager responsible for that area for having brought about that improvement, or should you sack him for not having improved it enough? Ratios allow clear targets to be set. For instance, the board of directors of a company can decide that it wants an after-tax return on shareholders' funds of 15% per year and a current ratio of 1.2.

Senior managers can then be given responsibility for achieving these targets, and be appraised on whether or not they have met their target (**controlling**). So, ratios provide targets against which the performance of managers and other employees can be measured.

D

BUSINESS ANALYSIS: AN EXAMPLE

Now that we know some of the tools of business analysis, let us put our knowledge to the test:

Epsilon Limited commenced trading several years ago, and has remained profitable, but the managing director has become concerned that the company has found itself increasingly obliged to borrow from the bank. He is of the opinion that finance of a more permanent nature is required if the company is to continue to expand, and accordingly you have been asked to look into the matter.

Abstracts of the audited accounts of the last four years have been presented to you, as follows:

Balance Sheets

As at 31 December	1976 £	1977 £	1978 £	1979 £
Fixed assets				
Building, at cost	182,000	182,000	182,000	182,000
Plant, at cost less depreciation	69,000	67,100	70,200	70,600
	251,000	249,100	252,200	252,600
Goodwill	29,000	29,000	29,000	29,000
Current assets				
Stocks	131,000	162,000	208,000	277,000
Debtors	52,000	68,000	89,000	140,000
Cash	600	700	500	400
	183,600	230,700	297,500	417,400
Current liabilities				
Creditors	51,000	55,000	59,000	81,000
Bank overdraft	12,000	23,000	57,000	99,000
Taxation	18,000	18,000	21,000	23,500
Proposed dividend	13,000	13,000	13,000	13,000
	94,000	109,000	150,000	216,500
Net current assets	89,600	121,700	147,500	200,900
	369,600	399,800	428,700	482,500
Financed by				
Issued capital	270,000	270,000	270,000	270,000
Reserves	87,600	102,800	124,700	159,500
Shareholders funds	357,600	372,800	394,700	429,500
Deferred taxation	12,000	27,000	34,000	53,000
	369,600	399,800	428,700	482,500

Profit and Loss Accounts

Year ended 31 December	1976	1977	1978	1979	
		£	£	£	£
Sales	900,000	980,000	1,200,000	1,520,000	
Purchases	720,000	800,000	1,000,000	1,280,000	
Increase in stocks	11,000	31,000	46,000	69,000	
	709,000	769,000	954,000	1,211,000	
Gross profit	191,000	211,000	246,000	309,000	
Directors' remuneration	8,000	9,500	9,500	9,500	
Depreciation	8,200	8,100	8,300	8,000	
Bank interest	1,900	4,000	8,000	15,500	
Other expenses	149,900	151,200	180,300	220,200	
	168,000	172,800	206,100	253,200	
Profit before taxation	23,000	38,200	39,900	55,800	
Corporation tax	11,000	14,000	9,000	12,000	
Profit after taxation	12,000	24,200	30,900	43,800	
Dividend	9,000	9,000	9,000	9,000	
Retained	3,000	15,200	21,900	34,800	
Selling price indices	100	120	150	200	

You are required to draft comments to the managing director on the following aspects of the company's affairs:

(1) Sales.
(2) Profits.
(3) Dividend cover.
(4) Investment in debtors.
(5) Investment in stocks.
(6) Future financing of the company.

Use any working schedules or ratios which you consider would prove helpful.

Source: The Institute of Bankers in Scotland, Associateship examination May 1980. Reproduced with permission.

D1 EXPLANATORY NOTES

The **selling price index** gives an indication of inflation during the period under investigation (the late 1970s were a period of exceptionally high inflation in Britain). The information presented in the balance sheets and profit and loss accounts should not present any problems, with the possible exception of the term 'goodwill'.

Goodwill arises if you buy a business for a price which exceeds the value of its net assets. Suppose the assets of a greengrocer's shop are worth £30,000; this figure includes the shop (£20,000), the shopfittings (£5,000), and the stocks (£5,000). Somebody who buys this shop may well be prepared to pay more than £30,000 for it, because by buying it he benefits not only from the shop's tangible assets, but also from its reputation, its regular customers, and so on. If somebody buys this shop for £40,000, he will record it in his balance sheet as follows:

shop	£20,000
shopfittings	£ 5,000
stock	£ 5,000
goodwill	£10,000
	£40,000

The usual practice now is to write off the goodwill over a number of years or even in the year of acquisition, rather than just to leave it in the balance sheet.

D2 SOLUTION

Let us now turn to the 'Epsilon Limited' question. Try to work out the answer for yourself before consulting the suggested answer given here. Probably no two people who have a go at such a question will use exactly the same methods, but they should still come up with similar conclusions.

Suggested answer

(1) Sales: in money terms the sales rise by about 69% during the period under investigation. Prices, however, double. Consequently, sales fall in real terms.

(2) Profits: No problems here. Gross profit moves roughly in line with sales. Profits before and after tax rise sharply, no matter whether one just considers the published figures or compares them with sales or shareholders' funds. Profits also rise considerably in real terms (that is, after allowing for inflation).

(3) Dividend cover: Since profits rise sharply and dividends stay the same, the dividend cover improves.

(4)(5)(6) Investment in debtors, stocks, and future financing: These items are best grouped together in this case. Stocks and debtors rise substantially during the period. While sales increase by 69% in money terms, stocks more than double and debtors nearly treble. This ties up a lot of liquidity.

In 1976, stocks and debtors together amount to just over 20% of sales. If they still amounted to that percentage of sales in 1979, Epsilon Limited would have just over £300,000 tied up in stocks and debtors that year. In fact, it had tied up £417,000 in those two assets. Going back to 1976 ratios would therefore allow the company to set free more than £100,000 of liquidity, and this is enough to pay off the entire bank overdraft. In other words, there is no need for more permanent finance. All that is needed is a better control of stocks and debtors.

E

RATIOS IN THE INSURANCE INDUSTRY

We have already seen in Chapter 13 that insurance brokers' accounts are very similar to the accounts of non-insurance businesses, whereas the accounts of insurance companies are rather special. That means that the accounts of insurance brokers can be analysed by using the usual accounting ratios we have discussed so far, whereas a different set of ratios is needed for insurance companies. The most widely used insurance company ratios are the following:

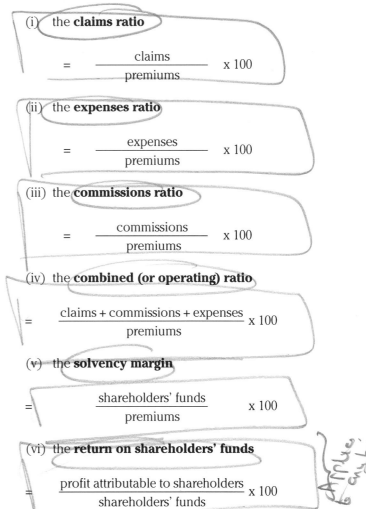

(i) the **claims ratio**

$$= \frac{claims}{premiums} \times 100$$

(ii) the **expenses ratio**

$$= \frac{expenses}{premiums} \times 100$$

(iii) the **commissions ratio**

$$= \frac{commissions}{premiums} \times 100$$

(iv) the **combined (or operating) ratio**

$$= \frac{claims + commissions + expenses}{premiums} \times 100$$

(v) the **solvency margin**

$$= \frac{shareholders'\ funds}{premiums} \times 100$$

(vi) the **return on shareholders' funds**

$$= \frac{profit\ attributable\ to\ shareholders}{shareholders'\ funds} \times 100$$

The first five of these ratios are specifically related to insurance companies, whereas the sixth can be applied to any business (we have worked it out for various companies in Chapter 13). 'Premiums' in the ratios mentioned above can be taken to mean either written premiums or earned premiums; one can find reasons for and against either approach.

? Do you remember the difference between written premiums and earned premiums? If not, see section 13G2B before you proceed.

While the use of earned premiums is more consistent with the general presentation of insurance company accounts (remember that the revenue account, the underwriting result and so on are based on earned premiums), one could well argue that commissions and expenses arise at the time when premiums are written, no matter when they are earned.

However, ratios are normally used to make comparisons, either to compare the performance of two or more companies in one particular year or to compare the performance of one company over a number of years. In all those cases, the main thing is to be consistent; that is, to use the same approach (no matter which one) throughout.

The first three ratios listed above express claims, commissions and expenses as a percentage of premiums. The combined (or operating) ratio is just a combination of the three previous ratios. These ratios can be worked out for several companies in one particular year, or for one company over a number of years, to compare the underlying performance, to discover any trends for the better or the worse, and to spot problem areas which require more attention from management. The lower these ratios are, the better: if you have lower claims or expenses in relation to premiums, you make a bigger profit. Insurance companies often quote the operating ratio, particularly in relation to their US business. For example, the Royal said in its interim report of August 1989, 'The second quarter statutory operating ratio…was 117.1%, an improvement from 119.0% in the first quarter.'

The return on shareholders' funds has already been discussed in section B1 and therefore needs no further discussion here.

The **solvency margin** compares shareholders' funds with premiums. What useful information does this ratio provide? Well, it gives some indication of how safe the company is. Suppose there is a series of exceptionally bad years, where losses amount to 10% of premiums each year. If company A has shareholders' funds amounting to 10% of premiums (so that its solvency margin is 10%), it can sustain one such year: after one such year its capital will be wiped out. If company B, on the other hand, has a solvency margin of 50%, only one fifth of its capital will be wiped out after one such catastrophic year, and theoretically it could endure four more such years. So, the higher the solvency margin, the safer the company (provided the underwriting is comparable: if one company writes more unpredictable business than others, it needs a higher solvency margin just to compensate for the riskier underwriting). In many countries there are legal regulations laying down minimum solvency margins.

Let us now use these ratios to compare the performance of the CU and the GRE in 1988. Using the accounts shown in section 13G2, we get the following ratios:

		CU	GRE
(i)	claims ratio	$\frac{1595}{2138} \times 100 = 74.6\%$	$\frac{1105}{1503} \times 100 = 73.5\%$
(ii)	expenses ratio	$\frac{274}{2138} \times 100 = 12.8\%$	$\frac{181}{1503} \times 100 = 12.0\%$
(iii)	commissions ratio	$\frac{398}{2138} \times 100 = 18.6\%$	$\frac{233}{1503} \times 100 = 15.5\%$
(iv)	combined ratio	$\frac{2267}{2138} \times 100 = 106.0\%$	$\frac{1519}{1503} \times 100 = 101.0\%$
(v)	solvency margin	$\frac{1269}{2138} \times 100 = 59.4\%$	$\frac{1261}{1503} \times 100 = 83.9\%$
(vi)	return on shareholders' funds	$\frac{131}{1269} \times 100 = 10.3\%$	$\frac{152}{1261} \times 100 = 12.1\%$

What do these figures tell us? By comparing the return on shareholders' funds we can see that the GRE was more profitable in 1988 than the CU; the GRE generated a profit of 12.1 pence for each pound of shareholders' funds, whereas the CU made only 10.3 pence for each pound of shareholders' funds. The cost ratios (ratios (i) - (iv) above) explain why the GRE was more profitable: all the main cost items made up a smaller percentage of premiums for the GRE than was the case with the CU. For instance, the GRE had 73.5 pence of claims for each pound of premiums earned, whereas the CU had 74.6 pence Taking the combined ratio, we can see that claims, commissions and expenses amounted to 106% of earned premiums for the CU, as against 101% for the GRE. No wonder, then, that the GRE was more profitable overall.

Q Now a question: how is it possible for these two companies to make any profit if claims, commissions and expenses add up to more than the premiums earned?

A The fact that the combined ratio exceeds 100% in both cases means that both companies make underwriting losses. However, the underwriting result is only part of the story. To get the total profit or loss, we have to add investment income and the shareholders' part of the life assurance profits to the underwriting result. In both cases, investment income and life profits are greater than the underwriting loss, so that both companies make profits overall. See the profit and loss accounts in section 13G2.

The GRE also has a considerably higher solvency margin than has the CU. Is this an advantage or a disadvantage?

There is no objective answer to this question. On the one hand, the solvency margin is an indicator of how safe a company is (as explained earlier). An investor, manager or director who is mainly interested in safety and minimising risk will therefore find the higher solvency margin of the GRE better than the lower one of the CU. On the other hand, a higher solvency margin means that a smaller amount of premiums has been earned for each pound of shareholders' funds.

The 83.9% solvency margin of the GRE means that 83.9 pence of shareholders' money was tied up to earn £1 of premiums, whereas the CU tied up only 59.4 pence of shareholders' funds to earn the same amount of premiums. This can also be expressed by saying that in the CU, £1 of shareholders' funds generated 1/.594 = £1.68 of premiums, whereas in the GRE £1 of shareholders' funds earned only 1/.839 = £1.19 of premiums. An investor, manager or director who is mainly interested in business growth may therefore wonder why the GRE earned a smaller amount of premiums per £1 of shareholders' funds than the CU did, and argue that it is better to earn £1.68 than it is to earn £1.19 of premiums for each pound of shareholders' funds. We can see, therefore, that which company you prefer on the grounds of the difference in solvency margins is not a matter of objective analysis, but one of personal preference, temperament and ideas of what aims a business should pursue.

Reference

1 Source: Companies' annual reports

14
SELF-ASSESSMENT QUESTIONS

1. For what reasons do people analyse company accounts?

   To see if targets have been met
   to compare one year with another
   to compare one Co with another — for pot. invest

2. What are the five standard categories of accounting ratios?

   Profitability   Gearing
   Productivity   Turnover
   liquidity

3. What is the difference between profitability and productivity?

   ① Profit looks at value of output
   Compared to value of input
   ② Prod. — is output compared to input

4. Why is it not sufficient to confine company analysis to analysing profitability?

   Because a company may be inefficient
   ② Changing shareholders funds into profit
   even though it makes a profit

5. Explain the importance of liquidity for the financial well-being of a company.

   Co must be able to meet its
   liabilities as they fall due otherwise
   it will be forced into bankruptcy

6. What is meant by 'gearing'? What are the advantages and disadvantages of a high level of gearing?

   Gearing is the extent to which a Co
   is financed by borrowing
   ①Advant — if profits inc —this can be passed
   on to Shareholders
   ② Disad — if profits fall bit, must still be
   paid before dividend paid

7. Comment on the links between shareholders' funds, sales and profits.

_____

_____

_____

8. How do:

(a) a more rapid turnover of debtors;

(b) a more rapid turnover of stocks;

(c) a more rapid turnover of creditors;

affect a company's liquidity?

(a) Inc

(b) decrease

(c) decrease

9. In what way can accounting ratios be used as a tool of planning?

aim to either reduce or increase particular ratios over a period of time

10. What is the difference between a liquid ratio and a liquidity ratio?

liquidity ratio shows ability to meet current liab @ a particular time

11. List the main ratios often used to analyse the performance of insurance companies.

Claims / Expenses / Comm / operating Solvency

12. What does the combined ratio indicate?

    Underwriting Profit/loss

13. What does the term 'solvency margin' mean?

    the amount by which Assets exceed liabs - thus the Co's Safety net in the event of Disastr year

    Shareholders funds expressed as % of Prems

14. What ratios would you use to analyse the performance of an insurance broking business?

    Same as non ins. biz

$$\frac{8}{1} = 8$$

$$\frac{2}{3} = 0.666$$

$$\frac{1}{2} = 0.5$$

$$\frac{4}{5} = 0.8$$

$$\overline{9.916}$$

$$\frac{9.966}{14} = 71\%$$

14

ANSWERS TO SELF-ASSESSMENT QUESTIONS

1.   Accounts are analysed to find out whether a company's performance meets certain targets; to compare the present performance of a company with its performance in previous years; to compare the performance of company with that of other companies; to compare the performance of different activities of a company; to decide whether or not to buy shares in a given company.

2.   Profitability, liquidity, productivity, gearing, and turnover (or activity) ratios.

3.   **Profitability** compares inputs and outputs in money terms (example: profit of £x; profit = y % of shareholders' funds). **Productivity** compares inputs and outputs directly (e.g. output per man-hour).

4.   No matter how profitable a company is, if it cannot pay its bills when due it may not survive.

5.   A company must have enough cash to pay creditors at the right time. If its liquidity is insufficient, it may not be able to pay its bills on time, which may lead to its being declared insolvent.

6.   Gearing indicates the extent of debt-financing. A highly geared company has a lot of debt. The higher the level of gearing, the more volatile will be the profitability of the company over time.

7.   Shareholders' funds are necessary to buy the equipment which will make sales possible. The sales then (hopefully) generate the profits.

8.   A more rapid turnover of debtors and stocks increases, and of creditors decreases, a company's liquidity.

9.   Ratios can be used to set targets for future performance.

10.   A liquid ratio is one particular kind of liquidity ratio: see section B3 for more details.

11.   Claims ratio; combined ratio; solvency margin; return on shareholders' funds.

12.   The combined ratio expresses the total of claims, commissions and expenses as a percentage of the premiums. If the combined ratio is less than 100, the insurance company makes an underwriting profit; a combined ratio of more than 100 indicates an underwriting loss.

13.   The solvency margin is the amount of shareholders' funds expressed as a percentage of premiums.

14.   The ratios normally used for non-insurance companies, like profitability, liquidity and turnover ratios.

You should work this assignment after studying Chapter 14. Answer any three questions, and allow yourself one and a half hours to complete it.

1.   Ratios are often used to analyse the performance of a business. Explain the reasons for using ratios, and outline the ways in which ratios can be used in the context of business analysis and planning.

2.   Analyse and compare the profitability of the following four airports. The information relates to the year ended 31.3.1989 (amounts in millions of £):

Airport	Revenue	Costs	Profits	Assets
London Heathrow	338.3	266.3	72.0	1,124.5
London Gatwick	159.8	134.3	25.5	712.5
Edinburgh	16.6	14.5	2.1	49.3
Glasgow	33.8	27.8	6.0	75.7

Source: BAA plc (formerly The British Airports Authority), annual report 1989.

3.   Explain the importance of liquidity to the financial well-being of a company. Why are ratios useful in analysing a company's liquidity position?

4.   What is meant by the term 'productivity'? Explain the difference between productivity and profitability.

15

CAPITAL MARKET FINANCE NEEDS

LEARNING OBJECTIVES

After studying this chapter, you should be able to:

▷ explain why businesses need short-term and long-term money;

▷ give examples of cases in which a business needs short-term money;

▷ give examples of cases in which a business needs long-term money;

▷ list some forms of short-term money;

▷ list some forms of long-term money;

▷ explain where money borrowed by businesses ultimately comes from;

▷ explain the role of financial intermediaries;

▷ outline the main uses and sources of funds for businesses in the UK.

A

THE NEED FOR SHORT-TERM MONEY

Suppose you are a textile manufacturer and have just received an order from a retailer or wholesaler for a thousand pairs of trousers. You will of course be paid for those trousers once you deliver them, but before you can deliver them you have to make them, and in that process you will have to spend money long before you will be paid by your customers. You will have to buy the material from which to make the trousers, you will have to pay your workforce, pay electricity bills and other overheads; and all this is weeks or even months before you can deliver the finished product and receive payment from your customers. In the meantime you have to find that money somehow. Either you have to invest money of your own, or you have to borrow. Needless to say, if you need money now to buy raw materials and can expect to be paid by your customers in, say, three months' time, you need not sell a long-term stake in your company to raise more money; all you need is money for three months. This example shows the need for short-term money in manufacturing industry: industry often has to spend money to get production going before it will be paid on or after delivering the finished goods. In the meantime, production has to be financed.

Much the same can be said of farming. A farmer will be paid when he sells his crop, but a few months before that he has to buy seeds and fertilisers. In the meantime he has to find the money to finance these outlays until the time when he will be paid for his crops.

In trading, traders can normally expect credit from suppliers when they buy goods for resale, but sometimes a trader has to pay his suppliers before he gets money from his customers after selling the goods. Again, this leads to a need for short-term finance. And then, there is the government: tax revenues are normally not spread evenly over the year, so the situation may arise that the government has to spend money now while the next important tax payment date is still a month away. In such a case, the government will have to borrow money for one month.

These examples indicate that many sectors of the economy have a demand for short-term money.

B
THE NEED FOR LONG-TERM MONEY

In addition to needing short-term money, companies and others often have a need for long-term money. If investment in fixed assets like machinery exceeds the amount generated from operations (see the section on source and application of funds statements), the excess has to be attracted from outside the business. This time, however, short-term money will not do. If a manufacturer or a farmer wants to buy a new machine, or an airline needs a new aeroplane, they will not be able to repay that money in a few months' time. Fixed assets, therefore, should be financed either from funds generated by the business itself or from long-term money raised outside the business. Such long-term money can either take the form of long-term loans (like long-term bank loans, or debenture issues), or the company can raise money by selling more shares. In Britain and most other European countries such new shares are usually offered to the existing shareholders first by a process known as a **rights issue;** this gives the existing shareholders the possibility of maintaining their stake in the company at the same level if they so wish. In North America, the new shares are sold in the stock market to whoever wants to buy them, although the existing shareholders have the right to set a limit to the total number of shares that may be issued.

Having said that companies and others may have a need of both short-term and long-term money

(generally speaking, the former is used to finance current assets and the latter is used to finance fixed assets), the logical next question to ask is: where is this money to come from?

C
PROVIDERS OF MONEY

At any time, there are some people and organisations in the economy who spend less than they earn (that is, they save), and others who spend more than they earn. Among the former are individuals who save from income, companies whose funds generated from operations exceed their applications of funds, and governments who run budget surpluses. Among the latter are individuals who buy a house, companies which invest heavily in new equipment, or governments which have a budget deficit. The personal sector (private individuals as a group) usually spends less than it earns while the business sector spends more than it earns. Government can be in either category, depending on whether it has a budget surplus or deficit.

Obviously, those who want to spend more than they earn can only buy their houses or equipment if they can attract the necessary finance—which ultimately has to come from those people or organisations who spend less than they earn. We can say therefore that it is necessary for the smooth functioning of the economy that funds be channelled from those who spend less than they earn to those who spend more than they earn.

? Which of these categories do you fall into, as an individual? Whichever it is, spend a moment thinking of the ways in which surplus funds are channelled from you to others, or to you from others, before reading on.

D
FINANCIAL INTERMEDIARIES

Usually, the channelling of funds described in the previous section is done through a variety of financial intermediaries. For example, an individual who saves can deposit his savings in a building society, which channels this money to housebuyers who want to spend more money than they have, in the form of mortgages. Banks also accept deposits and lend most of this money to industry and commerce. And then, savers can invest their savings in debentures, company shares or government securities; such investment will normally be done through the Stock Exchange.

Insurance companies also play a role in this process. Claims can only arise after premiums have been paid, and in the meantime the money can be invested. As we have seen earlier (see sections 5G and 5H), insurance companies are important investors in the capital markets, buying large amounts of company shares and interest-bearing securities and thereby financing other people's businesses.

We can summarise all this by saying that at any time some units in the economy spend less than they earn, while others spend more than they earn. If the economy is to function smoothly, the savings of the former must be channelled to the latter, and this channelling of savings is normally done through financial intermediaries like banks, building societies, insurance companies, the Stock Exchange, and others.

E
SOURCES AND USES OF CAPITAL FUNDS OF INDUSTRIAL AND COMMERCIAL COMPANIES IN THE UK

Let us now look at the amounts involved. The table below shows the main sources and uses of funds in the UK business sector for a number of years. In 1988, for example, industry and commerce invested a total of £76.9bn in a variety of assets. The most important single item among the uses of funds is investment in fixed assets in the UK; other items are current assets like stocks and liquid assets, as well as investment in other British companies and investment overseas.

How did the business sector get those £76.9bn? Well, £40.3bn were generated from the business sector's own operations, largely by means of retained profits and depreciation (see section 13D). Most of the rest was borrowed from financial institutions (mainly banks), though security issues and investment inflows from overseas also play a part. Logically, the total of the sources must be equal to the total of the uses. After all, every pound received must be used somehow (if only to increase liquid assets), and every pound used must have come from somewhere. However, nobody can ever keep track of all the money flowing into and out of the entire business sector. For this reason, the statistically recorded sources and uses often do not add up to the same total. In this case, an 'errors and omissions' item is brought into the statistics to make sources and uses equal again.

Sources and uses of capital funds of industrial and commercial companies in the UK (£ bn)

	1984	1985	1986	1987	1988
Uses of funds					
Investment in fixed assets in the UK	19.6	24.9	26.7	32.3	40.3
Increase in value of stocks	5.4	2.4	2.5	5.8	9.4
Investment in UK company securities	4.0	3.2	2.4	2.7	10.4
Investment overseas	5.8	6.2	4.2	19.6	10.1
Increase in liquid assets	2.2	4.8	10.6	8.9	5.3
Other items	0.3	0.5	0.7	0.6	1.4
	37.3	42.0	47.1	69.9	76.9
Sources of funds					
Generated from operations	30.1	32.1	27.9	38.7	40.3
Borrowings from financial institutions (mainly banking)	7.7	8.3	10.5	14.8	35.1
Securities issued in the UK	1.4	4.3	6.1	13.9	6.0
Overseas	-2.8	0.5	4.1	6.0	5.6
Other items	0.4	0.8	0.6	0.6	1.2
	36.8	46.0	49.2	74.0	88.2
Errors and omissions	0.5	-4.0	-2.1	-4.1	-11.3
	37.3	42.0	47.1	69.9	76.9

Source : CSO Financial Statistics, December 1989

The table also shows that reliance on bank borrowing increased sharply during the 1980s. In 1984, funds generated from operations amounted to about 80% of all funds used, whereas in 1988 that percentage was down to little more than 50%, with the balance coming largely from the banks.

15

SELF-ASSESSMENT QUESTIONS

1. What do businesses need short-term money for?

   To enable them to pay the costs of production prior to them receiving payment for their final product — 1/1

2. What do businesses need long-term money for?

   For the purchase of fixed assets — 1/1

3. Who are the ultimate providers of money used by businesses?

   the public, who spend less than they earn. i.e. savers — Owners + Lenders — 1/2

4. What role do financial intermediaries play in channelling funds to businesses?

   They use depositors savings + invest where they feel suitable — 1/1

5. In what way do insurance companies contribute to financing business activities?

   Ins Cos invest prem income in short term market prior to paying claims — 1/1

6. Give examples of financial intermediaries.

   *Bank
   Building Society
   Stock broker* — 1/1

7. What are the two main sources of finance for businesses in the UK?

1/1

① funds generated from operation (retained profit)

② Borrowing

8. How has the relative importance of the two main sources of finance for UK businesses changed during the last few years?

Borrowings increased rapidly ✗

6½
8

ANSWERS TO SELF-ASSESSMENT QUESTIONS APPEAR OVERLEAF

15

ANSWERS TO SELF-ASSESSMENT QUESTIONS

1. Short-term money is used to finance current assets, like stock or debtors.

2. Long-term money is used to finance fixed assets, like buildings or machinery.

3. Owners and lenders provide the money.

4. The channelling of funds from savers to users is normally done via financial intermediaries. For example, a saver may deposit his savings with a bank which then lends the money to a company that wants to buy new machinery.

5. Since claims can occur only after premiums have been paid, insurance companies have money for investment. The invest most of this money in interest-bearing securities, company shares and property, thus financing the activities of industry and commerce as well as government.

6. These include banks, building societies, insurance companies, the stock exchange, unit trusts, and so on.

7. These are funds generated from operations, and borrowing from banks.

8. Bank borrowing has increased more rapidly than have funds generated from operations, so relatively speaking the importance of bank borrowing has increased and that of funds generated from operations has decreased.

PART IV
THE LEGAL ENVIRONMENT

16

TRADING ORGANISATIONS

A   The different kinds of trading organisation

B   Corporations

C   Legal requirements of a registered company

LEARNING OBJECTIVES

After studying this chapter, you should be able to:

▷ name the different kinds of trading organisation found in Great Britain, and outline the characteristics of each;

▷ identify how a registered company differs from a partnership;

▷ outline the different kinds of registered company, and the characteristics of each;

▷ explain the procedures which are involved in forming a company and beginning to trade;

▷ give details of the documents which a company must file with the Registrar of Companies;

▷ explain how one may become a member of a company.

A

THE DIFFERENT KINDS OF TRADING ORGANISATION

The various kinds of trading organisations found in Great Britain can be listed as follows:

► sole traders;

► partnerships and other unincorporated associations;

► corporations;

► specialised types of business organisation.

A1   SOLE TRADERS

This term is used to describe natural persons engaged in business on their own, without being associated with others. A sole trader is an unincorporated trading organisation.

In principle, every person in England is free to engage in any kind of business activity. The system, adopted in many Continental countries, of registration of merchants or certain other classes of businessmen in a commercial register is, in general, unknown to English law. A sole trader may carry on business under a name other than his real name: this other name is known as a business name.

A2   PARTNERSHIPS AND OTHER UNINCORPORATED ASSOCIATIONS

The business associations that fall under this heading have one feature in common: **they do not have legal personality.** That is, they are not legal entities distinct and separate from the persons of which they consist. Associations which have legal personality are called corporations or bodies corporate.

A2A Ordinary partnerships

A partnership is defined by the **Partnership Act 1890** s.1 as 'the relation existing between two or more persons carrying on a business in common with a view of profit'.

In English law, the essential distinction between the partnership and the company is that the former has no legal personality, but the latter is a body corporate. Many important consequences flow from this fundamental distinction, as will be explained later.

There are two types of partnership: the ordinary partnership, which is governed by the Partnership Act 1890, and the limited partnership formed under the Limited Partnership Act 1907.

Since an English partnership is not a legal person, the partners themselves are the joint owners of the partnership property and are personally liable for the debts and liabilities of the firm.

Unless they are limited partners in a limited partnership, their personal liability is unlimited. Unless they have made other arrangements, their shares in the partnership are not transferable, and each of them is an agent of the others and, on behalf of the partnership, may make contracts, undertake obligations and dispose of partnership property in the ordinary course of the partnership business.

A2B Limited partnerships

The limited partnership, as admitted by the **Limited Partnership Act 1907,** is an importation from abroad; it is an adaptation of the type of business organisation known in French law as *societé en commandité* and admitted by most Continental legal systems. In Great Britain the limited partnership never took root and, indeed, offered little attraction, because in the same year in which it was introduced businessmen were offered the alternative of forming or joining a private company, with all the advantages and immunities conferred by the law on such companies.

In a limited partnership there must be one or more partners with unlimited liability. These partners are called 'general partners'; the other partners are the 'limited partners'. The latter contribute to the partnership assets a specified amount in money or money's worth, and enjoy immunity from liability beyond the amount so contributed. It is, however, an essential condition of this immunity that a limited partner shall not take part in the management of the business, and he is to have no power to bind the firm. He may inspect the books and may advise (that is, consult with the other partners as to the state and prospects of the business) but he must not go beyond this. If he does, even if through ignorance of the law, or inadvertently, or at the urgent request of the general partners, he forfeits his immunity from liability.

A2C Unincorporated companies

This type of business association made its first appearance in the seventeenth century and was much used in the eighteenth and the first half of the nineteenth centuries, when it developed into the so-called 'deed of settlement' company. The promoters of this kind of company attempted, by using the devices of contract and trust, to endow the unincorporated company with many of the privileges and advantages normally reserved to corporations without obtaining the status of a corporation, which in those days could only be obtained by royal charter or special Act of Parliament. In law, the unincorporated company has always been regarded as a large partnership with some special features, one of them being the transferability of its shares. Today the role of the unincorporated company is insignificant.

A2D Syndicates and mutual associations

While the characteristic feature of the partnership and the unincorporated company is that the members carry on business jointly, it may happen that persons combine without accepting joint liability to third parties; they may indicate in their contracts with them that their liability shall be several, not joint, and shall be restricted to a stated amount.

This type of association, which is neither a partnership nor an incorporated company, is met sometimes in insurance and banking. Syndicates of underwriters at Lloyd's and outside Lloyd's and some mutual assurance associations fall within this category. Further, banks providing finance by means of syndicated loans form syndicates.

In insurance, when underwriters' syndicates issue policies, which they do through managers or agents, it is customary to indicate on them the percentage of the total risk for which each underwriter holds himself responsible. It has been held that neither underwriters' syndicates nor mutual assurance clubs are partnerships and that, consequently, a member is not liable to a contracting party for a defaulting member's share.

B

CORPORATIONS

A corporation is an artificial person recognised by the law, with an entity apart from its members, for the purpose of preserving in perpetual succession rights which would fail if vested in a natural person.

B1   COMPANIES

A company is one of many kinds of corporation. Companies registered under the Companies Acts are the most numerous and important class of company. Such a company must particularly be distinguished from:

A partnership

(i) A firm is not a legal person distinct from the partners who compose the firm; a company is a different person altogether from its members. This is illustrated by the famous case of *Saloman v. Saloman & Co. Ltd (1897)*. S sold his business to a company which he formed. There were seven members: S with 20,000 fully paid shares, and members of his family with one share each. No other shares were issued. S also had, as part of the purchase price of the business, £10,000 in debentures; that is, he lent £10,000 to the company on mortgage. The company was later wound up, the assets amounting to £6,000 only, out of which it was necessary to pay £10,000 which was due to S

and secured by debentures, and £7,000 due to unsecured creditors. The latter contended that as the company was really the same person as S he could not owe money to himself, and they should be paid first. But the House of Lords held that the company was quite distinct from S, and that the £6,000 should be applied in part-payment of his secured debt.

(ii) A partner cannot transfer his share without the other partners' consent; shares in limited companies are normally freely transferable.

(iii) A partner is an agent of the firm; a shareholder is not an agent of the company.

(iv) Partners' liability is unlimited, except in the case of a limited partnership (where some, though not all, of the partners have limited liability); the liability of a shareholder may be limited by shares or by guarantee.

(v) The maximum number of members of a partnership is limited to 20 (ten in the case of a banking partnership), whereas there is no limit in the case of a company. The limitation on the size of membership dates from the **Companies Act 1862,** and was intended to avoid the difficulties which had been experienced by the public in dealing with large trading associations with a fluctuating membership. The result of the limitation was to compel business associations with numbers in excess of the statutory limit to organise themselves as companies subject to statutory control. Some professions have found this limitation irritating in practice and in their case the law has now been amended to allow larger partnerships. Under the **Companies Act 1985,** as amended by the **Companies Act 1989:**

► banking partnerships may have a maximum of 20 members, against ten previously;

► unlimited membership is available to partnerships of solicitors, accountants, members of a recognised stock exchange, or to other bodies which may be specified by the Department of Trade and Industry.

The Limited Partnership Act 1907 is similarly modified as regards partnerships of solicitors, accountants and stock-brokers, but not bankers.

A company incorporated by Royal Charter or by special Act of Parliament

A **chartered company** has all the powers of an ordinary individual. The powers of a **statutory company** are limited by the special Act creating it. The powers of a company registered under the Companies Acts are limited by its memorandum of association (see section C4).

B2   TYPES OF REGISTERED COMPANY

Registered companies may be divided into:-

▶ **Unlimited liability companies.** The liability of members is not limited at all. These companies are not numerous. Such a company may have share capital, and must have a memorandum and articles of association. Several land investment companies are of this type, though the total number is very small.

A company registered as unlimited may be re-registered as limited. Similarly, a company registered as limited may be re-registered as unlimited. An unlimited company is exempted from the requirement to annex accounts to the annual return, subject to certain conditions.

▶ **Companies limited by guarantee.** Each member undertakes to be liable to pay the company's debts up to a certain amount in the event of a winding-up; an example is a golf club where no working capital is required on formation.

▶ **Companies limited by shares.** These companies, which comprise the vast majority of trading companies, are the subject of the remaining sections of this chapter.

B2A   Public and private companies

A second way of dividing registered companies is the division into public companies and private companies.

Before 1980, private companies were defined by reference to certain restrictive provisions contained in their articles of association, and a public company was any company whose articles did not contain those provisions. The pendulum has now swung so that since 1980 it is the public company which is specifically defined and the private company which is the residual category.

A public company is defined as any company:

▶ which is limited by shares (or limited by guarantee and has a share capital);

▶ whose memorandum states that the company is to be public;

▶ whose name ends with the words 'public limited company' (plc); and

▶ which has complied with the registration provisions of the **Companies Act 1985** as amended.

In some cases, companies which were public companies before the legislation was passed have not wished to meet the last of these requirements and have re-registered as private companies. Those companies that have chosen the new public company status have been attracted by the advantage that their members are generally able to freely transfer their shares, and any member of the public willing to purchase them may normally become a member. In the absence of a market place, with adequate flows of information to prospective sellers and buyers, the advantage of transferability would be less significant.

The market place for transactions in the shares (and debentures) of public companies is provided by the Stock Exchange. Public companies whose shares are dealt in and 'quoted' (or 'listed') on the Stock Exchange are commonly referred to as 'quoted public companies'. By no means all public companies are quoted companies. Those that are quoted have to meet certain strict requirements laid down by the Council of the Stock Exchange.

A private company is any company which is not a public company. While the former prohibition on the offering of shares to the public still applies, the other two requirements for a private company, which limited the number of members to 50 and required the articles to restrict the right to transfer shares, have been removed. Nevertheless, it is likely that where the private company is used as the vehicle for running a family business the right to transfer shares will still be restricted in order to

[handwritten note: Promoter is the person wishing to start a company. He can only make provisional contracts on its behalf and these must be confirmed by the company]

retain family control over the business.

? Think back over the information given so far in this chapter. What kind of trading organisation do you work for? Try to think of organisations you come into contact with in each (or most) of the categories outlined. Some will be obvious; others may take a minute or two to identify.

C
LEGAL REQUIREMENTS OF A REGISTERED COMPANY

There are several of these, which we will deal with individually in detail.

C1 FORMATION OF A COMPANY

[handwritten: done by promoter]

This requires a promoter, which is a term not of law but of business. A promoter is a person who undertakes to form a company with reference to a given object, and to set it going, and who takes the necessary steps to accomplish that purpose. People assisting in promotion, even if only in a subordinate position, may be held by the courts to be promoters and to have incurred the heavy responsibilities attaching to that position.

A promoter is not an agent or trustee for the company, as it has not yet come into existence, but he stands in a fiduciary relation towards it; he is a quasi-trustee. He is not permitted to make secret profits and must account for all profits made without the company's knowledge and consent. If he wishes to sell his own property to the company, he must furnish it with an independent board of directors or make a full disclosure to intended members. A promoter has no power to bind the company prior to its incorporation.

A company cannot make a binding contract before it is incorporated. A preliminary contract may be made between the vendor and a promoter professing to act on behalf of the company about to be formed. As the company does not exist, the promoter is not an agent and, therefore:

▶ the company, when it comes into existence, is not bound by the contract;

▶ the company cannot sue the vendor on the contract;

▶ the promoter is personally liable on the contract (unless it expressly excludes his liability), even if it is afterwards satisfied by the company;

▶ after incorporation, the company must enter into a fresh contract with the vendor; ratification of the promoter's contract is not sufficient.

Promoters are primarily liable for the preliminary expenses of formation. They cannot, in the absence of a contract made after incorporation, recover from the company, but where they are called upon to account for profits they may first of all deduct promotion expenses.

C2 REGISTRATION

The following documents must be filed with the Registrar of Companies:

▶ memorandum of association;
▶ articles of association;
▶ a statement as to directors, secretary and registered office;
▶ statutory declaration that the requirements of the Act have been complied with.

The Registrar enters the company on the Register and issues a certificate of incorporation. The company is then in existence, but if it is a public company it cannot commence business until certain other formalities have been complied with.

The certificate of incorporation is conclusive evidence of the company's existence, and conclusive evidence that the requirements of the Act as to registration have been complied with.

C3 COMMENCEMENT OF BUSINESS

Commencement of business is subject to the following conditions:

▶ A private company may commence business on the issue of the certificate of incorporation.

▶ A public company cannot commence business until:

(i) shares up to the amount of the minimum subscription have been allotted (not applicable where there is no prospectus);

(ii) directors have taken up their qualification shares and paid on each the same amount as the public is liable to pay;

(iii) where necessary, permission has been applied for or obtained to deal on a stock exchange with shares or debentures of the company offered for public subscription, and no money is liable to be repaid in respect of such shares or debentures because of failure to obtain such permission;

(iv) a statutory declaration that these conditions have been complied with has been filed;

(v) listing particulars have been filed. These are full details of the company, which are available for public inspection before the public subscribe for shares. This applies if the company is obtaining a stock exchange listing.

When these conditions have been fulfilled, the Registrar will certify that the company is entitled to commence business, by issuing a Trading Certificate.

Contracts made by the company before it is entitled to commence business are provisional only, and are not binding on the company until that time. But this does not affect offers of shares or debentures and the receipt of money for these.

The following points concerning **minimum subscription** should be noted:

▶ Where a company offers shares to the public for subscription, the promoters must determine beforehand the minimum amount of capital they need to carry on business successfully. This amount is the minimum subscription, and

must be stated in the listing particulars.

▶ The minimum subscription must provide for the purchase price of any property to be acquired, preliminary expenses, underwriting commission, repayment of money borrowed for these purposes, and working capital.

▶ If not subscribed within 40 days of the issue of the listing particulars, all money received from applicants must be repaid, and if not repaid within 48 days after issue, the directors are personally liable to repay it with 5% interest.

▶ These provisions only apply to the first allotment of shares offered for public subscription, and do not apply to private companies.

C4 THE MEMORANDUM OF ASSOCIATION

The memorandum of association of a company limited by shares is the document which defines the constitution of the company, the scope of its intended objects and its general external relationship. Such a memorandum must contain the following six clauses.

C4A The name of the company

Any name may be chosen subject to the following restrictions:

(i) It must end with the words 'limited' or 'Public Limited Company' as appropriate. This condition may be dispensed with by licence of the Department of Trade and Industry in the case of certain kinds of cultural non-profit-making associations.

(ii) No company may be registered with a name which the Department of Trade and Industry considers 'undesirable'. Thus, names which resemble those of existing companies will not be permitted; nor will names such as 'royal', 'municipal', 'chartered', and 'co-operative', except in proper cases.

(iii) Under the **Companies Act 1985,** the Department of Trade and Industry can direct a company to change its name if, in the opinion of the Department, it gives so misleading an indication of the nature of its activities as to cause harm to the public. The company may appeal within three weeks of the direction.

The Registrar has power to refuse registration, and if a company is registered with a name resembling that of any existing company, the Department of Trade and Industry may within six months of registration order the name to be changed, or the company may voluntarily change it. In any event, a person prejudiced by registration of a name may take legal proceedings to restrain its use.

A change of name requires a special resolution.

The name must be shown outside the company's offices and on all letters, notices, cheques, orders, and similar documents. This ensures that anyone dealing with the company has notice of the members' limited liability.

C4B   The registered office

The memorandum must state whether this is to be in England, Wales or Scotland. This fixes the company's nationality, which cannot be altered without the consent of Parliament. The situation of the office may be changed within the country of registration by giving notice to the Registrar.

Every company must have a registered office on commencing business or within 14 days of incorporation, whichever is the earlier. Writs and other documents must be served at the office, and the register of members is kept there.

C4C   The objects of the company

The statement of the objects determines the powers of the company. The company cannot do anything outside the powers given in the memorandum. Anything so done is said to be ultra vires and is void. It cannot be made valid even if every member assents.

The powers in the memorandum are not strictly construed, however, and the company may do anything reasonably incidental to them. For example, a company formed to run a railway was permitted to let as workshops arches upon which the railway had been erected.

It must be noted that if the act was outside the powers of the directors or the articles only, the shareholders could validate it by ratification or by alteration of the articles respectively.

Powers not expressly mentioned may be implied if warranted by the company's constitution; for example a trading company has implied power to borrow.

The objects must not be illegal; for example in restraint of trade, or contrary to the Companies Acts.

The objects clause may be altered by special resolution to enable the company to:

▶ carry on business more economically or efficiently;

▶ attain its main purpose by new or improved means;

▶ enlarge or change the local area of its operation;

▶ carry on some other business which may be conveniently combined with its own;

▶ restrict or abandon any of its objects;

▶ sell or dispose of the whole or part of its undertaking;

▶ amalgamate with another company.

C4D   The limitation of liability.

The mere statement 'the liability of members is limited' is usually inserted. This means 'limited by shares', and no member can be called upon to pay more than the nominal amount of his shares which remains unpaid. For example, a company might issue £1 nominal shares, 30 pence partly paid. A member's liability would then be limited to 70 pence per share. Thus, if his shares are fully paid, his liability is nil.

C4E   The capital clause

This states the amount of nominal capital, the

number of shares, and the amount of each. There is no legal limit to the amount of capital, or the amount of each share. The amount of capital depends on the cost of starting the business and providing sufficient working capital.

The shares may be divided into two classes (such as ordinary and preference) or more, with various rights and conditions attached to each. Rights of preference shareholders are usually stated in the articles only, but may be stated in the memorandum in order to give them additional security.

If the rights are set out in the memorandum and are unalterably attached to a particular type of share, they cannot be altered except by virtue of a scheme sanctioned by the court under the Companies Act 1985. If the memorandum provides a method of alteration, that method must be used.

C4F Association clause and subscription.

In the association clause, the subscribers declare that they wish to be formed into a company, and agree to take shares. This clause is followed by a tabular form containing the names, addresses and descriptions of the subscribers, together with the number of shares taken by each.

There must be at least two subscribers, who must each subscribe for at least one share. The signature must be attested by a witness.

Anyone may subscribe; this includes minors, corporations, and aliens.

The duties of the subscribers are:

▶ to pay for the shares for which they have subscribed;

▶ to sign the articles of association;

▶ to appoint the first directors (if not named in the articles);

▶ usually, to act as directors until such appointment.

? Before going any further, make sure that you can name the six clauses contained

in the memorandum, and that you remember the basic ingredients of each. Checking these at this stage should help you to keep them separate, in your mind, from the articles of association, which we are about to cover.

C5 THE ARTICLES OF ASSOCIATION

The articles are the rules of the company relating to internal management. Where there are no separate articles, the form set out in the Companies (Tables A to F) Regulations 1985 and called Table A is implied and becomes the company's articles. This may be adopted in part only if appropriate.

The articles must be printed, divided into numbered paragraphs, signed by the subscribers to the memorandum, and attested.

The articles are subject to the memorandum and cannot give powers not given by the memorandum. Any articles that contain anything illegal or ultra vires the company are inoperative, and anything done thereunder is void and incapable of ratification. But where the memorandum contains an ambiguity, the articles may be looked at to explain it.

The articles usually deal with (i) definitions (ii) exclusion or modification of Table A (iii) preliminary contracts (iv) shares and transfers (v) calls (vi) increase and reduction of capital (vii) meetings (viii) directors (ix) dividends (x) accounts (xi) audit (xii) notices (xiii) winding-up (xiv) registers.

The articles and any new regulations bind the company and the members as if they had been signed and sealed by each member and contained covenants by each member to observe them. From this it follows that:

▶ each member is bound to the company;

▶ the company is bound to the members as members;

Thus, a member is entitled to insist on rights given to him by the articles (for example, a right to certain dividends), but where the rights are not given to him as a member he cannot enforce them.

▶ neither company nor members are bound to outsiders;

▶ members are bound to each other.

There is no contract in terms between the individual members, although the articles regulate their rights inter se. It is for the company, not an individual shareholder, apart from exceptional cases, to sue for breach of the articles.

The articles can be altered by special resolution. The company may freely alter the articles provided that:

▶ altered articles are not illegal or *ultra vires*;

▶ a member's liability is not increased without his written consent;

▶ the alteration does not constitute a fraud on the minority, or sacrifice the rights or interest of the minority, unless clearly for the company's benefit.

Thus it could be said that, if it would be to the advantage of members of the company collectively, an alteration of the articles operating retrospectively is permissible.

A company cannot deprive itself of the power to alter its articles. This is so even if the alteration causes a breach of contract with third parties; the remedy of the latter is damages for breach of contract and not an injunction to restrain the alteration.

The memorandum and articles are registered with the Registrar of Companies, and may be inspected by anyone. Any person dealing with the company is deemed to have notice of their contents, and therefore of the powers of the company and the directors, and he must make sure that the proposed dealing is not inconsistent with these. Thus,

if the articles provide that cheques must be signed by two directors, he must see that a cheque is so signed, otherwise he cannot claim under it.

C6   MEMBERSHIP OF A COMPANY

The right to be a member of a company is generally open to all persons, natural or legal. Thus company X may hold shares in company Y. Indeed, if company X holds more than half of the 'equity share capital' of company Y, then company Y is a **subsidiary** of company X, its **holding company.** (Equity share capital will generally be the company's issued ordinary shares.) In this case, one restriction upon membership of a company would be that company Y could not hold shares in company X, since the Companies Acts provide that a subsidiary may not be a member of its holding company. Although it was a long-established rule that no company could purchase its own shares or be a member of itself, this policy has been modified to allow greater freedom, particularly to private companies, to buy back their shares. Similar relaxation has been granted in respect of a company which provides financial assistance to third parties to buy its own shares.

There are three ways in which a person may become a member of a company:

▶ by subscribing to a memorandum of association;

▶ by agreeing, as a director, to take and pay for any shares which under the articles any director is required to hold; and

▶ by agreeing to become a member and by having his name entered in the register of members.

By far the most usual way of becoming a member is the last method.

16

SELF-ASSESSMENT QUESTIONS

1. Define a partnership

   two or more sole traders/ individuals comming together to form a business (cont all the capital + accept all the loss/profit)

2. What is a limited partner?

   One who
   (a) plays no part in running of Co
   (b) liability is limited to a specified amount

3. Define a public company.

   One whose shares are available for any body, natural or legal, to buy

   limited by share name ends Plc mem Share pub

4. What is a promoter?

   Somebody who initiates the formation of a registered Co.

5. What documents must a private company file with the Registrar of Companies before it can commence business?

   Articles of Assoc
   Memorand of Assoc
   Dec Regs complied with

6. What six clauses must a memorandum of association contain?

   Name Reg Office Objectives
   Capital Clause
   Subscription limits on liab

7. What are the articles of association of a company?

   The Internal management of company rules reg. Shares/directors/audit/winding up

   5·75
   7

16

ANSWERS TO SELF-ASSESSMENT QUESTIONS

1. A partnership is the relation existing between two or more persons carrying on a business in common with a view of profit.

2. A limited partner is a partner in a limited partnership (which must contain at least one general partner) who contributes a specified amount to the partnership assets. He enjoys immunity from liability beyond the amount so contributed but, in return, is prevented from taking part in the management of the business.

3. A public company is any company:

   ► which is limited by shares (or limited by guarantee and has a share capital);
   ► whose memorandum states that the company is to be public;
   ► whose name ends with the words 'public limited company';
   ► which has complied with the registration provisions of the Companies Act 1985, as amended.

4. A promoter is a person who undertakes to form a company with reference to a given object and to set it going, and who takes the necessary steps to accomplish that purpose.

5. A private company file the following documents with the Registrar of Companies:

   ► memorandum of association;
   ► articles of association;
   ► a statement as to directors, secretary and registered office;
   ► a statutory declaration that the requirements of the Companies Act have been complied with.

6. The memorandum of association must contain the following clauses:

   (i)   name;
   (ii) registered office;
   (iii) objects;
   (iv) limitation of liability:
   (v)   capital clause;
   (vi) association and subscription.

7. The articles of association are the rules of a company relating to internal management.

17

COMPANY MANAGEMENT

A   Internal management

B   Directors

C   Company secretary

D   Chairman

E   Takeovers

LEARNING OBJECTIVES

After studying this chapter, you should be able to:

▷ explain the management structure of a company;

▷ explain how directors of a company may take up and vacate office;

▷ detail the regulations affecting directors, their powers and their interests;

▷ explain the ways in which directors may be liable;

▷ explain the differing roles of the company secretary and chairman;

▷ explain how a take-over of a company may be effected.

A
INTERNAL MANAGEMENT

In the case of a sole trader, a partnership or a private company, ownership of the business is not divorced from the management function and the owners will not need to exert their control over a separate management team. This is not the situation in the case of a large public company, the shareholders of which will be concerned that their interests are protected. To ensure that management does not disregard the interests of shareholders, the internal structure of a company will consist of two organs: a board of directors and a meeting of shareholders.

A1   BOARD OF DIRECTORS

The board of directors of a company will be a comparatively small group of people who have been appointed directors by the general meeting. Under the articles of association of the company, the directors, as a board, will usually be given extensive powers, including control of the day-to-day management of the company. The board, in turn, may delegate all or any of these powers to one of themselves as managing director.

The division of responsibility for the control of management between the board and the general meeting will be determined largely by the articles. Where the board is given powers under the articles, the general meeting cannot interfere with the board's exercise of those powers. However, the general meeting will be able to exert some control over the board's use of its powers by removing directors from office. The general meeting can also act in areas reserved for the board if the directors are in deadlock or their number has fallen below that required for a quorum at board meetings. Moreover, if the directors exceed their powers, or use them for improper purposes, the general meeting may decide not to ratify their actions.

A2   MEETINGS OF SHAREHOLDERS

By exercising their rights to attend and vote at general meetings, shareholders as a body may exert some control over the running of their company.

The **Companies Acts** lay down various provisions for the calling, holding and conduct of general meetings. General meetings can be broadly classified as:

► annual general meetings (AGM); and
► extraordinary general meetings (EGM).

The **annual general meeting** must be held every calendar year, with an interval of not more than 15 months between one AGM and the next. This gives the shareholders the opportunity to question the directors on the company's performance each year. Twenty-one days' notice in writing must be given of an AGM to every member, specifying the place, date and hour of the meeting and, if there is to be any special business, the general nature of that business.

Extraordinary general meetings are any general meetings of a company other than an annual general meeting. The calling of such meetings will depend upon the articles. Most provide that the directors may convene an EGM whenever they think fit. Normally, the articles require that they must call an EGM if asked to do so by the holders of not less than one tenth of the paid-up capital of the company carrying voting rights. Failure by the directors to do so within 21 days gives those asking for the meeting the right to convene it themselves. Not less than 14 days' notice in writing must be given of an EGM, unless a special resolution is to be proposed, in which case at least 21 'days' notice must be given. Notice of the business to be conducted must give the member such information as will allow him to make up his mind whether to attend or not and, at the same time, to appreciate the consequences if he decides not to go.

A2A   Resolutions

A company in general meeting acts by the passing of resolutions of which due notice has been given

to the members. There are three types of resolution:

► the ordinary resolution;
► the extraordinary resolution; and
► the special resolution.

An ordinary resolution is a resolution passed by a simple majority of the members present and voting (in person or by proxy) at the meeting.

An extraordinary resolution is defined in the 1985 Act as a resolution passed by at least a three fourths majority of the votes of the members present and voting (in person or by proxy) at the meeting.

A special resolution is defined as a resolution passed by at least a three fourths majority of the votes of the members present and voting (in person or by proxy) at a meeting of which at least 21 days' notice has been given.

The length of notice required for ordinary or extraordinary resolutions will depend on the kind of meeting being held.

In the absence of any contrary provision in the Companies Act 1985, or in the memorandum or articles, a company will act by ordinary resolution (for example on an increase of capital). However, special resolutions are required for any major constitutional change such as alteration of memorandum or articles. Extraordinary resolutions are less common, and are normally used where speed is essential, as in winding-up proceedings. A printed copy of special and extraordinary resolutions must be registered with the Registrar of Companies within 15 days of their being passed.

B
DIRECTORS

Directors need not necessarily be called 'directors' (there are many alternatives, such as 'managing committee'), but the provisions of the 1985 Act apply to anyone in the position of director. They are agents for the company and to some extent trustees.

B1 AGENTS

The general principles of the law of principal and agent apply to their relationship with the company. When they make contracts for the company, they are not personally liable, (except where an agent would be liable,) as where they contract in their own names. Where they contract in their own names but really on behalf of the company, the other party may, on discovering the real principal, sue either the directors or the company. Where the directors contract beyond their powers but within those of the company, the company may ratify the contract.

B2 TRUSTEES

Directors are not in the same position as trustees of a marriage settlement or a will, and the strict rules applicable to such trustees do not apply in all respects to directors, but in some cases they are trustees for the company. They are trustees of the power of approving transfer, allotting shares, declaring shares forfeited, and making calls. They are trustees of the company's assets under their control, and may be liable for breach of trust.

B3 APPOINTMENT OF DIRECTORS

The first directors are usually named in the articles. Such appointment is invalid unless each proposed director has signed and delivered to the Registrar a consent to act, and has:

▶ signed the memorandum for his qualification shares (those shares which the articles require directors to hold; see below), if any;

▶ taken up and paid or agreed to pay for them;

▶ filed with the Registrar a signed undertaking to take up and pay for them; or

▶ filed with the Registrar a statutory declaration that qualification shares are registered in his name.

Where the articles do not appoint the first directors, they usually provide that the directors may be appointed by the subscribers to the memoran-

dum. Unless the articles otherwise provide, such appointment must be made either by writing signed by all the subscribers, or by the majority at a meeting of subscribers.

Where there is no provision in the articles for appointment of the first directors, they may be appointed by the company in general meeting, subject to certain restrictions. The articles may empower the vendor or another outsider to appoint one or more directors. The articles usually specify the way in which subsequent appointments are to be made, for example by the company in general meeting, or by continuing directors.

A register containing names and former names, address, nationality, business or occupation of each director, particulars of other directorships, and date of birth for those over the normal age limit of 70, must be kept at the registered office. Where the director is a corporation, the corporate name and the address of its registered office must be entered in the register, which is to be open to inspection by members free, and to others for a fee not exceeding five pence. A return containing the above particulars must be made to the Registrar within 14 days of appointment of the first directors or of any change in the register.

No share qualification is required by the law, but the articles may require it. Any share qualification must be disclosed in the listing particulars, and the company (unless a private company) cannot commence business until the directors have taken up their qualification shares and paid on them the same proportion as the public have had to pay.

The qualification must be obtained within two months of appointment, or any shorter time fixed by the articles. The office of director is vacated if the qualification is not obtained within the prescribed time, or if the director at any time afterwards ceases to hold the qualification.

Although normally the articles specify holding of shares by the director 'in his own right', the director may nevertheless hold them as trustee unless the articles expressly forbid this. As long as the company may safely deal with the director as owner of the shares, the requirement of holding in his own right is satisfied.

A director taking his qualification shares as a present from the promoter(s) is guilty of a breach of trust and must account to the company for any damages sustained thereby. Although directors may be acting invalidly because of defective appointment or qualification, the irregularity does not affect third parties dealing with the company through the directors, provided that such third parties had no notice of the irregularity.

B4 VACATION OF OFFICE

A director may vacate office by:

▶ Disqualification as provided by the articles, for example by holding another office of profit under the company.

▶ Failure to take or keep qualification shares.

▶ Resignation. The articles may provide for this; in other cases, a director can resign on reasonable notice, but his resignation need not be accepted. Once accepted, a resignation is irrevocable. A verbal resignation accepted by a general meeting is effective, although the articles provide that writing is necessary.

▶ Removal by the company. Power is usually given by the articles, and the 1985 Act provides that a director may always be removed by ordinary resolution.

▶ Retirement by rotation, as provided by the articles.

▶ Death or mental illness.

▶ Bankruptcy.

▶ Assignment of office.

▶ Retirement on attaining the age limit. The 1985 Act provides that a director must retire at seventy, but this limit may be varied by the company.

▶ Disqualification by court order. The **Company Directors Disqualification Act 1985** and the **Insolvency Act 1986** give the court power to restrain certain persons from managing companies.

The powers of directors cease on appointment of a liquidator.

B5 REMUNERATION

There is no right to remuneration, unless the articles so provide. Table A (see section 16C5) gives the company power to fix remuneration in general meeting. Provisions as to remuneration must be disclosed in the listing particulars. The aggregate amount of directors' emoluments (including emoluments from subsidiary companies) must be stated in the accounts, distinguishing fees as directors, other emoluments, pensions and compensation for loss of office.

In addition, the following details in respect of directors' emoluments are required by the 1985 Act:

▶ emoluments of chairman (unless his duties were wholly or mainly outside the United Kingdom);

▶ number of directors whose emoluments fall in any of the following brackets:

(i) receiving nil to £5,000 per annum;

(ii) receiving £5,000 to £10,000 per annum and upwards in brackets of £5,000 per annum unless their duties as directors were wholly or mainly discharged outside the United Kingdom;

(iii) also emoluments of highest paid director where not the chairman, unless his duties as director were wholly or mainly discharged outside the United Kingdom;

▶ number of directors who have waived rights to receive emoluments; also the aggregate amount so waived.

Emoluments under these three headings **exclude** contributions paid under any pension scheme. Where a company is neither a holding company nor a subsidiary, it is exempted from showing details where the total of the directors' emoluments does not exceed £60,000.

Where remuneration is provided for, it is a debt due from the company and may be sued for, and paid out of capital if there are no profits. Travelling and other expenses cannot be paid in addition to the remuneration, unless expressly provided.

Disclosure under the **Companies Act 1985** is also required of emoluments of employees receiving more than £30,000 per annum, excluding pension scheme contributions, stating the number of employees whose emoluments fall in each bracket of scale in multiples of £5,000 commencing at £30,000. Employees working outside the United Kingdom are excluded.

Despite decisions to the contrary, it appears that a director may always recover a proportionate share of remuneration in the absence of a contrary provision, if he vacates office before the end of a current year. Compensation for loss of office may not be paid unless full particulars of the proposed payment are disclosed to and approved by the members of the company.

B6 POWERS OF DIRECTORS

These are generally defined in the articles, which usually give the directors powers of management and all powers not required, by statute or the articles, to be exercised by the company in general meeting. Directors are in a fiduciary position and must exercise their powers for the benefit of the company. Where they do some act outside their powers but not *ultra vires* the company, the shareholders may ratify the act.

The directors must act at a duly summoned board meeting, unless the articles permit decisions to be made informally.

Because of conflicting interests, a director cannot contract or have any interest in a contract with the company, except a contract to take shares or debentures. A director who is in any way interested in a contract or proposed contract with the company is under a statutory duty to declare the nature of his interest. But the articles may provide that a director may contract upon full disclosure of his interest to the board; in such a case he is usually prohibited from voting at a board meeting, but may vote at a shareholders' meeting. Where a contract is made contrary to the provisions of the Act or of the articles as stated above, it is voidable irrespective of fairness or unfairness, and the com-

pany may have it set aside and may sue the director for damages for breach of duty.

B7 DIRECTORS' INTERESTS

The **Companies Act 1985** requires that all directors of a company shall declare all interests in any type of share or debenture of the company or group, whether held by themselves or their family. All changes in their interests must also be disclosed within 14 days. A properly indexed register must be kept of the information provided, with entries for each director; entries are to be made within three days of receipt of the details.

The register is to be open to any person at the company's registered office or wherever the register of members is kept, and is to be available to anyone attending the annual general meeting.

Q Which document establishes the whereabouts of the registered office? Briefly, what regulations are there concerning setting up the office?

A The office's whereabouts is fixed by the memorandum of association. The regulations, should you need to check them, are mentioned in section 16C4B.

A broad definition is given in the Act of what is meant by 'interested in shares and debentures of a company'. Among other matters, an interest is to 'be construed so as not to exclude any interest on the ground of its remoteness or manner in which it arises'.

Every company must have available to members copies of each director's current service contract with the company. If this information is not in writing, a memorandum setting out the terms of the contract is required. These agreements are to be available for inspection free of charge during business hours, at the registered office of the company.

A director of a company is guilty of an offence if he (or a spouse or minor children) purchases an option to buy or sell the right to quoted shares or debentures of the company, or of companies in its group. However, the buying of a right to subscribe for shares in or debentures of a company, and the purchase of debentures carrying a subscription or conversion option, are allowed.

Anyone (including a director) who holds or subsequently acquires an interest in three per cent or more of the nominal value of the voting share capital of a quoted company must disclose within 14 days the amount of his interest to the company. The interpretation of the term 'interest' is the same as that indicated for disclosure of directors' interests, with the omission of the reference to debentures. The interests of a spouse and minor children are also omitted. The onus to make the disclosure is placed on the holder or purchaser of the interest. A properly indexed register of any interests must be kept at the place where the company's register of directors' interests is kept, and in a similar manner. Details supplied are to be entered within three days of receipt. The register is to be available to anyone within ten days of application.

B8   LIABILITY OF DIRECTORS

Directors may be liable under any of the following heads:

B8A \ To third parties\

Contract: as agents, the directors are not usually personally liable on contracts made in the company's name. They may be liable (i) for breach of warranty of authority (ii) where an agent would be liable, as on bills endorsed, drawn or accepted without the words 'per pro' or 'for and on behalf of'. Where a director contracts without using the word 'Limited', he is personally liable, as also if he does not disclose the company's name.

Tort: a director is liable for torts committed or authorised by him, even if committed or authorised as an agent of the company.

Fraudulent trading: if guilty of knowingly carrying on business fraudulently, directors may be ordered by the court to pay all or part of the company's debts.

B8B \To subscribers for shares\

Directors may be liable for misrepresentations or omissions in the listing particulars.

B8C \ To the company\

Negligence: a director must act honestly and exercise a reasonable degree of skill and diligence in performing his duties. His skill need not be of a specialised character, so that a director of a life assurance company need not have the skill of an actuary or a doctor, and he is not bound to give continuous attention to the company's affairs.

Breach of trust: such as accepting qualification shares as a present from the promoter.

Wrongful application of the company's funds: the term 'breach of trust' may be used to cover this. It includes payment of dividends out of capital, and application of funds for *ultra vires* purposes.

Misfeasance: this term may be confined to wrongful acts not involving misapplication of funds, or may be used to cover all wrongful acts in the nature of breach of trust or breach of duty. Examples of the first are giving a creditor a fraudulent preference, and committing a breach of the articles involving the company in loss.

Directors cannot contract out of any liability imposed on them by the law: any clause in the articles or special contract to that effect is absolutely void.

Directors are not liable for mere errors of judgment unaccompanied by negligence. If in any proceedings for negligence, breach of duty, breach of trust or default, the court considers that the director has acted honestly and reasonably and may fairly be excused, it may relieve him from liability even if his acts have been *ultra vires*.

The only proper plaintiff in an action to enforce the liabilities of the directors to the company is the company itself, as long as it is not being wound up. But where the directors control a majority of the votes, a minority shareholder may bring an action on behalf of all the shareholders. On winding up, the liquidator or any creditor or member may bring proceedings.

Any director who has had to pay for misfeasance or misrepresentation is entitled to contribution from the others if they have also been in default.

C

COMPANY SECRETARY

Every company must have a secretary. A sole director may not also be the secretary; anything that is required to be done by a director and the secretary cannot be done by one person acting in the two capacities. The secretary is the leading servant of the company and is responsible to the directors for the company's internal organisation. He is **not** the agent of the company to contract for it, borrow money for it, register transfers, issue writs in its name, or do other acts on its behalf, without express authority from the directors.

Particulars of the present and any former name, and the residential address, of the secretary must be entered in the register of directors and secretaries. The Registrar must be notified of any change of secretary and the date of such change, within 14 days.

D

CHAIRMAN

The chairman of the board under most articles is appointed by the board, and both the chairman and the managing director can hold their offices only while they are directors. The chairman, by virtue of his appointment, is also the chairman of the shareholders' meetings.

The main function of the chairman is to preside at meetings; if he is not present or leaves the meeting, any director present can take over. The direc-

tors present have to settle who should preside among themselves, and commonly there is some protocol laid down by the board minutes, with one director being named as the vice- or deputy chairman. Some companies allow the managing director to fulfil this function, if he is not already chairman. Others avoid this, on the principle that the chairman's function is to supervise management and not to be part of it.

The chairman's duty is to keep order and see that business is properly conducted. In the absence of formal standing orders to regulate meetings, apart from rules as to the form in which resolutions are to be put on the agenda and decided, the proceedings are very much in the hands of the chairman, who tends to follow traditional debating procedures. This is in fact the practical legal requirement: that **meetings should be conducted so that views of shareholders may be properly heard.** There is a presumption that the decisions of the chairman on points of order and incidental questions are correct, and his decision is usually said in the articles to be conclusive as to whether a person has a valid vote, or whether a proxy vote is valid. Except in the case of special or extraordinary resolutions where a poll is demanded, a declaration by the chairman is conclusive evidence that a resolution has been carried, but only if the declaration does show it was passed by the proper majority.

On a show of hands, a poll can still be demanded formally, and the chairman must declare the result in accordance with the poll. The chairman must accept that the meeting continues during the taking of the poll, and cannot close the poll or the meeting until voting is concluded, although he may adjourn it for the voting to take place on a subsequent day. A chairman can even arrange for a postal vote if he considers it to be the fair procedure. In any event either the chairman or the meeting can appoint scrutineers.

The articles usually give the chairman a casting vote, except in the case of some private companies which are divided between two or more groups and in which it is intended that in cases of equality there should be a deadlock position or some arrangement for decisions by an outside umpire or arbitrator. In such cases, as in a partnership, provision is usually made that resolutions fail automatically if they are not agreed.

The chairman, or some other members of the board according to ordinary practice, may propose resolutions, and these are then put by the chairman to the meeting for discussion. For this reason, where private copies of resolutions are required by the Companies Registry, such copies are signed by the chairman. By law the minutes of the meetings, if signed by him, are presumed to be a correct record of the meeting until the contrary is proved. A chairman does not need the approval of anyone to authenticate the minutes although it is customary either to circulate the minutes or to read them out at the next meeting, and only then to sign them. It is also possible for the chairman of the next succeeding meeting to sign. This rule applies not only to meetings of directors and shareholders, but also to meetings of committees. When extracts of minutes are required, for example as instructions to operate accounts by banks, it is requested that they should be signed as correct extracts from the minute book by the chairman and the secretary.

It is for the same reason, namely his power of authentication of authority, that many people in commerce prefer to correspond or communicate with the chairman on important or unusual business, particularly if there is no managing director.

In some companies, the chairman and managing director are the same person, which gives him autocratic powers in practice. Conversely, many companies will have as chairman someone who will maintain a dialogue with the executive directors outside the boardroom. Such a chairman may be a full-time executive appointment. Where the chairman is not so appointed, this can be an advantage from the point of view of the shareholders since the chairman can provide a detached view on situations.

E
TAKEOVERS

A takeover is the acquisition by one company of the whole or a significant proportion of the share capital of one or more other companies. The consideration involved may be the issue of shares in the acquiring company or payment of cash, or a combination of both of these.

It is possible for a takeover to be made by an individual, although this is rare in practice: the individual would be more likely to effect a takeover through a company which he controls. An increasing occurrence in modern times, however, has been the management buy-out, in which the directors of the company basically buy out a majority of the shares. This practice could arise, for instance, in an ailing company in which the management has confidence that prosperity does lie ahead, but has been constrained by a controlling (often corporate) shareholder from expanding into further markets. The latter, perhaps at its own volition, is thus bought out. A major problem for the management in these cases is obtaining the necessary finance to carry through the transaction, although certain financial institutions are becoming increasingly inclined to provide this.

? You should keep your eye on the insurance and business press, to see the kinds of takeover bid which are common at the moment. Insurance companies and brokers are by no means strangers to the practice, and you should try to spot any trends which develop in the market.

There are several methods by which a takeover may be effected.

► Individual agreement with members of the company being taken over.

► Purchase of shares by private treaty or on the Stock Exchange, or by both of these methods. This may not immediately involve the acquisition of the whole of the share capital of the company taken over, but may be a gradual process or a preliminary step in an offer for the remainder of the share capital.

► An offer to all or to a significant number of the members of the company can be made to acquire all or a large proportion of their shareholdings.

The first of the above methods may simply involve the exchange of consideration in return for executed transfers and share certificates, but more often a formal agreement will be drawn up. Meetings of both companies will then be necessary to approve the agreement and any transfers and appointments. The Registrar of Companies will need to be notified in regard to changes in the officers of the company taken over and in regard to allotment of shares. Appropriate notifications will also be necessary in regard to various registers and the like.

If a takeover bid is made by a company whose securities are listed on the Stock Exchange, or the securities of the company to be taken over are so listed, then the relevant rules require that the offer document be forwarded to the Stock Exchange Quotations Department for examination and approval.

The contents of offer documents are covered by the City Code on Takeovers and Mergers and are regulated by Rule 24 of the Code. In addition to financial information on the offeror and offeree companies, certain other information should be disclosed including the following:

▶ the offeror's intentions regarding the offeree company's business and its employees;

▶ details of shareholdings in the offeree by the offeror, its directors and persons acting in concert with the offeror, and details of any dealings by those persons in the offeree's shares in the twelve months prior to the offer period;

▶ in the case of a securities exchange offer only, whether and in what manner the emoluments of the offeror's directors will be affected by the acquisition; and

▶ details of any agreement, arrangement or understanding between the offeror (or any person acting in concert with it) and any of the directors, recent directors, shareholders or recent shareholders of the offeree, having any connection with or dependence upon the offer.

What usually happens in a takeover bid is that one company makes an offer to the shareholders of another company to buy their shares for cash or the offeror company's securities (or a combination of these). The offer made by the first company is mostly made conditional on acceptance by a particular proportion of members. Under the normal type of offer the members of the 'target' company who accept the offer become bound to sell, but the offeror company is bound only when the condition (namely acceptance by a particular proportion) is fulfilled.

Often the takeover bid is used by the offeror company to acquire a controlling interest in the target company, and the latter will become a subsidiary. In the case of listed companies, bids are made to existing shareholders for their shares at a higher price than on the market.

The possible reasons behind a takeover are many and varied. The intention may be to eliminate a competitor (although this may run serious risks of a reference to the Monopolies and Mergers Commission), to acquire production facilities, patents or skilled personnel, or to reduce particular costs. It is certainly unrealistic to think that take-overs are mostly used to join two companies that are going concerns. The target company may for a number of reasons (including inefficient management) have shares listed at a price far below the actual or possible value of the business. The intention may be to take over an inactive company as a 'shell company' and eventually obtain its large assets: this involves the practice of 'asset-stripping'.

SELF-ASSESSMENT QUESTIONS

1. What is the purpose of the annual general meeting of a company?

   ½ ~~Elect new directors~~
   ~~Agree dividends~~
   ~~Agree necessary changes for future of Co~~

2. Name the three types of resolution passed by a company in general meeting.

   ~~Ordinary — majority~~
   ~~Extraordinary ¾ maj — @ meeting with 21 days notice~~
   ~~Special — ¾ maj~~

3. How may a director vacate office?

   ~~Resignation, liquidation, shares no held below~~
   ~~Retirement, death, bankruptcy, mental~~
   ~~illness, death~~

4. What is the main duty of the chairman of a company?

   ~~Keep order @ meetings — ensure~~
   ~~fair running of company~~

5. What is a takeover?

   ~~When someone or Co. buys all~~
   ~~or large proportion of another Cos~~
   ~~share capital~~

   $\frac{4.5}{5}$

17
ANSWERS TO SELF-ASSESSMENT QUESTIONS

1. The annual general meeting of a company gives its shareholders the opportunity to question the directors on the company's performance each year.

2. The three types of resolution passed by a company in general meeting are ordinary, extraordinary and special resolutions.

3. A director may vacate office by:

   ▶ disqualification as provided by the articles;
   ▶ failure to take or keep qualification shares;
   ▶ resignation;
   ▶ removal;
   ▶ retirement by rotation;
   ▶ death or mental illness;
   ▶ bankruptcy;
   ▶ assignment of office;
   ▶ retirement on attaining the age limit;
   ▶ disqualification by court order.

4. The main duty of the chairman of a company is to preside at meetings, keeping order and seeing that business is properly conducted.

5. A takeover is the acquisition by one company of the whole or a significant proportion of the share capital of one or more other companies.

18

INSURANCE COMPANIES

A   Insurance Companies Act 1982

B   Financial Services Act 1986

C   Classification of insurance business

D   Important provisions and requirements

E   DTI returns

F   Solvency margins and policyholder
    protection

A
INSURANCE COMPANIES ACT 1982

Companies carrying on certain forms of insurance business, in addition to being subject to the Companies Acts, are also governed by the **Insurance Companies Act 1982.**

Under s.2 of the Act, no person shall carry on any insurance business in the UK unless authorised to do so by the Secretary of State for Trade and Industry. However, by virtue of s.2(2) the above requirement does not apply to insurance business (other than industrial insurance business) carried on:

▶ by a member of Lloyd's;

▶ by a body registered under the enactments relating to friendly societies; or

▶ by a trade union or employers' association where the insurance business carried on is limited to the provision for its members of provident benefits or strike benefits.

There are further exceptions for certain industrial assurance business carried on by a registered friendly society, general insurance business carried on solely in the course of banking business, and for insurers who exclusively or primarily provide benefits in kind.

Under s.3 of the 1982 Act, the Secretary of State may authorise a body to carry on in the UK such of the classes of insurance business listed in section C below, or such parts of those classes, as may be specified in the authorisation.

In s.4 of the Act there is an exception which allows certain insurance companies which carried on business prior to the coming into force of the Act to carry on business in corresponding classes. Section 6 contains the general principle that the Secretary of State shall not authorise a body to carry on both long-term and general business unless:

LEARNING OBJECTIVES

After studying this chapter, you should be able to:

▷ state and explain the main provisions of the Insurance Companies Act 1982;

▷ detail the circumstances in which authorisation may be granted to carry on insurance business in the UK;

▷ outline how the Financial Services Act 1986 affects insurance companies;

▷ list the different classes into which insurance business is divided;

▷ explain what information has to be submitted to the DTI, and why.

▶ the long-term business is restricted to reinsurance; or

▶ the body is, at the time the authorisation is issued, already carrying on in the UK both long-term business and general business (in neither case restricted to reinsurance).

The terms 'long-term' and 'general' business will be explained in section C below.

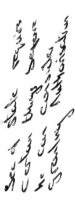

A1 CONDITIONS OF AUTHORISATION

The Secretary of State under s.5 shall not issue an authorisation under the 1982 Act unless certain detailed information (proposals, financial forecasts and so on) has been submitted and he is satisfied that authorisation should be granted. Generally he is required to decide on an authorisation application within three months.

The conditions on which authorisation is granted differ for applicants whose head office is situated in the UK, in other EC member states and in countries outside the EC.

Basically, for a **UK** applicant:

▶ it must be a company as defined under the Companies Act 1985, a registered society, or a body corporate established by Royal Charter or Act of Parliament and already authorised under s.3 or s.4 to carry on (other) insurance business;

▶ it must not have any share capital issued after the coming into force of s.7 (January 1983) but not fully paid-up;

▶ it must appear to the Secretary of State that any director, controller, manager or main agent of the applicant is a fit and proper person to hold the position held by him.

For an applicant from another **member state:**

▶ there must be a suitable representative (complying with s.10) resident in the UK;

▶ it must appear to the Secretary of State that any relevant executive or main agent is a fit and proper person to hold the position;

▶ where the applicant seeks authorisation restricted to reinsurance business, among other things the Secretary of State must be satisfied that the applicant is a body corporate entitled under the law of the member state to carry on insurance business there.

For an applicant from **outside the EC,** the Secretary of State must be satisfied that:

▶ the applicant is a body corporate entitled under the law of the place of situation of its head office to carry on long-term or general business there;

▶ the applicant has in the UK assets of the prescribed value;

▶ the applicant has made a deposit of this amount with the prescribed person.

In addition, no authority will be granted to a body from outside the EC unless it has a general representative, who is a fit and proper person, resident in the UK: he must be authorised to accept service on behalf of the applicant.

B

FINANCIAL SERVICES ACT 1986

The **Financial Services Act 1986** affects insurance companies only to the extent that their insurance business is **investment business,** and the authorisation and prudential regulation provisions of the **Insurance Companies Act 1982** continue in force under the supervision of the insurance division of the Department of Trade and Industry.

Paragraph 10 of Schedule 1 to the 1986 Act provides that rights under a contract which constitutes long-term business under the 1982 Act are an investment. Reinsurance contracts are excluded, as are rights under a contract which is in effect a life assurance contract with no savings (that is investment) characteristics. Thus insurance companies' general (or indemnity) business is not caught by the 1986 Act.

By s.22 of the 1986 Act, a body which is authorised

under s.3 or s.4 of the 1982 Act to carry on insurance business which is investment business, and carries on such investment business in the UK, is an authorised person as regards:

► any insurance business which is investment business; and

► any other investment business which that body may carry on without contravening s.16 of the 1982 Act ('Restriction of business to insurance').

Part II of the 1986 Act deals with insurance business. Section 129 provides that Schedule 10 has effect with respect to the application of the Act to 'regulated insurance companies'; that is:

► insurance companies to which Part II of the 1982 Act applies (namely insurance companies carrying on business in the UK, subject to certain exceptions); and

► insurance companies which are authorised persons (under the 1986 Act) by virtue of s.31 ('Authorisation in other Member States').

Schedule 10, para. 2 to the 1986 Act deals with the authorisation of insurance business which is investment business, whether authorised under s.22 or s.31 or otherwise, and specifically provides that none of the provisions of the 1986 Act regulating investment business is to be taken as authorising any person to carry on insurance business in any case in which he could not lawfully do so apart from those provisions.

C

CLASSIFICATION OF INSURANCE BUSINESS

Schedules 1 and 2 (Part I) of the **Insurance Companies Act 1982** cover the types of insurance. Schedule 1 deals with long-term (life assurance etc.) and schedule 2, Part I, with general business.

Long-term business is divided into seven classes:

Life and annuity   Tontines
Marriage and birth   Capital redemption
Linked long-term   Pension fund management
Permanent health

General business is now divided into 18 classes:

Accident   Motor vehicle liability
Sickness   Aircraft liability
Land vehicles   Liability for ships
Railway rolling stock   General liability
Aircraft   Credit
Ships   Suretyship
Goods in transit   Miscellaneous financial loss
Fire and natural forces   Legal expenses
Damage to property   Assistance

For the purpose of authorisation to transact insurance, the classes of general business are divided into groups in Schedule 2, Part II:

(1) Accident and health - Classes 1 and 2.

(2) Motor - Class 1 (to the extent that the relevant risks are risks of the person insured sustaining injury, or dying, as the result of travelling as a passenger) and classes 3, 7 and 10.

(3) Marine and transport - Class 1 (to the said extent) and classes 4, 6, 7 and 12.

(4) Aviation - Class 1 (to the said extent) and classes 5, 7 and 11.

(5) Fire and other damage to property - Classes 8 and 9.

(6) Liability - Classes 10, 11, 12 and 13.

(7) Credit and suretyship - Classes 14 and 15.

(8) General - All classes.

D

IMPORTANT PROVISIONS AND REQUIREMENTS

The 1982 Act contains a number of provisions and requirements which we will now consider.

D1 SOLVENCY

Section 32 of the 1982 Act sets out the solvency requirements for insurance companies.

A distinction is adopted, as elsewhere, between insurance companies whose head office is situated in the UK, those from other member states of the EC and those from countries outside the EC. The prescribed margins of solvency (contained in regulations) vary according to which of these types the company is.

A distinction is drawn between the UK margin of solvency and the Community margin of solvency. The former is computed by reference to the assets and liabilities of the business carried on by the company in the UK, and the latter by reference to the assets and liabilities of the business carried on by the company in all member states, taken together. Companies from outside the EC are often required to provide a deposit in the UK.

Solvency margins are dealt with in more detail in section F.

D2 INTERVENTION BY THE SECRETARY OF STATE

Under ss.38 to 45 of the 1982 Act, the Secretary of State has certain powers to intervene in the affairs of insurance companies. There are many circumstances detailed where he may exercise these powers. He may require the company not to make investments of a specified class or description; he may require that a certain value of assets be maintained in the UK. He may require a company to take steps that the aggregate of premiums do not exceed a certain amount; he may order certain actuarial investigations or he may speed up the supply of information required by the accounting provisions. He may, among other powers, require a company to furnish him with such information and documents as he orders. There is also a residual power in the Secretary of State to require a company to take such action as he considers appropriate for the purpose of protecting policyholders (or potential ones) against the risk that the company may be unable to meet its liabilities or to fulfil expectations.

There are requirements for written notice (stating reasons and pointing out that representations may be made), and the order or any subsequent withdrawal must be gazetted.

D3 WINDING-UP

Sections 53 to 64 of the Insurance Companies Act 1982 contain special provisions for the winding-up of insurance companies.

An insurance company can be wound up by the court (leave having been granted) on the petition of ten or more policyholders owning policies of an aggregate value of not less than £10,000.

Under s.54, the Secretary of State may present a petition for the winding-up of an insurance company. The grounds include inability to pay debts under the **Insolvency Act 1986,** failure to comply with an obligation under insurance company legislation and failure to keep or produce accounting records.

D4 APPROVAL OF APPOINTMENTS

Under ss. 60 to 64 of the 1982 Act notice of the appointment of certain officers must be given to the Secretary of State and he must approve them or three months must elapse after the service of the notice.

Notice of subsequent changes must also be given.

D5 CONDUCT OF BUSINESS

Under Part III of the 1982 Act there are wide powers for regulations governing the conduct of insurance business: dealings with advertisements, intermediaries in insurance transactions, notices, and withdrawals.

D6 ACCOUNTS, STATEMENTS ETC.

Sections 17 to 31 cover accounts and other statements, and application of assets. Every insurance company must, for every financial year, prepare a revenue account, a balance sheet and a profit and loss account or, in the case of a company not trading for profit, an income and expenditure account.

Certain periodic investigations are required, under s.18 of the 1982 Act, of companies with long-term business.

There are a number of other provisions dealing with actuaries, statements of business, audit, deposit of accounts with the Secretary of State, application of assets and allocation of surplus to policyholders, and certain restrictions on transactions. The Insurance Companies (Accounts and Statements) Regulations 1983 prescribe the precise form and contents for the annual returns of insurance companies authorised to carry on business in the UK.

E
DTI RETURNS

The assets of a composite insurer which relate to its long-term business must be kept separately from the assets relating to its general business. In this way, the interests of both categories of policyholder can be safeguarded.

? Can you remember how many classes of general business there are, and how many of long-term? If not, remind yourself from section C. You should aim to be able to name them all, and to explain what kind of insurance every one covers.

Separate solvency requirements apply to the two classes of business and must be satisfied from the assets separately maintained. Similarly, proprietary life offices must segregate the assets relating to their insurance business from those assets which represent shareholders' funds, and from which the relevant solvency requirement must be demonstrated.

Section 28 of the **Insurance Companies Act 1982** requires a company authorised for long-term business to establish a separate insurance fund into which is paid all receipts relating to that business. The liabilities attaching to the ordinary long-term business must be set against the assets of the fund. A separate fund must be established if a company is also authorised for industrial assurance business. The company must maintain all records and accounts which identify the long-term business assets and liabilities.

Composite insurers are therefore required to separate the assets and liabilities relating to their long-term and general business, and life offices to separate the assets and liabilities relating to their insurance business and shareholders' funds.

There are usually at least two long-term funds maintained by most life offices; one for with-profits business and one for non-profit business. Within a long-term fund there may be notionally segregated funds for particular classes of business: this is usually the case with unit-linked business.

Section 29 imposes restrictions on the uses to which the long-term assets of a company may be put. With two exceptions, the long-term assets of a company must be used for the purposes of the long-term business. It is not permissible for long-term assets to be sold in order to settle general business liabilities, but the converse does not apply. The two exceptions are:

▶ that assets in the long-term fund may be used for purposes other than the long-term business to the extent that such assets exceed the long-term liabilities, as disclosed by an actuarial valuation: the 'free reserves' may thus be used for the purposes of the business generally.

▶ that long-term assets may be exchanged for other assets of the company, provided the exchange is at fair market value. Inter-fund investment transfers are thereby permitted, and often take place if an investment held by one fund is found to be more appropriate to the needs of the other fund.

As a further protection for long-term policyholders, no dividend may be declared by any company authorised for long-term business unless it has established by a valuation of its long-term assets and liabilities that the assets are at least equal to the liabilities.

The **Insurance Companies Act 1982** requires insurance companies to submit annual returns to the Department of Trade and Industry.

All insurance companies must prepare a revenue account, profit and loss account and balance sheet in prescribed form, together with additional statements prescribed by regulations. In addition, all companies authorised for long-term business must appoint an actuary, and the appointed actuary must carry out a valuation of the long-term fund once a year.

The form and content of the accounts and statements to be submitted are set out in the **Insurance Companies (Accounts and Statements) Regulations 1983.**

The accounts must be audited and submitted to the DTI within six months of the end of the financial year concerned. Shareholders and policyholders have a statutory right to receive copies on request.

For general insurers, the returns that must be completed under the regulations are as follows:

▶ Balance sheet and profit and loss account.

▶ General business: review account and additional information and statements about major reinsurers and major cedants.

▶ Certificates by directors and auditors.

The emphasis of the returns is directed towards demonstrating the solvency of the insurer and testing the soundness of reserving policies.

The forms supplied by the Department of Trade and Industry (see Appendix I) must be followed precisely. Some additional information has to be provided by way of notes to the returns, but in general terms the statement of accounting policies and other notes which appear in the accounts prepared for shareholders are not required. The extent of the returns to be completed by a general insurer or a composite insurer in respect of its general business depends upon its corporate status, as follows:

▶ **United Kingdom company:** a 'global' return, pertaining to the company's business worldwide;

▶ **European Community company:** a 'branch' return, pertaining to the company's business carried on in the United Kingdom;

▶ **external company:** a 'branch' return pertaining to the company's business carried on in the United Kingdom, and a 'global' return pertaining to the company's business worldwide;

▶ **United Kingdom deposit company:** a 'global' return pertaining to the company's business worldwide and a 'Community branch' return pertaining to the company's business carried on in the United Kingdom and any other member state;

▶ **Community deposit company:** a 'branch' return pertaining to the company's business in the United Kingdom.

With respect to premiums and claims, insurers must prepare separate forms for each 'accounting class' of business carried on. Separate returns are also required for each country in which business is transacted, each 'risk group' forming a sub-division of the accounting class, and each currency in which business is transacted. Any country producing less than 2.5% of a company's gross premium income, or gross premium income of less than £100,000, is excluded from the territorial analysis, as it is not material to an overall appreciation of the company's business. Companies transacting 'Community co-insurance' business are required to provide an analysis of this business by accounting class and country of risk.

E1   ACCOUNTING CLASSES

For the purposes of the DTI returns, insurers have to classify their business according to the accounting classes defined in the 1983 Accounts and Statements Regulations. The Insurance Companies Act 1982 subdivides non-life business into 18 classes of general business for the purpose of authorisation. These authorisation classes are grouped together in eight groups. For accounting purposes, however, ten different classes apply and it is essential for the accounting system of insurers to ensure that their underwriting classification records can satisfactorily transpose the appropriate figures into the divisions needed to complete the returns according to the accounting classes.

The ten accounting classes and the corresponding authorisation classes are:

Accounting class	Corresponding authorisation class
(1) Accident and health	(1) Accident
	(2) Sickness
(2) Motor vehicle (including damage to other land vehicles); damage and liability	(3) Land vehicles
	(10) Motor vehicle liability
(3) Aircraft, damage including liability	(5) Aircraft
	(11) Aircraft liability
(4) Ships, damage and liability	(6) Ships
	(12) Liability for ships
(5) Goods in transit	(7) Goods in transit
(6) Property damage	(4) Railway rolling stock
	(8) Fire and natural forces
	(9) Damage to property
(7) General liability	(13) General liability
(8) Pecuniary loss	(14) Credit
	(15) Suretyship
	(16) Miscellaneous financial loss
	(17) Legal expenses
	(18) Assistance
(9) Non-proportional treaty reinsurance	
(10) Proportional treaty reinsurance	

Marine and aviation business is not dealt with on quite the same basis as other insurance. Accounting classes 3, 4 and 5 have to include treaty reinsurance business of the corresponding classes. Accounting classes 9 and 10 are used for treaty reinsurance business of any other class.

A company underwriting an aviation account only may include hovercraft business in accounting class 3, if it has no other business which would fall within that class. Goods in transit business attached to motor policies can be included in accounting class 5 instead of class 2, if the basic motor cover does not include damage to vehicles.

It therefore follows that an insurer must keep adequate records of premiums and claims under **at least** these headings if a complete and proper return is to be provided. In practice, insurers tend to keep very much more sophisticated records so that patterns and trends can be monitored and rating become more sophisticated.

You will see that one apparent omission is the combined or package policy. Insurers are bound to identify premiums and claims under the DTI headings. This can be achieved case by case,

though it is more common to find that an insurer will make as realistic as possible an assessment of the percentage breakdown between the various classes combined in the package for **premium** purposes. Claims, of course, are a more straightforward proposition, and these are classified individually.

As with returns for general business, the extent of returns to be completed by life companies depends upon the corporate status of the insurer concerned:

▶ **United Kingdom company:** a 'global' return pertaining to the company's business worldwide;

▶ **European company:** a 'branch' return pertaining to the company's business carried on in the United Kingdom;

▶ **Community deposit company:** a 'branch' return pertaining to the company's business carried on in the United Kingdom;

▶ **pure reinsurer:** a 'global' return pertaining to the company's business worldwide;

► **United Kingdom deposit company:** a 'global' return pertaining to the company's business worldwide, and a 'Community' return pertaining to the company's business carried on in the United Kingdom and other member states taken together;

► **external company:** a 'global' return pertaining to the company's business worldwide, and a 'branch' return pertaining to the company's business carried on in the United Kingdom.

E2 DOCUMENTATION

The forms to be completed are prescribed in the 1983 Accounts and Statements Regulations and comprise:

► balance sheet and profit and loss account;

► long-term business:
  (a) revenue account;
  (b) additional information;

► actuary's valuation report on long-term business: abstract of report;

► statement of ordinary long-term business;

► certificates by directors, the appointed actuary and auditors.

The general approach of the forms is similar to that for non-life business, in that separate revenue statements are required for the main classes of life business, divided between a number of risk groups, but the extensive geographical analysis applied to non-life business is not followed through to long-term business.

For the purposes of the forms, the allocation of business into United Kingdom and overseas is to be made on the basis of the place where the contract is made, or in the case of treaty acceptances, where the head office of the ceding company is found. There is a detailed division of business between with- and without-profits, linked and non-linked, group and individual. Figures shown in the returns for premiums must include amounts recoverable from the Inland Revenue under the Life Assurance Premium Relief regulations.

The annual valuation report of the appointed actuary, contained in the returns, is not subject to audit. The DTI examines the returns and may raise queries with the company, but does not audit the company's records. However, the DTI has wide-ranging powers of intervention if a company fails to comply with its legal obligations, and can order it to cease writing new business. As part of the supervisory procedure, insurers have to notify the DTI of changes in controlling shareholders, directors, chief executives, managers and main agents.

F

SOLVENCY MARGINS AND POLICYHOLDER PROTECTION

The concept of a minimum solvency margin - **a minimum amount by which the assets of an insurer must exceed its liabilities** - was first introduced by the **Assurance Companies Act 1946.** Specific solvency margins are now imposed by law on both life and non-life insurers, and are an important aspect of insurance company supervision, and so of security for policyholders.

The solvency margins required by the **Insurance Companies Act 1982**, and elaborated in statutory regulations, are monitored by the DTI. These margins reflect those required by European Community Directives. Generally, the calculation and assessment of solvency margins is complicated, requiring expert knowledge of the regulations and actuarial advice in the case of life companies. The margin by which assets must exceed liabilities varies with the type of company, the classes of cover it writes and certain other factors. For all companies there is a minimum margin, the 'minimum guarantee fund', which is a fixed sum, expressed in European Currency Units, set at different levels for different types of company.

For general insurers, the required solvency margin is the greatest of the minimum guarantee fund and two other amounts; one calculated by reference to gross premiums for the year and the other by reference to gross claims for either the last three or last seven years, with both figures modified to a limited extent for reinsurance recoveries.

In a life company, the calculation of the required solvency margin is the responsibility of the company's appointed actuary. The required margin is the greatest of the minimum required guarantee fund, the sum of percentages applied to actuarial reserves and the net 'capital risk' (the latter being sums payable on death less amounts provided), modified to a limited extent by reinsurance cover.

Newly authorised insurers have special requirements imposed on them so that their activities during early trading years can be closely monitored by the DTI. These requirements can also apply if there is a change in control of an insurance company.

There is a formal application procedure for new companies entering the market, which involves the submission of complete business plans for three years and discussions with the DTI on all aspects of the business. The application process takes a minimum of six months. For new insurance companies, and for others where the DTI considers it advisable, quarterly returns must be submitted.

Under the **Policyholders' Protection Act 1975,** a board appointed by the government can raise funds by making levies on insurance companies. The fund formed by these levies is available to meet the claims of policyholders if an insurer becomes insolvent and is unable to meet its contractual obligations.

Q Certain insurance cover is compulsory: can you name the main types?

A The main examples of compulsory insurance in the UK are motor and employer's liability insurance.

In the case of compulsory insurance the compensation fund would meet claims in full. In most other classes of insurance the fund would meet 90% of the policyholder's claim, or 90% of the value of a life policy.

The compensation fund does not cover marine, aviation, transit or reinsurance policies, or the claims of non-life policyholders which are companies.

18
SELF-ASSESSMENT QUESTIONS

1. List the classes into which long-term insurance business is divided.

    _____

    _____

    _____

2. Explain the requirements of s. 28 of the Insurance Companies Act 1982.

    _____

    _____

    _____

3. What are the restrictions placed on the use of the long-term assets of an insurance company by the Insurance Companies Act 1982?

    _____

    _____

    _____

4. List the accounting classes into which general insurers must classify their business under the Insurance Companies (Accounts and Statements) Regulations 1983.

    _____

    _____

    _____

5. What is a solvency margin?

    _____

    _____

    _____

6. Explain how the Policyholders' Protection Act 1975 assists policyholders whose insurers become insolvent.

    _____

    _____

    _____

18
ANSWERS TO SELF-ASSESSMENT QUESTIONS

1. Long-term business is divided into the following classes:

    ► life and annuity;
    ► marriage and birth;
    ► linked long-term;
    ► permanent health;
    ► tontines;
    ► capital redemption;
    ► pension fund management.

2. Section 28 of the Insurance Companies Act 1982 requires a company authorised for long-term business to establish a separate fund into which is paid all receipts relating to that business.

3. Section 29 of the 1982 Act restricts the use to which the long-term assets of a company may be put so that, with two exceptions, they may only be used for the purposes of the long-term business.

4. General insurers must classify their business into the following accounting classes:

    (1) Accident and health.
    (2) Motor vehicle; damage and liability.
    (3) Aircraft, damage including liability.
    (4) Ships, damage and liability.
    (5) Goods in transit.
    (6) Property damage.
    (7) General liability.
    (8) Pecuniary loss.
    (9) Non-proportional treaty reinsurance.
    (10) Proportional treaty reinsurance.

5. A solvency margin is the maximum amount by which the assets of an insurer must exceed its liabilities.

6. Under the Policyholders' Protection Act 1975, a board appointed by the government can raise funds by making levies on insurance companies. The fund formed by these levies is available to meet the claims of policyholders if an insurer becomes insolvent and is unable to meet its contractual obligations.

18
ASSIGNMENT 8

You should work this assignment after studying Chapters 15 to 18. Answer any three questions, and allow yourself one and a half hours to complete it.

1. Distinguish a company from a partnership.

2. Explain the information to be found in a company's memorandum of association.

3. Explain the various methods by which one company may effect a takeover of another.

4. Briefly outline the ways in which UK insurance companies are supervised by the Department of Trade and Industry.

APPENDIX 1

Form 9
(Sheet 1)

Returns under Insurance Companies Legislation

Statement of solvency

Name of Company

Global business

Financial year ended

		Company registration number	Global/ UK/CM	Period ended day month year		Units	For official use
	F9				19	£000	

		As at the end of the financial year 1	As at the end of the previous year 2	Source Form Line Column

GENERAL BUSINESS
Available assets

Other than long term business assets allocated towards general business required minimum margin	11			

Required minimum margin

Required minimum margin for general business	12			12.49
Excess (deficiency) of available assets over the required minimum margin (11-12)	13			
Implicit items admitted under regulation 10(4) of the Insurance Companies Regulations 1981	14			

LONG TERM BUSINESS
Available assets

Long term business admissible assets	21			10.11
Other than long term business assets allocated towards long term business required minimum margin	22			
Total mathematical reserves (after distribution of surplus)	23			
Other insurance and non-insurance liabilities	24			
Available assets for long term business required minimum margin (21+22−23−24)	25			

Implicit items admitted under regulation 10(4) of the Insurance Companies Regulations 1981

Future profits	31			
Zillmerising	32			
Hidden reserves	33			

Total of available assets and implicit items (25+31+32+33)	34			

Required minimum margin

Required minimum margin for long term business	41			60.13
Explicit required minimum margin (1/6 x 41, or minimum guarantee fund if greater)	42			
Excess (deficiency) of available assets over explicit required minimum margin (25−42)	43			
Excess (deficiency) of available assets and implicit items over the required minimum margin (34−41)	44			

V5409

1

APPENDIX 1

Liabilities (other than Long Term business)

Name of Company

Global business

Financial year ended

	Company registration number	Global/ UK/CM	Period ended day	month	year	Units	For official use
F15					19	£000	

			As at the end of the financial year 1	As at the end of the previous year 2	Source Form	Line	Column
General business technical reserves	Unearned premiums	21					
	Additional amount for unexpired risks	22					
	Claims outstanding (less amounts recoverable from reinsurers) — Reported claims	23				See Note below	
	Claims incurred but not reported	24					
	Expenses for settling claims outstanding	25					
	Funds	26					
	Claims equalisation	27					
	Other	28					
	Total (21 to 28)	29					
Other insurance liabilities	Amounts due in respect of direct insurance and facultative reinsurance contracts accepted except amounts which must be included in line 29	31					
	Amounts due to ceding insurers and intermediaries under reinsurance treaties accepted except amounts which must be included in line 29	32					
	Amounts due to reinsurers and intermediaries under reinsurance contracts ceded	33					
Other liabilities	Loans secured	41					
	Loans unsecured	42					
	Subordinated loan stock	43					
	Taxation	44					
	Recommended dividend	45					
	Cumulative preference share dividend accrued	46					
	Other creditors	47					
Total (29 to 47)		59					

		As at the end of the financial year 1	As at the end of the previous year 2			
Amounts included in line 59 attributable to liabilities to related companies, other than those under contracts of insurance or reinsurance	61					

Note The sources are as follows:

Line 21 All forms 21.29.6 + 21.31.6 —(22.23.3 + 22.24.3 — 22.25.3)
Line 22 Summary form 20.23

Line 23 All forms 22.31.3 + 22.41.3
Line 24 All forms 22.32.3 + 22.42.3

Line 25 All forms 22.21.3 + 22.22.3
Line 26 All forms 24.42.5 + 27.46.3

APPENDIX 1

Returns under Insurance Companies Legislation

Form 21
(Sheet 1)

General business: Analysis of premiums for direct insurance and facultative reinsurance business

Name of Company

Global business

Financial year ended

Accounting class

Company registration number	Global/UK/CM	Period ended day month year	Units	Accounting class	For official use
F21		19	£000		

Premiums receivable (less rebates and refunds) in the financial year		Gross		Reinsurance premiums payable		Net of reinsurance	
		Earned in previous financial years 1	Unearned at end of the financial year 2	Earned in previous financial years 3	Unearned at end of the financial year 4	Earned in previous financial years 5	Unearned at end of the financial year 6
In respect of risks incepted in previous financial years		11					
		Earned in the financial year 1	Unearned at end of the financial year 2	Earned in the financial year 3	Unearned at end of the financial year 4	Earned in the financial year 5	Unearned at end of the financial year 6
In respect of risks incepted in previous financial years		12					
In respect of risks incepted in the financial year for periods of less than 12 months	expiring by the end of the financial year	13					
	expiring after the end of the financial year	14					
	commencing prior to the last 12 months of the financial year	15					
In respect of risks incepted in the financial year for periods of 12 months	commencing in each of the last 12 months of the financial year	Month 1	16				
		Month 2	17				
		Month 3	18				
		Month 4	19				
		Month 5	20				
		Month 6	21				
		Month 7	22				

Note

– for the normal financial year of 12 months, the amounts for each month are entered at lines 16 to 27 commencing with the first month at line 16;

– when there are more than twelve months in the financial year, the total amounts for the months before the last 12 months in the financial year are entered at line 15, the amounts for each of the last 12 months are entered at lines 16-27, starting with the first of the last 12 months at line 16;

– when there are less than 12 months in the financial year, amounts should be entered for each month with the amounts for the last month of the financial year at line 27, with preceding months at lines 26, 25 etc.

APPENDIX 1

Returns under Insurance Companies Legislation

Form 22

General business: **Analysis** of claims and expenses for direct insurance and facultative reinsurance business

Name of Company

Global business

Financial year ended

Accounting class

		Company registration number	Global/ UK/CM	Period ended day month year	Units	Accounting class	For official use
	F 22			19	£000		

			Amount brought forward from previous financial year 1	Amount payable/ receivable in the financial year 2	Amount carried forward to next financial year 3	Amount attributable to the financial year 4
Claims arising from incidents occurring in previous financial years	gross	11				
	recoverable from reinsurers	12				
	net (11–12)	13				
Claims arising from incidents occurring in the financial year (including claims reported in the reconciliation return on Form 33)	gross	14				
	recoverable from reinsurers	15				
	net (14–15)	16				
Expenses	expenses for settling claims arising from incidents occurring in previous financial years	21				
	expenses for settling claims arising from incidents occurring in the financial year (including claims reported in the reconciliation return on Form 33)	22				
	management expenses	23				
	commission payable	24				
	reinsurance commission receivable	25				
	expenses in respect of the financial year (22 + 23 + 24 – 25)	26				
	total (21 + 26)	29				

Amount included in line 13 attributable to	reported claims	31				
	claims incurred but not reported	32				
Amount included in line 16 attributable to	reported claims	41				
	claims incurred but not reported	42				

Notes

1 Any amounts included in 14.1, 15.1, 16.1 and 22.1 relate only to claims included in the reconciliation return on Form 33

2 The values in column 4 are calculated as follows:

for lines 11 to 22, values in columns 2 + 3 – 1
for lines 23 to 25, values in columns 1 + 2 – 3

APPENDIX 1

Returns under Insurance Companies Legislation

Form 23

General business: Analysis of claims outstanding net of reinsurance recoveries for direct insurance and facultative reinsurance business

Name of Company

Global business

Financial year ended

	Company registration number	Global/ UK/CM	Period ended day month year	Units	For official use
F23			19	£000	

Year of origin ended month / year	Accounting class code		Claims outstanding(net) as at end of year of origin 1	Total claims paid (net) in all years since year of origin 2	Claims outstanding (net) at end of financial year 3

Accounting class

19		11			
19		12			
19		13			
19		14			
19		15			
19		16			
19		17			
Previous years		18			
Reconciliation		19			
Total		29			

Accounting class

19		11			
19		12			
19		13			
19		14			
19		15			
19		16			
19		17			
Previous years		18			
Reconciliation		19			
Total		29			

Notes
1 All figures are net of reinsurance recoveries
2 Line 19 relates to claims reported in the reconciliation return on Form 33. These claims are not included in lines 11 to 18.
3 23.29.3 = 22.13.3 + 22.16.3

APPENDIX 1

Returns under Insurance Companies Legislation

Form 25

General business (three year accounting): Additional information relating to premiums

Name of Company

Global business

Financial year ended

Accounting class

Division of premiums between UK and overseas

	Company registration number	Global/ UK/CM	Period ended day	month	year	Units	Accounting class	For official use
F 25					19	£000		

Premiums on Form 24 attributed to		UK 6	Overseas 7
	receivable under direct insurance and facultative reinsurance contracts	11		
	receivable under reinsurance treaties accepted	12		
Premiums	payable to reinsurers and retrocessionaires to reinsure business of a kind shown at line 11	13		
	payable to retrocessionaires to reinsure business of a kind shown at line 12	14		
	amounts receivable net of retrocessions in respect of outstanding claims and loss portfolios	15		
	receivable net (11+12−13−14+15)	19		

Note   25.19.6+25.19.7=24.19.5

Grossed-up premiums (only to be completed if values in the first part of the form are net of commission).

Grossed up values of entries shown at lines 11 to 14 on Form 24		Insurance business incepted in:				
		All years prior to the second year preceding the financial year 1	Second year preceding the financial year 2	First year preceding the financial year 3	The financial year 4	Total (1+2+3+4) 5
	receivable under direct insurance and facultative reinsurance contracts	71				
	receivable under reinsurance treaties accepted	72				
Premiums	payable to reinsurers and retrocessionaires to reinsure business of a kind shown at line 71	73				
	payable to retrocessionaires to reinsure business of a kind shown at line 72	74				
	Balance (71+72−73−74)	79				

APPENDIX 1

Returns under Insurance Companies Legislation

Form 31

General business: Analysis of exposure to risk measured by premiums

Name of Company

Financial year ended

Country   Currency

Accounting class

		Company registration number	Period ended — day month year	Monetary units	Country	Accounting class	For official use
	F31		**19**				

Gross premiums receivable (less rebates and refunds) on direct insurance and facultative reinsurance business		Additional exposure attributable to previous financial years **1**	Exposure in the financial year **2**	Exposure carried forward to following financial years **3**	Total gross premiums (1+2+3) **4**	Total gross premiums expressed in sterling (£000) **5**

Risk group

in previous financial years		**11**					
in the financial year in respect of risks incepted in	previous financial years	**12**					
	the financial year	**13**					
Total (11 + 12 + 13)		**19**					

Risk group

in previous financial years		**11**					
in the financial year in respect of risks incepted in	previous financial years	**12**					
	the financial year	**13**					
Total (11 + 12 + 13)		**19**					

Risk group

in previous financial years		**11**					
in the financial year in respect of risks incepted in	previous financial years	**12**					
	the financial year	**13**					
Total (11 + 12 + 13)		**19**					

Risk group

in previous financial years		**11**					
in the financial year in respect of risks incepted in	previous financial years	**12**					
	the financial year	**13**					
Total (11 + 12 + 13)		**19**					

APPENDIX 1

Returns under Insurance Companies Legislation

Form 33

General business: Analysis of claims by number and cost

Name of Company

Financial year ended

Country   Currency

Accounting class

Risk group

	Company registration number	Period ended			Monetary units	Accounting Country class		For official use	
		day	month	year					
F33				**19**					

For direct insurance and facultative reinsurance business			Number of claims	Amounts of payments made in the financial year	Amounts of payments made in previous financial years relating to claims in column 1	Estimates of payments remaining to be made	Total gross amount paid and outstanding (2+3+4)
		month year					
Claims attributable to year of origin ended	**10**	**19**	1	2	3	4	5
Claims closed in the financial year	at no cost (other than reopened claims)	**11**					
	at some cost (other than reopened claims)	**12**					
	reopened claims	**13**					
Claims outstanding at the end of the financial year	reported (other than reopened claims)	**14**					
	incurred but not reported (IBNR)	**15**		▓▓▓	▓▓▓		
	reopened claims	**16**					
Claims closed in previous financial years (excluding those reopened claims shown at lines 13 and 16)		**17**		▓▓▓			
Total claims attributable to the year of origin (11 to 17)		**19**					
Line 19 expressed in sterling (£000)		**29**	▓▓▓		▓▓▓		▓▓▓

		month year					
Year of origin ended	**10**	**19**					
Claims closed in the financial year	at no cost (other than reopened claims)	**11**					
	at some cost (other than reopened claims)	**12**					
	reopened claims	**13**					
Claims outstanding at the end of the financial year	reported (other than reopened claims)	**14**					
	incurred but not reported (IBNR)	**15**		▓▓▓	▓▓▓		
	reopened claims	**16**					
Claims closed in previous financial years (excluding those reopened claims shown at lines 13 and 16)		**17**		▓▓▓			
Total claims attributable to the year of origin (11 to 17)		**19**					
Line 19 expressed in sterling (£000)		**29**	▓▓▓		▓▓▓		▓▓▓

Instructions for completion of this form are included in the Appendix

LIST OF STATUTES

Assurance Companies Act 1946, 18F

Companies Acts 9C4, 16B1, 17A2
    1862, 16B1
    1985, 12C, 13A2, 13F1, 16B1, 16B2A, 16C4A, 17B
    1989, 16B1
Company Directors Disqualification Act 1985, 17B4

Data Protection Act 1984, 11D

Finance Act 1989, 7D4
Financial Services Act 1986, 4C4, 10D1, 18B

Insolvency Act 1986, 17B4
Insurance Brokers (Registration) Act 1977, 9C4
Insurance Companies Acts, 4D, 9C4, 13G2A
    1982, 10C2, 18

Limited Partnership Act 1907, 16A2B, 16B1

Partnership Act 1890, 16A2A
Policyholders' Protection Act 1975, 9C4, 18F

INDEX

INDEX

INDEX

insurance
 brokers' accounts, 13G1
 companies, 18
 company accounts, 13G2
 international nature, 8I1
Insurance Companies (Accounts and
 Statements) Regulations 1983, 18E
interest, 8B
 cover, 14B4
 rates, 7B4, 7B5, 7D2, 8G2
investment, 5G2
 by insurance companies, 5G3
 in real capital, 5E3A
invisible
 earnings, 5E1A
 hand, 1C
invisibles, 8B

labour, 5F
level of production, 5A
liabilities, 13A1
liability of directors, 17B8
life assurance, 3A6, 4C4
limitation of liability, 16C4D
limitations on supply of insurance, 3B2
limited companies, 9B3C, 10C
liquid
 assets, 13D, 14B3
 ratio, 14B3
liquidity ratios, 14B3
Lloyd's, 10C2,16A2D
location, 4C3
long-term
 insurance business, 18C
 money, 15B

management, 12B1
 buyout, 17E
 structures, 10C2
 of companies, 17
Maritime Telegraph and Telephone, 4D
market
 accessibility, 4B4
 economy, 1B, 2I, 7C1
 transparency, 4B3
membership of a company, 16C6
memorandum of association, 16C4, 16C5,
 17A2A, 17B3
minimum subscription, 16C3
minority interests, 13F1, 14B4
mixed economy, 1B1
monetary policy, 7, 8F
 definition, 7A
money, 15
 supply, 7B

and the insurance industry, 7D
 control, 7B3, 7B4
Monopolies and Mergers Commission, 17E
motor insurance, 3A5
motorcycle insurance, 3B2
multiple counting, 5E1B
mutual organisations, 9B3D, 16A2D

national income, 5
National Insurance, 3A5
natural resources, 5F
net current assets, 13B
non-business organisations, 9A
non-executive directors, 10C1
non-profit-making organisations, 12A1
notice of meeting, 12C1

OECD, 9C2
one best way to structure a business, 10A
opening hours, 4C3
operating ratio, 14E
ordinary resolution, 17A2A
output, 5
 per capita, 5A

partnerships, 9B3B, 10B, 16A2, 16B1
 limited, 16A2B
 ordinary, 16A2A
planned economy, 1B
policyholder protection, 18F
powers of directors, 17B6
premiums
 earned, 13G2B
 unearned, 13G2B, 13G2D
 written, 13G2B
price
 competition, 4C1
 of insurance, 3A3, 3B2
 regulation, 4D
private
 companies, 16B2A, 16C3
 sector organisations, 12A3
production, 5E1A
 and insurance, 5H
 processes, 9B1
productivity ratios, 14B2
professional indemnity cover, 3A5
profit, 8B
 and loss account, 12C5, 13C, 13G2C
profitability ratios, 14B1, 14B6
promoter, 16C1
Proposition 103, 3B2
providers of money, 15C
PSBR, 7C2
PSDR, 7C2

INDEX

INDEX